Tris Speaker and
the 1920 Indians

Tris Speaker and the 1920 Indians

Tragedy to Glory

GARY WEBSTER

McFarland & Company, Inc., Publishers
Jefferson, North Carolina, and London

All unattributed game notes, including those in text, are from the Cleveland *Plain Dealer*.

All photographs in this book are from the Library of Congress.

LIBRARY OF CONGRESS CATALOGUING-IN-PUBLICATION DATA

Webster, Gary.
   Tris Speaker and the 1920 Indians : tragedy to glory / Gary Webster.
      p.   cm.
   Includes bibliographical references and index.

   ISBN 978-0-7864-6796-9
   softcover : acid free paper

   1. Speaker, Tris. 2. Baseball players — United States — Biography. 3. Cleveland Indians (Baseball team) — History. 4. Nineteen twenty, A.D. I. Title.
GV865.S72W94 2012
796.357092 — dc23
[B]   2012024871

BRITISH LIBRARY CATALOGUING DATA ARE AVAILABLE

© 2012 Gary Webster. All rights reserved

No part of this book may be reproduced or transmitted in any form or by any means, electronic or mechanical, including photocopying or recording, or by any information storage and retrieval system, without permission in writing from the publisher.

Front cover: Tristram E. Speaker (photograph by Charles Conlon); cover design by David K. Landis (Shake It Loose Graphics)

Manufactured in the United States of America

McFarland & Company, Inc., Publishers
  Box 611, Jefferson, North Carolina 28640
    www.mcfarlandpub.com

For my father, Richard, who introduced me to baseball in general and the Indians in particular; my mother, Betty, who always encouraged me to pursue my interests; my writing mentors, William Brown and Linda Rome; and the 1920 Cleveland Indians, who, as Yogi Berra would've said, made this book necessary.

Table of Contents

Preface	1
1. Twenty Years in the Making	5
2. Way Down Yonder in New Orleans	28
3. They're Off!	38
4. All Aboard!	49
5. Summertime Blues	62
6. And Then There Were Three	76
7. Come a Little Bit Closer	96
8. Chappie	113
9. Thank You, Miss Jamieson	130
10. Cleveland's Time to Win	161
11. There's No Place Like Home	174
12. Aftermath	201
Appendix A: 1920 Indians Statistics	209
Appendix B: 1920 Indians Game by Game	212
Notes	217
Bibliography	223
Index	225

Preface

There it was on the Cleveland Indians' website, just hours after the team had won another game at Progressive Field en route to a 30–15 start to the 2011 season. In the fan comment section, someone wrote a note of caution:

"Enjoy it while you can, Cleveland. Don't you know the Indians invented the June swoon?"

Whether or not the Indians invented the habit of starting a season like a house afire and then hitting the skids, they certainly perfected it. During my time as a fan of the Tribe, which began on the day in August of 1964 when my dad took his eight-year-old son (me) to his first major league game at cavernous Municipal Stadium (with the Indians winning, 16–8, over the Minnesota Twins), the team has sprinted from the starting gate like Secretariat many times, only to cross the finish line miles behind the winner and wheezing like an old plow horse.

An example occurred in 1966, when the Indians tied the existing American League record by winning their first ten games. They improved that to 14–1 and stayed in first place until mid-June before swooning and finishing fifth. Or in 1972, when, after having lost 102 games the previous season, the Indians stood atop the Eastern Division at 18–10 in mid-May. When all was said and done, they came home fifth.

Then there was the strike year of 1981. It was whispered that the teams in first place when the players hit the bricks would be declared the first-half division winners and would meet the second-half division winners in a special play-off (since we all knew the season would resume, we just didn't know when). The Indians were in first place on the day the strike was to have begun, but negotiations between the players and owners seemed to be making progress, so the strike deadline was extended by a week. By the time the talks broke down, the Yankees had taken over first place and were declared the first-half division winners. The Milwaukee Brewers won the second-half title.

In 1988, fresh off another 100-plus defeat season the year before, the Indians astonished their fans (and everyone else) by winning 16 of their first 20 games. Local sportswriters (who should've known better) were dreaming of the League Championship Series. Unfortunately, there were 142 games left on the schedule, and the Indians lost 80 of them. That added up to a 78–84 record and sixth place.

I often wondered why my dad didn't get excited over those quick starts. Baseball had been an important part of Dick Webster's life since my grandfather moved his family from the small coal mining town of Osceola Mills, Pennsylvania, to Cleveland in 1929, just before the stock market crash. In 1936, when my dad was 11 years old, the family moved into a house on East 66th Street, one block from League Park, where Cleveland's teams had played their home games since 1891. My dad remembers being able to see the ballpark from his front porch. The elementary school he attended was across the street. He joined the kids who stood along Lexington Avenue, outside League Park's 40-foot-high right field wall, during batting practice, hoping to retrieve a ball slammed over it. Returning a ball meant free admission to that day's game. How could a kid not become an Indians fan, a trait my dad passed along to me, which has been both a blessing and a curse.

The reason dad didn't get excited over those fast starts was because he'd seen them before. The Indians spent his formative years as a fan, the 1930s, promising plenty and delivering little. They wrote the book on sprinting out of the starting gait, holding the lead until early-to-mid June, tantalizing their fans, then hitting the skids. When the final statistics were tallied, the Tribe would have 80 to 85 wins and a comfortable third or fourth-place finish, well behind the accursed Yankees. It took a lot to impress my dad as far as baseball was concerned.

There are two magic numbers in my hometown. The first is 1964, the year the Cleveland Browns shocked the heavily-favored Baltimore Colts to win the National Football League championship. It was the last "world championship" to be claimed by a Cleveland team, although fans of the American Football League champion Buffalo Bills will give you an argument about the validity of that claim.

The other is 1948, the year in which maverick owner Bill Veeck's upstart Indians vaulted from fourth place the previous season to tie the

Boston Red Sox for first place after 154 games, forcing the first one-game, winner-take-all play-off in American League history. To the surprise of many, the Tribe spanked the Red Sox, 8–3, at Fenway Park, to win the second pennant in club history. In an almost anti-climactic World Series, the Indians trimmed the Boston Braves in six games to win their second world championship.

Clevelanders are still waiting for the third, explaining why Veeck remains an icon despite selling the team and blowing town a year after ending the city's 28-year title drought and why the 1948 Indians have become almost mythical in their accomplishments. You'd be hard-pressed to find an Indians fan of legal drinking age who couldn't identify Veeck. Ask an Indians fan about James Christopher Dunn, however, and you're likely to be the recipient of a blank stare. And that shouldn't be.

Nobody expected the 1948 Indians to seriously challenge the mighty Red Sox and Yankees for the pennant, making their meteoric rise to the top all the more the stuff of legend. Just the opposite was the case in 1920, when "Sunny" Jim Dunn's Tribe was the odds-on favorite to "cop the flag," in the lexicon of the era. The pages to come will reveal that the Indians had, by 1920, already achieved a well-earned reputation for letting their fans down. And no one could've blamed the 1920 Tribe if it had gone the way of its predecessors, given the obstacles fate threw in its path.

It can be argued that few, if any, World Series winners have had to endure more adversity than Tris Speaker's boys in 1920. The list included the following events:

— The unexpected death of the team's star pitcher's wife in late May.

— The first (and, as of the writing of this book, the only) fatal injury ever sustained by a major league player on the field of play.

— A disagreement between the Protestant and Catholic players over how and where their beloved teammate, Ray Chapman, was to be buried, a conflict that threatened to tear the club apart.

— Or the nervous breakdown suffered by Speaker, the team's manager and star player, as a result of his close friend's death. At least, that was what the newspapers reported. In truth, when Speaker was supposedly bedridden thanks to his shattered nerves (which may have been true to an extent) he was actually recovering from injuries sustained when he came to blows with the team's catcher, Steve O'Neill, over the arrangements for Chapman.

— No other team had ever been required to deal with the almost super-human force that was Babe Ruth, who hit baseballs where no one had ever hit them before and transformed the Yankees from a non-descript also-ran into an offensive force the likes of which baseball had never seen and changed the way the game was played forever.

— Lastly, there remain to this day the taunts of those who insist the Indians wouldn't have been anywhere near first place had not the Chicago "Black Sox," who'd conspired with gamblers to throw the 1919 World Series to the Cincinnati Reds, remained in the pockets of those gamblers. They continued tossing games in 1920, since those gamblers had bet heavily on the Indians to take the pennant.

When Dunn bought the seventh-place Indians in February of 1916, he brashly promised a pennant within three years. He was a year overdue by 1920, but the "dope," to use another term from the period, said that the Indians would deliver, in spite of strong competition from the White Sox and Yankees.

And deliver the Indians did. Here's how.

1

Twenty Years in the Making

It would be a cold day before major league baseball returned to Cleveland.

A strong case can be made that baseball of major league caliber left Cleveland after the 1898 National League season. The Spiders, Cleveland's entry in the league since 1889, came in fifth, winning 81, losing 68, and finishing a dismal 21 games behind the pennant-winning Boston Beaneaters.

More dismal to Spiders owner Frank DeHaas Robison were the attendance figures. Cleveland's home attendance of 70,496 was easily the lowest in the 12-team league. No other team drew fewer than 103,000 spectators. So disgusted with Cleveland's response to his team was Robison that he transferred all but three of the Spiders' scheduled home games in the season's final two and a half months to the visiting team's ballpark, believing that his team's share of the gate receipts as the visitor would exceed the amount it would earn as the home team, with crowds averaging about 900 per game.

Robison, a Cleveland streetcar magnate, had tried everything to interest his hometown in the Spiders. Beginning with the 1892 season, the club was consistently competitive, always winning more games than it lost and qualifying for postseason play in 1892, 1895 and 1896. The 1895 Spiders had captured the Temple Cup, a best-of-seven series pitting the National League's pennant-winner against the runner-up (a forerunner of today's wild card?) for the mythical "world championship." The Spiders humbled the pennant-winning Baltimore Orioles in five games to grab the brass ring. Thirty thousand fans attended the three games played in Cleveland's

League Park (capacity 9,000), giving Robison reason to believe baseball had finally caught on with the populace.

The Spiders met the Orioles in a Temple Cup re-match in 1896, and not only was the outcome reversed (Baltimore swept Cleveland in four straight), but the only game played in Cleveland (with the Spiders trailing three games to none and the outcome of the series all but decided) drew a paltry 1,500 fans to the ballpark at the corner of East 66th Street and Lexington Avenue. Such crowds, and considerably smaller ones, were the rule rather than the exception during Robison's ownership. The Spiders never finished higher than fifth in the league in attendance and came in last or next-to-last six times (including the playoff seasons of 1895 and 1896).

Robison's final hope was Sunday baseball, which was forbidden by Ohio law. The state left enforcement up to individual communities, however, and the law was ignored in Cincinnati, where the Reds had played on the Sabbath for years. Playing on Sunday had resulted in the expulsion of the original Cincinnati franchise from the National League after the 1880 season. Robison convinced Cleveland's city council to take advantage of the home rule provision in Ohio's constitution and pass a local ordinance allowing his Spiders to play on Sunday. Cleveland's religious leaders pressured the police and elected officials to ignore the ordinance and put a stop to such debauchery, which they did. Robison challenged the Sunday baseball ban in court in 1897, losing his case in Cleveland's Municipal Court, securing a reversal of that decision in Cuyahoga County's Common Pleas Court, and ultimately having the reversal reversed by Ohio's Supreme Court. There would be no Sunday baseball in Cleveland. Soon, there would be no major league baseball at all.

The Spiders' 1898 road show was a preview of coming attractions. Bound by an agreement that all National League owners had signed in 1892, committing each club to its home city for ten years, Robison, unable to move the team, did the next best thing. He and his brother, Stanley, purchased controlling interest in the sad-sack St. Louis club and, in March of 1899, transferred all of Cleveland's best players, including future Hall of Famers Cy Young and Jesse (The Crab) Burkett, a two-time .400 hitter, to the team that would eventually become known as the Cardinals. Owning controlling interest in two franchises, while unethical, was legal and was known as syndicate baseball. It was also happening in Baltimore and Brooklyn, where a group that included Orioles manager Ned Hanlon bought a majority of stock in the Dodgers, who were then known as the Superbas, while maintaining control of the Orioles. Hanlon moved north to manage Brooklyn, where many of the players who won pennants in

Baltimore in 1895 and 1896 won pennants in 1899 and 1900. The Orioles were weakened but not reduced to a laughingstock, as the Spiders were by the Robison brothers machinations.

The once-proud Spiders, though still carrying the "major league" label, won just 20 games in 1899. They played only 41 games in Cleveland and drew a mere 6,088 fans for the abbreviated season, an average of about 150 per contest. Few Clevelanders cared that the Spiders spent all of July, August, September and October on the road.

Contraction was on the agenda when National League owners met on March 17, 1900. A 12-team league wasn't working, and it was a foregone conclusion that the pathetic Spiders would be terminated, along with the weak franchises in Baltimore (league champions as recently as 1896 and runners-up in a frantic pennant race in '97), Washington and Louisville. That opened the door for Byron Bancroft (Ban) Johnson, a former sportswriter from Cincinnati who had taken over as president of the minor Western League in 1894, largely due to the machinations of John T. Brush, the Indianapolis businessman who owned the Reds and chafed at Johnson's constant criticism of Brush's management style. Forsaking his typewriter for a management position of his own, Johnson's Western League had become the strongest minor league in the country. Johnson knew the National League would eventually collapse under the weight of a dozen franchises, and when it finally did, he pounced. His ultimate ambition had been to elevate the Western League to major league status, and with Cleveland, Baltimore and Washington about to be abandoned by the National League, he prepared to make his move.

On February 29, 1900, Johnson visited the office of Davis Hawley, a Cleveland banker who'd been part-owner of the Spiders since their inception in 1889. His message was simple. "There's room for a second major league in this country, Mr. Hawley," Johnson said. "Cleveland should be in it."[1]

And so the city would be, although Hawley declined to become involved in the franchise's ownership, citing his advanced age. Hawley introduced Johnson to a pair of wealthy young men, John F. Kilfoyl and Charles W. Somers, who were none too happy about the prospect of spending the coming summer without a professional baseball team in their hometown. Although no less of an authority than the editorial board of the Cleveland *Press*, in the wake of the 1899 Spiders fiasco, declared the city to be "a dead baseball town," Kilfoyl and Somers weren't buying it. Neither was Johnson. What Somers did buy was the Western League's club in Grand Rapids, Michigan, a team that he immediately transferred to

Cleveland. It had been a busy year for the Grand Rapids team, which started the 1899 season in Columbus, Ohio, before being uprooted and moved north in July. Somers also bought League Park from Robison, who no longer needed it since Cleveland no longer had a National League team. Fans riding Robison's trolley cars to the intersection of East 66th and Lexington to watch a ballgame put money in Robison's coffers, and while Robison and his fellow National League owners were concerned about Johnson's plan to elevate the newly re-named American League to major status, they were busy hatching a scheme they were certain would scuttle Johnson's plan. The National League's idea of controlling its competition by reviving the late and unlamented American Association, a major league from 1882 through 1891 that the NL had swallowed up eight years earlier, never got off the ground.

Cleveland's playmates in the American League in 1900 were Chicago, Detroit, Milwaukee, Minneapolis, Indianapolis, Kansas City and Buffalo. Each of those cities, with the exception of Minneapolis, had once been a member of the National League (Chicago, of course, still was). After a one-year shakedown cruise (Cleveland posted a 63–73 record in the American League's only season as a minor league), Johnson was ready to end the monopoly on major league baseball that the National League had enjoyed since 1892. When the National League sneered (as established leagues invariably do at the efforts of upstarts to challenge them), Johnson declared war. He started by lopping off Kansas City, Minneapolis, Indianapolis and Buffalo. He wanted to replace Milwaukee with St. Louis for 1901 but had to back off when brewer Zachary Tinker, the that owner Johnson recruited, got cold feet at the 11th hour and backed out of the deal.

The American League's primary weapon in its battle for baseball supremacy (Johnson wasn't willing to settle for mere equality with the National League) was money. Much of that money came from Cleveland and the sizable bank account of Charley Somers. First, Somers paid Tom Loftus $2,500 for the Grand Rapids franchise. Loftus was a baseball lifer who had a stop in Cleveland on his lengthy resume, having managed the Spiders to a sixth place (61–72) finish in 1889, their first season in the National League. Then, Somers forked over $10,000 for League Park. He then, in the words of historian Norman L. Macht in his book *Connie Mack and the Early Years of Baseball,* "opened his bankroll to fund Johnson's plans for the rest of the family."[2] And Johnson had grand plans for his new major league.

Johnson wanted the American League to include franchises in Philadelphia, Boston and Washington. Why Johnson coveted Philadelphia was obvious. Philadelphia's population of 1.2 million had supported the city's usually non-contending National League clubs enthusiastically for nearly 20 years. When the 1895 squad finished third and led the league with 1,068 runs scored (an average of eight runs per contest during the "dead ball" era), nearly 475,000 fans poured through the gates to watch the pain their heroes inflicted on opposing pitchers, establishing a major league record that no other team had come close to matching or surpassing by 1901. Connie Mack didn't have the money required to start a team in Philadelphia, however, so Somers loaned it to him. Charley thought it was the least he could do after Mack, at Johnson's behest, visited Cleveland to offer Somers and Kilfoyl advice on how to construct a championship team. Mack would build five such teams in Philadelphia before Cleveland would enjoy its first, and that would happen after Somers and Kilfoyl were out of the ownership picture.

Johnson encountered the same problem in Boston, where anyone with money was reluctant to challenge the firmly established Beaneaters (soon to be re-named the Braves). The Beaneaters had been a charter member of the first professional league, the National Association of Professional Base Ball Players, and had operated continuously since 1871, joining the National League for its maiden voyage in 1876. They'd won five pennants in the 1890s, and their battles with the rough and tumble Orioles were the stuff of legend. The Beaneaters captured the hearts and loyalty of New England's rabid baseball fans. What chance did an American League team have against such a track record? Reluctantly, Somers turned the operation of the Cleveland club over to his partner Kilfoyl (to avoid the stench of syndicate baseball, which Johnson despised) and financed the Boston team, assuming the club presidency. In his honor, the franchise was named the Somersets.

Why Johnson desired Washington is less clear, unless the league president craved the prestige of fielding a franchise in the nation's capitol, whose support for its (admittedly lousy) National League club had been lukewarm. Washington had joined the National League in 1886 and finished last, seventh, last and last again before dropping out after the 1889 season. After one season without baseball (the city's few fans were probably thankful for the respite) and one miserable season in the American Association, Washington's team was welcomed back by the National League in 1892, perhaps because the other 11 owners were searching for a punching bag to provide their clubs with a few guaranteed victories each year. The reborn Washingtonians never finished higher than seventh (and that only once) between 1892 and 1899 and twice failed to attract 100,000 fans to their home games. Washington's population of 279,000 made it the smallest city in the majors, and there was also the minor matter of having to compete with Baltimore so close to the north. Still, Johnson wanted Washington in his new league, and when, as in Philadelphia and Boston, no local owners stepped forward, Somers wrote the checks that got the team up and running.

When the American League took the field as a major circuit in 1901, 111 of its players (well over half) had worn National League uniforms the previous year, lured away by big contracts, some of which Somers' money had made possible. As if Somers hadn't done enough to get the infant league on its feet, he answered the call yet again in 1902, when the owners of the new St. Louis franchise, which had finally been transplanted from Milwaukee, found themselves short of cash, a condition that would be common to the Brown Stockings during their regrettable 51-year existence. Somers opened his checkbook, and the Browns were in business.

According to David Q. Voigt, author of *The League That Failed*, Somers had contributed $4 million turn-of-the-20th-century dollars to Johnson's cause by the time the two leagues declared a truce in January of 1903.[3] In the opinion of Franklin Lewis, whose 1949 book, *The Cleveland Indians*, remains the definitive history of the first half-century of the franchise, without Somers and his money, there would have been no American League.[4] Johnson had the ambition and the brains, but not the cash.

As for Cleveland's franchise in the American League, it was almost short-lived. The 1901 Blues (nicknamed, according to history books, for the team's bright blue road uniforms, though none of the Cleveland papers ever used the nickname) staggered through the season in seventh place, finishing ahead only of the pathetic Milwaukee Brewers, who were banished to St. Louis. Cleveland's response to the Blues was underwhelming. The club's home attendance of 131,380 was the lowest in the major leagues, and in late July, Johnson made a public statement that the city was likely to be stripped of its franchise. Speculation that the team would be moved to St. Louis, Cincinnati or Pittsburgh proved to be unfounded, and Somers returned home to take the reins after selling the Somersets in the fall of 1902 to former Brewers owner Henry Killilea. Attendance improved steadily, as did the club's performance, although the Naps (so named by a vote of the fans in 1902 to honor the team's star player, future Hall of Fame second baseman Napoleon Lajoie) always found a way to come up short. In 1904, led by the potent bat of Lajoie, the Naps led the league in runs scored (647) and outscored their opponents by 165 runs, the largest margin in the league, but finished fourth, seven and a half games behind

Boston. In 1906, the Naps again paced the American League offensively (663 runs) and outscored their opponents by a whopping 181 runs, and still managed to finish five games behind the "Hitless Wonder" Chicago White Sox, who batted a miserable .230 as a team (the Naps' team average was a robust .279) and whose pitchers allowed just 22 fewer runs than Cleveland's. What did a team have to do to win a pennant?

It's little consolation to Cleveland fans that no team will ever again lose a pennant the way the Naps lost in 1908, finishing half a game behind the Detroit Tigers. The Naps played all 154 scheduled games, winning 90 and losing 64. The Tigers played only 153 games, winning 90 and losing 63. A late August game in Washington that was rained out wasn't re-scheduled. No league rule specified that a game cancelled by weather had to be made up if it had a bearing on the pennant race, as the Tigers' game against the Senators certainly did. Detroit manager Hughie Jennings, a hard-bitten veteran of the legendary Orioles teams of the 1890s that would resort to anything, legal or not, to win a game, wasn't about to volunteer to re-schedule the game to give the Naps the chance to tie for the pennant and force a play-off. The Senators, who finished seventh with a 67–85 record, would most likely have lost the make-up game anyway, although they would've had a fighting chance if manager "Pongo" Joe Cantillon had sent future Hall of Fame pitcher Walter Johnson to the mound. Johnson, in his second major league season in 1908, hadn't yet blossomed into the dominant pitcher he'd soon become, but he did author six of his 110 career shutouts that season.

The Naps somehow managed to blow the pennant despite allowing just 457 runs, fewest in the league and 90 less than Detroit's pitchers permitted. They outscored their opponents by 111 runs, again the largest margin in the league.

The Naps and the city took the agonizing loss in stride. Although it resulted in a rule change requiring teams to make up games postponed for whatever reason, neither the players, the fans, nor the sportswriters shed any tears about the injustice of it all. It was simply accepted that rained out games weren't required to be made up, and that was that.

The *Cleveland Plain Dealer* reported on October 7, the day after the season ended:

> For the first time in the history of the league, the club finishing second has won as many games as the champions. Cleveland, however, was unlucky enough to have been able to play every game on the schedule, and that was what hurt.
>
> Just suppose it had rained three days in Washington when the

Naps were last in the east instead of only two days. Then Cleveland would have lost two games less [the Naps blew the pennant by losing 14 of 22 games to the hapless Senators] and the pennant would have come to Cleveland. Just suppose it had not rained on the last day of the Tigers' stay in Washington on that same eastern trip. Suppose the Tigers and Washington had been able to play that game. The [Senators] were going strong then and that game might have gone to them. In that case, a tie would exist today. But there is no consolation in "if." The season is over, Cleveland has lost by a nose, and the Naps must wait another year for their revenge.

Cleveland would have to wait much longer than that, if "revenge" is defined as winning the pennant.

Although the Naps were the favorites to grab Cleveland's first flag in 1909, they stumbled so badly that a discouraged Lajoie requested the word "manager" be removed from his title as player-manager. Somers granted the request. Cleveland didn't contend again until 1913, when it chased Mack's Athletics into late August before fading (a nasty habit displayed by far too many Cleveland teams) and limping home a distant third. At least that team didn't add to the frustration by leading the league in any important category.

The bottom fell out both on and off the field in 1914. The Naps collapsed, finishing last for the first time, dropping 102 games. Lajoie, the face (and name) of the franchise since 1902, reached the end of the line and was released at season's end after batting just .258, 80 points below his lifetime mark. In the front office, Somers, whose vast fortune and willingness to spend it had made the American League possible, was revealed to be $1,750,000 in debt.

There was scant improvement in 1915. A seventh place (57–95) finish cost manager Joe Birmingham his job early in the season, and when it was over, the lawyers who'd taken control of Somers' financial affairs ordered him to sell the team at once. Divesting himself of the Indians would prove for Somers to be far easier said than done.

It had been so simple 15 years earlier. Ban Johnson walked into Davis Hawley's office, Hawley arranged a meeting with Somers and Kilfoyl (who sold his stock to Somers when the 1908 pennant race proved to be too much for his nerves), the two young entrepreneurs expressed their interest, and the American League's future was assured, although no one in the room knew it at the time. Johnson would have a much more difficult time finding the team's second owner than its first. But the second owner would succeed where the first, in spite of his enormous wealth, had failed.

1. Twenty Years in the Making

Johnson's preference was for Clevelanders to take the Indians off Somers' hands, and it appeared early in 1916 that he'd get his way, as Johnson usually did. Henry P. Edwards, who'd covered the team for the *Plain Dealer* since 1901, reported on New Year's Day that a syndicate representing the Cleveland Athletic Club, headed by W.E. Telling, G.A. Schneider, and Dr. John H. Quayle, was negotiating with Somers' attorneys to purchase the club.

"Our object is to prevent the ownership of the Cleveland club going outside the city," Edwards quoted Quayle as saying. "We feel it would be a taint upon the reputation of the sixth city [Cleveland's population was the sixth largest in the United States] to have to peddle our ball club among out of town capitalists when we can finance the thing right here. As long as Mr. Somers had a chance to retain the club, we were willing to sit still as we had confidence in his coming through all right, but now that the team has been ordered sold and we have been assured that if Clevelanders do not buy it, outsiders will, we are going to try to buy it."

Edwards considered the Indians a good investment, noting "Cleveland has been a moneymaker with the exception of two years since it entered the American League." The bankers and lawyers overseeing Somers' financial affairs had valued the franchise at $560,000. At that price, the Cleveland Athletic Club's interest quickly waned. Another local group, called the Hofbrau syndicate, also expressed an interest in owning the Indians, and both potential buyers were willing to pay $460,000 for the franchise Somers had purchased for $2,500 in 1900. Although there was talk of the Cleveland Athletic Club and Hofbrau groups pooling their resources and making a joint bid, both instead decided to withdraw on January 5.

Johnson clung to the hope that Clevelanders would own their baseball team, but the league president admitted on January 10 that "Cleveland men seemed reluctant to invest."[5] With local ownership apparently out of the picture, the question of who would own the Indians became the city's hottest topic of discussion.

Within days after the Cleveland Athletic Club and Hofbrau groups threw in the towel, it was reported that the next owner of the Indians would be...

A) Former Boston Red Sox manager Jake Stahl, who had guided the Sox to the 1912 world's championship, and then retired from baseball the next year and was managing a bank in Chicago, or...

B) Oil millionaire Harry Sinclair and partners Ed Gwinner and C.B. Comstock, who had owned franchises in the soon-to-be defunct Federal League, which tried to become the third major league in 1914, or...

C) John Bruce, former secretary of the National Commission, Organized Baseball's ruling body, who had recently sold his interest in the Browns. Bruce reportedly planned to buy the Indians, quickly revive the team, and sell it at an enormous profit within three years. Or...

D) Theatrical entrepreneur Sam Harris, who had dispatched his Cleveland representative, John Hogarty, to Johnson's office to inquire as to the precise down payment needed.[6]

After a flurry of activity, and rumors, during the first two weeks of January, all of the parties alleged to be interested in the Indians laid low, with the asking price proving the major stumbling block. Even Sinclair, a man of immense wealth, was reluctant to part with better than half a million dollars for a bad baseball team. The front office tried to proceed with business as usual. Vice president Ernest Barnard announced the club's 1916 schedule of exhibition games on January 30, based on the assumption that someone would come forward with the cash and that the players would gather in New Orleans in early March for spring training.

"If not," Edwards wrote, "there's no telling what will happen to Barnard's carefully prepared schedule." With Somers broke, Johnson was faced with the possibility that the league would have to operate the Indians until a buyer could be found. Johnson found that buyer at Chicago's Comiskey Park.

At a meeting of the Woodland Bards, a group of baseball executives and fans who gathered regularly at a bar in the home of the White Sox to talk baseball, Johnson turned to James C. (Sunny Jim) Dunn and announced, "You're going to own the Cleveland ball club!"[7] How many rounds had been consumed before Johnson came to that conclusion isn't known. It also isn't known if Dunn, an Iowan who'd earned a small fortune in the railroad business, protested or responded enthusiastically. A protest would've been in vain. Johnson had made his decision, and Dunn would be the new owner of the Indians.

In a scene that eerily foreshadowed the 1970s, when, in the absence of a single candidate with deep pockets, the Indians were owned by a large number of people who contributed a minimal amount of money in exchange for the prestige of being able to say they were part-owners of a big league baseball team, Johnson, on that cold winter day, cobbled together a consortium that could scrape up the money needed to take the Indians off Somers' hands.

As Franklin Lewis explained it, Dunn told Johnson that he could lay his hands on $15,000 in cash immediately. Dunn's business partner, Pat

McCarthy, pledged $10,000. John Burns, who was tending bar that day, wanted a piece of the action. So did Tom Walsh, whose major league career had consisted of one hitless at-bat in two games with the National League champion Chicago Cubs in 1906. Johnson loaned Dunn $100,000 on behalf of the league, and White Sox owner Charlie Comiskey kicked in a second $100,000 loan. Comiskey hadn't forgotten that Somers provided the money needed to expand the White Sox' home park 15 years earlier. Dunn said that he thought he could interest friends and relatives back home in Iowa in purchasing stock. No Clevelanders would be involved in the deal.

On February 17, J.C. Dunn was introduced to the baseball writers of Cleveland's four daily newspapers as the new majority owner and president of the Indians.

"I will not stand for a tail-ender," Dunn told the assembled reporters. "If I thought the Cleveland club was destined to remain a second division team, I would not buy it, but I believe it can be turned into a first division team with the expenditure of some money, and that is what I intend to do. We will go after the best there is in the market and will spare no expense to bring Cleveland a winner."

Dunn had considered buying a big league team before Johnson selected him to bring an end to the Cleveland dilemma. He'd made overtures to Comiskey regarding the White Sox, but Comiskey assured Dunn he'd never sell the club. Cubs owner Charles Murphy wanted too much for his team, and Dunn rejected offers to buy a team in the Federal League because he was certain the venture would fail, as it did after two seasons.

Dunn had a Cleveland connection. He'd lived in the city in 1907 and 1908. He watched fans stream into League Park during the summer of 1908 as the Naps battled Detroit and Chicago, falling agonizingly short of capturing the city's first American League championship. His promise to the press to turn the Indians into a winner wasn't the public relations blather required of every new owner in order to ingratiate himself with the fans, particularly a fan base as turned off by its baseball team as Clevelanders had been by the Indians in 1914 and 1915. Dunn meant every word he said, and he wasted no time proving it.

When word came from Boston that Red Sox owner Joe Lannin was anxious to trade his star center fielder, Tris Speaker, in the spring of 1916, Dunn leapt at the opportunity to put Speaker in a Cleveland uniform. With the possible exception of Detroit's Ty Cobb, Speaker was the American League's brightest star. He'd led the Red Sox to World Series titles in 1912 and 1915, and few people took seriously Lannin's threat to dispose of

Speaker when the hard-headed owner and strong-willed outfielder found themselves embroiled in a contract dispute. But Lannin meant business, and Speaker, a proud Texan, didn't care to be pushed around.

With the Federal League threat eliminated, Johnson ordered American League owners, who'd doled out extended contracts worth big money to keep their best players from defecting, to slash salaries drastically. No one was exempt from the league president's edict. Thus, Lannin felt he was only following orders when he cut Speaker's 1916 salary from $18,000 to $9,000. He justified the low-ball offer by noting Speaker's 1915 batting statistics had declined appreciably from his 1914 numbers. Speaker argued that while his offense may have slackened, he was still baseball's best defensive outfielder. Neither man budged and Speaker held out briefly before reporting, reluctantly, to spring training without a contract. Through channels, Lannin let his fellow owners know that Speaker could be had, for the right price.

It appeared at first that Lannin had a deal with the New York Yankees, but it fell through at the last minute, leaving the door open a crack for Dunn, who promptly kicked it in. Speaker was just the player Dunn wanted. The Indians were a bad, dull team, devoid of a star since the decline of Lajoie. Speaker was not only a player that fans would pay to watch, but he was a star of the first magnitude, a talent entering his prime around whom Dunn could build the contending team he'd promised. But where would the seventh-place Indians find players that the defending world champion Red Sox would accept in exchange for Speaker?

By allowing the Red Sox to decide which players they wanted. The Indians placed their entire roster, with the exception of rising star shortstop Ray Chapman, at Boston's disposal. In the end, however, money talked.

Just hours after Speaker, still without a contract, belted a ninth inning home run that defeated the Brooklyn Dodgers in Boston's final exhibition game, he received an unexpected visitor in his hotel room. Bob McRoy, Cleveland's club secretary who knew Speaker from his days in the Red Sox' front office, asked Speaker how he'd like to play for the Indians. Speaker dismissed the thought as preposterous and told McRoy that Lannin had assured him after that day's game that his contract demands would be met.

And they would be, McRoy promised Speaker. But by Dunn, not by Lannin. In the biggest deal in baseball history, the Indians had acquired Speaker for $55,000. Dunn had said he'd spend money to improve the Indians, and he meant it. The Red Sox were also given the choice of (almost) any two players on the Tribe's roster. Manager Bill (Rough) Carrigan's first selection was pitcher "Sad" Sam Jones, whose record in 1915 had been an unimpressive 4–9. Carrigan chose Jones on the basis of a 1–0 game he'd pitched against the Red Sox in a losing effort the previous year. Jones didn't win a game for Boston in 1916 or 1917, but notched 64 victories from 1918 through 1921, before he was dispatched, as all of Boston's best players eventually were during that era, to the Yankees.

With the second pick, Carrigan was expected to pluck promising young second baseman Bill Wambsganss. Instead, much to the relief of the Indians, Carrigan, who had been a catcher in his playing days, chose receiver Fred Thomas. Thomas would play only 44 games for the Red Sox, after Carrigan had retired. Wambsganss would be Cleveland's regular second baseman through the 1923 season.

Speaker, an icon in Boston, was understandably reluctant to leave the world champions and admitted as much to Dunn. One of Speaker's biographers, Charles Alexander, quotes the outfielder as telling his new boss shortly after arriving in Cleveland that "When I came to Cleveland, I came with a bad taste in my mouth. I will guarantee to give my best work to you and do all I can toward making your proposition a success."[8] Dunn soon came to rely heavily on Speaker's baseball judgment, and the taste in their mouths five years later would be that of champagne.

It didn't take long for Speaker to become acclimated to Cleveland. Another biographer, Timothy Gay, says that "Almost immediately, he felt at home in Cleveland in a way he never experienced in Boston."[9] Speaker also felt at home in his new home park almost immediately, tying teammate Jack Graney for the league lead in doubles with 41, many of them clanging off League Park's inviting right field wall. Speaker's .386 batting average paced the circuit, 15 points better than Ty Cobb, who saw his nine-year streak of batting championships snapped. And it didn't take long for Speaker's new teammates to become acclimated to their leader. The Indians sprinted out of the gate and led the American League well into June. They couldn't maintain the pace, but their final record of 77–77 represented a 20-game improvement over 1915. Dunn had been right. The Indians could be built into a contender, and the process had begun.

Interestingly, sportswriter Grantland Rice, shortly after Speaker had been banished to Cleveland, estimated that the loss of his bat and glove would cost the Red Sox ten victories in 1916. Rice's prediction was accurate. Boston's record slipped from 101–50 to 91–63, but the Red Sox overcame Speaker's absence to win another pennant and defeated Brooklyn in the World Series.

"I found Tris to be not only a wonderful ballplayer, but a man of his word," Dunn told an audience at a postseason dinner celebrating the team's resurgence and Speaker's first (and only) batting championship, "and today I regard him as one of my very best friends, a man who has my interests at heart all the time."[10]

Speaker had words of praise for his manager, Lee Fohl, who recognized the asset he had in his center fielder and relied heavily on Speaker's judgment and instincts. By the end of his first campaign in Cleveland, Speaker was the Tribe's assistant manager, in fact if not in title. Speaker told the gathering that he never wanted to play for a manager other than Fohl, who had taken over from Birmingham 27 games into the 1915 season. Dunn debated briefly after purchasing the Indians whether to retain Fohl or try to make a publicity splash by hiring a "name" manager. The trio of Dunn, Fohl and Speaker, having had a full season (in Fohl's case, almost two full seasons) to evaluate the talent on hand, set out to make Dunn's promise of a pennant winner a reality.

The 1917 Indians featured a re-vamped infield. Gone were first baseman Arnold (Chick) Gandil, sold to Chicago for a paltry $3,500. The rough-hewn Gandil had antagonized enough of his teammates during his one season in Cleveland to make his departure a case of addition by subtraction. Gandil would play on a pair of pennant winners with the White Sox (1917 and 1919) and would be among the ringleaders of the infamous Black Sox. Also gone was second baseman Ivy Howard, whose .187 batting average neither Fohl nor Speaker could stomach. Wambsganss was shifted to second base and Chapman, whose 1916 season was limited to 109 games by injuries, returned to his normal position of shortstop after bouncing around between short, second and third. Terry Turner, an infield mainstay since 1904, surrendered third base to Joe Evans, who held it all season despite a .190 batting average. The outfield of right fielder Bobby (Braggo) Roth, Speaker and left fielder Graney returned intact, and Steve O'Neill remained the starting catcher.

Pitching carried the 1917 Indians to a third-place finish. Jim Bagby and Stan Covelskie emerged as the team's top two starters, combining for 42 victories. Ed Klepfer added 14 wins, and the Tribe's 2.52 ERA was the third-lowest in the league. Fohl guided the team to an 88–66 record, 12 games behind the champion White Sox. Dunn's rebuilding project was making progress.

The 1918 season may have been the most chaotic in major league history. America's entry into World War I in the spring of 1917 left the game's owners uncertain of the course they should follow. Unlike the spring of

1942, shortly after the United States became embroiled in the Second World War, when commissioner Kenesaw Mountain Landis asked for and received a ringing endorsement for the sport to continue from President Franklin D. Roosevelt, the government took no position as to whether or not baseball should play out the 1918 season or suspend operations for the duration. Baseball was not on the list of industries that were given Washington's sanction to continue because they provided needed entertainment for the folks on the homefront, such as theater, vaudeville and motion pictures, and were therefore considered essential to the nation's morale. With able-bodied men from the ages of 18 to 31 subject to being drafted into military service, Johnson, aware of the drain on manpower that baseball would experience, was willing to cancel the 1918 season. Despite Johnson's near dictatorial power over the American League, he was over-ruled by the owners.

In May, Provost Marshal General Enoch Crowder issued a "work or fight" order, requiring every man of draft age to find employment in a war-related industry or register for the draft, effective July 1. Crowder's order had been issued "after a series of conferences with [Secretary of War] Newton D. Baker," according to the *Plain Dealer*. The newspaper noted that Baker, a former mayor of Cleveland, "added that it was his understanding that the large majority of ball players attached to the major league teams 'were more mature and did not come within draft age.' Telegrams apprising him that the regulation, if applied to ball players, will wreck practically every big league club in the country ... were a surprise to the secretary."

Johnson again broached the idea of suspending operation of both major leagues until the end of the war, rather than giving fans "minor league ball at major league prices," but the owners mandated the games continue while they petitioned the War Department for an exemption from Crowder's order through October 15, which would allow for completion of the regular season and a World Series. While baseball waited for a decision, it was estimated that the "work or fight" order would apply to 20,000 men in Cuyahoga County, in which Cleveland was located, by itself.

The Indians continued to shuffle personnel in 1918. For the third straight season, they had a new first baseman, as Wheeler (Doc) Johnston replaced Joe Harris, who'd replaced Gandil. Wambsganss and Chapman were firmly established as the team's double-play combination, and Evans stayed at third base, by virtue of having raised his batting average 73 points over the previous season. Former Red Sox pitcher "Smoky" Joe Wood, who turned to the outfield after his pitching arm gave out, took over for Graney in left field. Roth stayed in right. O'Neill remained behind the plate, catching Bagby, Coveleskie, Guy Morton and Fritz Coumbe, who combined for 66 of the Tribe's 73 victories during the war-shortened season.

"All in all, it looks as if the big fight will be between Boston, New York and Cleveland," Edwards wrote in the *Plain Dealer* on June 2. At the time, the Tribe was mired in fourth place with a mediocre record of 21–20, four and a half games in back of the Red Sox. Edwards had more to say at month's end.

> It will be hard luck for the Cleveland baseball club if the government insists that big league ball players must fight or go to work at some essential occupation after tomorrow, for if there ever was a time when it looked as if the Cleveland team would win the pennant, this is the time. It looks as if the American League championship could be brought to Cleveland this year — this, if the government permits players to finish the season. There are but between 200 and 300 players of draft age in the two big leagues affected by Crowder's order. But those same 200 or 300 are entertaining several million persons each year, as did the actors in the movies or on the spoken stage.

"I should hate to see anything done that would interfere with the great national game," Baker said in early July, a week after Crowder's order became effective and while baseball's request for a temporary exemption was still pending. "But I do not want this to be taken as my decision in the matter."[11] Instead of agreeing with Edwards that baseball players provided entertainment to millions of weary workers, Baker expressed the opinion that the exemption granted to entertainers should be re-considered. It wouldn't be.

While the games continued, enforcement of Crowder's order was taken seriously. A newspaper account of a July 12th doubleheader between the Cubs and Braves at Chicago's Weeghman Park (now Wrigley Field) noted that "a corps of federal agents guarded the gates of the north side park today, and every attendant of draft age was forced to show his registration card. A number who were without cards were held for investigation."[12] To be called a slacker was the most vile insult that could be directed toward an able-bodied man in the summer of 1918, while America's best and brightest were fighting for their lives and for the freedom of the folks back home against the bloodthirsty hordes of Kaiser Wilhelm.

The War Department denied baseball's petition for an exemption from the "work or fight" order in late July, and Dunn immediately announced that League Park's gates would close and that the Indians would suspend operations following their game on July 22 against Philadelphia. The Indians were in second place, six games behind Boston. Echoing Johnson, Dunn said he wouldn't give Cleveland "the brand of baseball that is furnished by men under or beyond draft age."[13] Despite the wave of patriotism sweeping the nation, Dunn found himself alone on that particular bandwagon. After much wrangling, the government allowed baseball to continue until September 1. That deadline was extended by one day to allow teams to play the traditional (and profitable) Labor Day doubleheaders. The players would be given ten-days to find jobs in war-related industries or report to their draft boards at the conclusion of the season, and the two pennant winners would be permitted to decide the world's championship before the "work or fight" order applied to them.

Franklin Lewis contends that the Indians would've won the 1918 pennant had the season been played to its regularly scheduled conclusion. The abbreviated schedule favored Boston, which opened a three-week homestand on August 10. The Indians played their final home game two days later, and then embarked on a road trip that took them to each of the seven cities in the league. Their visit to Fenway Park produced two losses in three games August 17 through the 20, and they left trailing the Red Sox by three games — a deficit they were unable to overcome in the season's 12 remaining days. The Tribe could come no closer than two and a half games on August 27. Boston clinched the pennant August 30, splitting a doubleheader with Philadelphia while the Indians were edging the White Sox in Chicago, 2–1. Had the season's final scheduled weeks been played, the Red Sox had only seven home (where they won 70 percent of the time) games remaining, and faced 21 contests on the road. Boston's record away from Fenway Park was an underwhelming 26–30. The early end to the campaign wiped out 25 games for the Indians, 17 of which would've been played at League Park, where they posted a 38–22 record. Lewis theorized that September would've been Boston's Waterloo and that the Indians, had they continued to win at a 63 percent pace at home, would've caught and passed the Red Sox and hoisted Cleveland's first pennant. Thanks to the war, that event would have to wait.

After the Red Sox defeated the Cubs in a six game World Series, major league baseball officially shut down ... forever, in the opinion of many doomsayers. It was a foregone conclusion that the 1919 season would be cancelled if war continued to rage across the Atlantic Ocean, since the government had already determined the game's entertainment value was insufficient to label it essential to the country's morale. And even if it had been, where would the warm bodies have come from to form 16 teams? Able-bodied men were being sent off to Europe to battle the Central Powers as quickly as they could be trained and issued uniforms.

With the armistice of November 11, 1918, the soldiers began returning from "over there," and major league baseball owners, in their infinite wisdom, chose to ignore the pundits who'd declared the game deceased after the World Series and instead plunged ahead with preparations for the 1919 season, which would be shortened to 140 games. Buoyed by their near-miss in 1918, Fohl and Speaker met with Dunn to discuss what (and who) was needed to put the Tribe over the top.

Specifically, the manager and his aide-de-camp felt the Indians needed a third baseman and a spare outfielder. Dunn obliged by sending Bobby Roth to the Athletics for veteran third sacker Larry Gardner. Outfielder Charlie Jamieson and pitcher Elmer Myers were included in the deal. Speaker remembered Gardner well from their days as teammates in Boston, where they'd helped the Red Sox win world championships in 1912 and 1915. Gardner's sacrifice fly against New York Giants ace pitcher Christy Mathewson had plated the World Series' winning run in 1912. Gardner hung around for Boston's 1916 World Series triumph and was grateful to be liberated from Philadelphia, which finished in the American League's basement in 1916 and '17 (without Gardner) and 1918 (with Gardner), establishing residency there through 1921. Myers had won just

Charlie Jamieson was coming off a terrible season with a miserable Athletics team when he was traded to the Indians before the 1919 season. Jamieson never wore another uniform and retired in 1932 with a .303 career batting average.

1. Twenty Years in the Making

four of 12 decisions for the Athletics, and Jamieson had batted a miserable .202 with an equally abysmal 11 runs batted in. Myers would prove to be a disappointment with the Tribe, but Jamieson would wear a Cleveland uniform through 1932, compiling a .303 lifetime average.

The rebuilding process was over. Fohl and Speaker had the players they wanted.

Those players had the Indians in second place, trailing the rampaging White Sox, with a somewhat disappointing record of 44–33 on the afternoon of July 18, 1919. The shortened season had passed the halfway point a week earlier. Providing the opposition at League Park on that Friday afternoon were the Red Sox, the defending world champions who'd fallen upon hard times and had been Cleveland's favorite punching bags up to that point. The Tribe had won all nine of its games against Boston and appeared on the verge of making it ten straight when a four-run eighth inning rally snapped a 3–3 tie and gave the Indians a 7–3 lead.

The Red Sox cut the lead to 7–4 and loaded the bases with two out against Myers. There were no ninth inning "closers" in that era, and Fohl had three pitchers warming up in the bullpen. Stepping up to the plate was Babe Ruth, formerly Boston's ace pitcher, who was well on his way to setting a new major league single-season home run record with 29. Ruth had already connected for a homer earlier in the game against Cleveland starter Henry (Hi) Jasper. League Park's tantalizing right field wall, a mere 290 feet away, beckoned seductively to the left-handed batting Ruth.

Fohl looked to center field for a sign from Speaker. The pair, during their three and a half seasons together, had devised a set of more than a dozen secret signals they used to exchange information. Befitting Speaker's status as assistant manager, it figured that Fohl would glance toward the outfield for Speaker's input on such a crucial decision. Speaker signaled that he wanted a right-handed pitcher to replace Myers. Instead, Fohl walked to the mound and gestured for left-hander Fred (Fritz) Coumbe.

Coumbe had been with the Indians since 1915. He'd been a spot starter and reliever and was coming off his best season, 13–7 with an ERA of 3.00 in 1918. Coumbe managed to achieve those numbers while allowing more hits than innings pitched and walking more batters than he'd struck out. He'd pitch in just eight games for the Tribe in 1919, and his record was 1–0 as he walked to the mound to take the ball from Fohl. As had been the case the previous year, Coumbe in limited duty in 1919 had allowed more hits than innings pitched and walked more batters than he'd fanned. Nonetheless, he was Fohl's choice to pitch to the game's mightiest slugger with the bases loaded. Or did Fohl mistakenly think Coumbe was Speaker's choice?

Within the cozy confines of League Park, Speaker could be heard moaning, "No, no, not Coumbe!"[14] Heard by everyone except Fohl (and, presumably, Coumbe) Speaker didn't know if Fohl hadn't seen his signal for a right-hander, or possibly had misinterpreted it. Or, Fohl may have exercised his prerogative as manager to over-rule his center fielder and play the situation according to baseball's unwritten "book," which would call for a left-handed pitcher to face a left-handed batter. The confused Speaker considered asking for time and dashing to the dugout to confront Fohl, but deferred to the manager's judgment.

Coumbe's bread and butter pitch was a slow curve that Fohl may have felt would disrupt Ruth's timing. The first one did. O'Neill, noting that the pitch had been high in the strike zone and fearful that Ruth wouldn't be fooled again, rushed to the mound and reminded Coumbe to keep the ball down, in the dirt, if necessary. Walking Ruth would only have cut the Indians' lead to two runs, and Boston's main offensive weapon would've been disposed of. Speaker, meanwhile, heaved a sigh of relief. Maybe Fohl had been right.

Coumbe wound up and threw another slow curve. Ruth was ready, and, according to Edwards' game story in the next morning's newspaper, "the second ball Coumbe pitched, the colossus knocked out of the lot, over the right field screen, across Lexington

Fritz Coumbe wasn't a member of the 1920 Indians, and although he's shown here swinging a bat, it was the pitch he threw to Babe Ruth in a 1919 game that wound up on Lexington Avenue that led to Tris Speaker's elevation to manager.

Avenue, and nearly over the houses on the opposite side of that thoroughfare." Ruth's grand slam gave Boston an 8–7 lead that the shell-shocked Indians couldn't overcome in their half of the ninth inning. A certain victory had slipped away. It was the kind of game a team like the Indians, chasing a juggernaut like the White Sox, couldn't afford to lose.

Coumbe's final pitch as an Indian had cost his team a game. The aftermath, however, may have led to the final piece of the team's 1920 championship puzzle being put into place.

Speaker was summoned to Dunn's office shortly after the game. "Lee has resigned," he was told by the owner. "We want you to take over as manager." Speaker resisted at first, then agreed, provided the request came from Fohl. "I don't want him to think I asked for the job," Speaker told Dunn.[15] Fohl assured Speaker that he had resigned and wanted Speaker to accept the promotion. The Indians had a new manager.

Alva Bradley, one of the group known as "the millionaires" who owned the Indians from 1928 until 1946, was often quoted as saying, "I hire the manager. The public fires him." Cleveland became known as baseball's "graveyard of managers" during Bradley's stewardship. For the record, he hired five managers: Roger Peckinpaugh (twice), Walter Johnson, Steve O'Neill, Oscar Vitt, and Lou Boudreau. Fohl undoubtedly would've agreed with Bradley's claim that it was the fans who ran managers out of town, based on his comments in the *Plain Dealer* the day after his resignation.

"I have failed to win the confidence of the fans, although I have done my best to make the club a winner," Fohl was quoted as telling Dunn. "I want you and Cleveland to have a winner, but if the fans think you ought to have someone else running the team, I think I should step aside." The Indians had improved significantly and steadily under Fohl, although that improvement didn't begin until Dunn bought the team and acquired Speaker. Dunn insisted to the press and the fans that he didn't demand Fohl's resignation in the wake of the Coumbe/Ruth debacle, but according to Timothy Gay, he didn't waste any breath trying to talk the manager out of his decision.

"Owner Dunn and Fohl were apparently on the outs. Dunn had come to believe that Fohl had lost the respect of the players in the clubhouse,"[16] according to Gay, in which case Fohl's strategic gaffe may have given Dunn a graceful way to extricate himself from what was becoming an untenable situation. Fohl was a competent manager, calling the shots for Cleveland, the Browns and the Red Sox over an 11-year career. His 1922 St. Louis team established a franchise record for victories (93) and finished one game behind the pennant-winning Yankees. Fohl's lifetime record of 713–792 was dragged down by the fact that he spent his final three years in the dugout at Fenway Park, managing hopeless Red Sox teams which had traded all of their talent to the Yankees and received less in return than the natives who'd sold Manhattan Island to Peter Minuit.

Was Fohl a good enough manager to have led the Indians to a world's championship, as Speaker did? Or was Dunn correct about Fohl having lost the respect of his players? We'll never know. But any manager who could win 93 games and guide the woebegone Browns to within a single game of a pennant must've had something in terms of smarts.

Coumbe cried when he learned of Fohl's resignation and Speaker's promotion, and with good reason. Speaker's first decision as manager was to send Coumbe to the minor leagues. That was in keeping with the description of the new field boss by Edwards in the *Plain Dealer*. Though Edwards hadn't called for Fohl's scalp as the Indians continued to languish in second place, he felt the change would be beneficial.

"There is no doubt of Speaker being more aggressive than Fohl," Edwards wrote. "He is more of a fighter than his predecessor. Fohl is of the phlegmatic type. Speaker is an enthusiast. Fohl cannot be accused of not trying, but he is a more graceful loser than Speaker. Tris is as hard a loser as there is in the game." Edwards added that Speaker replayed defeats repeatedly in his head, searching for ways the outcome might have been reversed.

Despite being aggressive, Speaker said he had no plans for personnel changes, aside from dispatching Coumbe to the bush leagues. "Cleveland has a good ball club, and one that will win many games,"[17] he said. He was right. The Indians would win 40 of the 61 games they'd play with Speaker at the helm, but it wouldn't be good enough to catch a White Sox team that historians still rank among the best of all time. Cleveland trailed Chicago by five games when Speaker took over, slumped briefly and fell to fourth place, and then closed with a rush that included a ten-game winning streak ... after the issue had all but been decided. The Tribe's 84–55 record was good for its second straight second-place finish, but the three and a half game deficit behind the White Sox is slightly misleading. After losing two of three to the White Sox in Comiskey Park in early September, the Tribe limped out of town trailing by seven with 17 games remaining, and the deficit increased to eight games with just 16 to play when the Indians were rained out in New York while Chicago won its next two games. When the pennant was in doubt, the White Sox were firmly in control of the race. No one could have imagined at the time the disgrace that eight members of that team would bring to themselves and the sport in the weeks to come.

On the morning of the season's final day, Edwards told his readers where many of Cleveland's players planned to spend their off-seasons. Pitchers Ed Klepfer and George Uhle (a native Clevelander signed by the Tribe off the city's sandlots), shortstop Chapman, second baseman Wambsganss and outfielders Graney and Elmer Smith (from nearby Milan) would stay in town for the winter. Chapman's marriage to the daughter of a prominent Cleveland businessman (his manager and closest pal, Speaker, would serve as best man) promised to be the social event of the autumn season. Speaker planned to commute between his home in Hubbard, Texas, and Cleveland "preparing his team for 1920."

Had Edwards been psychic, he might have added, "as best he could." Or, maybe, "good luck." No one, with the possible exception of the father of psychology, Dr. Sigmund Freud, could have prepared the Indians for the journey that awaited them.

2

Way Down Yonder in New Orleans

Tris Speaker's biggest fan, Nancy Jane (Jenny) Speaker of Hubbard, Texas, confided to Henry Edwards in March of 1920 that "Tris did not want to be manager, but now that he has taken the position, he will leave nothing undone to be successful."[1] It was the only way Jenny Speaker's son knew how to play, and it was the only way he knew how to manage. And Jenny's mother's intuition told her that the Indians were on the verge of something big.

"Tris just can't go wrong this year, when he has a birthday on such a day as Easter, just ten days before the season opens,"[2] she told Edwards. Speaker would celebrate his 32nd birthday on April 4. Even a team with abundant talent such as the Indians could benefit from some positive omens.

Speaker's main concern, aside from pitching, which is every manager's main concern, involved when his full squad would assemble in New Orleans to begin working out the kinks following a long winter of doing whatever each player did to supplement his baseball salary. The era of professional sports as a full-time, year-round occupation would not arrive for decades. Although Jim Dunn was among baseball's more generous owners, three Tribe mainstays, catcher Steve O'Neill, jack-of-all-trades Joe Evans, and first baseman Joe Harris, hadn't agreed to contracts by March 2, when Speaker presided over the team's first workout. O'Neill's and Evans' holdouts weren't expected to last long, and they didn't. Baseball was vastly preferable to just about anything else a man could do to earn a living in 1920, to say nothing of being more lucrative.

Harris's salary demands were another matter, and the Indians prepared to replace the bat that had produced a .375 average in limited action in 1919. The Indians were hoping that Larry Gilbert could fill the void that would be created if Harris chose to sit out the season. They had obtained Gilbert during the winter but never dreamed that convincing him to sign a contract would be just as difficult as convincing Harris.

"Larry, as Cleveland fans well know, is the new acquisition to the Indians' outfield," wrote the Cleveland *News* on March 3. "He was sold to Cleveland by the New Orleans club during the off-season, but has been debating with himself whether to report to the 'big time' or ask to remain with the Pelicans and, incidentally, look after his oil business; his gasoline station being located close to Heineman park [the Pelicans' home field] and having proved very profitable to date."

Edwards described Gilbert as "the champion batsman, base runner and outfielder of the Southern Association."[3] Gilbert's .349 batting average had paced that minor league in 1919, and his contributions to the Pelicans' offense included 31 doubles, ten triples, five home runs and 42 stolen bases. Ed Bang, sports editor and baseball writer of the *News,* was even more effusive in his praise, calling Gilbert the "Tris Speaker of the minors."[4] The 28-year-old Gilbert had played in 117 games for the Boston Braves in 1914 and 1915, and reminded no one of Speaker, who was plying his trade nearby with the Red Sox. Gilbert contributed a .268 batting average and drove in 25 runs in 1914 as the Braves vaulted from last place in the National League on the Fourth of July to an improbable pennant and the first four-game sweep in World Series history as Boston overwhelmed the heavily favored Athletics. Gilbert played in just 45 games for the Braves in 1915, hitting .151, and had toiled in the minor leagues ever since.

Gilbert had pocketed $2,800 as his share of the World Series loot in 1914, and he said only the promise of cashing another sizable check in October could lure him to Cleveland. The effort to convince Gilbert to sign a contract became almost comical as spring training progressed, particularly for readers of the *News*. Edwards followed the saga closely. Ross Tenney, the Cleveland *Press*'s baseball writer and sports editor, treated Gilbert as an afterthought. As far as the *News* was concerned, Gilbert may as well have been the Holy Grail, and the Indians' pursuit of his services was treated accordingly.

Back home, anticipating a banner year based on the Tribe's 1919 showing, Dunn was studying plans to increase League Park's seating capacity. "Work will begin as soon as the weather will permit," the *Plain Dealer* reported. "The outside work will continue while the team plays at home. Work inside the park will be done while the club is on its first eastern trip and it is planned to have the additional 3,500 seats ready for spectators for the game Sunday, May 23."[5] It wouldn't be the only time that League Park would expand its seating capacity in 1920.

Speaker's primary concern was sorting out his pitching staff. He knew the Indians would generate plenty of offense, even if they failed to sign Gilbert. "Manager Speaker hopes to have all 14 of his pitchers ready to go nine innings when the season starts," Edwards reported. Fourteen was the total number of pitchers the Indians had in camp, though Speaker wouldn't be bringing that many hurlers north with him. In the current era of specialization, it isn't uncommon for a team to carry nearly that many pitchers on its 25-player roster at any given time.

"Speaker is counting on retaining eight or nine pitchers for the regular season and says every one of the 14 will receive a thorough trial,"[6] Edwards concluded. None of them received a thorough trial the day Edwards sent that report to Cleveland. Practice was cancelled due to 45 degree weather. When the cold weather persisted the next day, rather than scrubbing practice again, Speaker let the pitchers work on their batting skills. They'd need those skills since the designated hitter was still more than half a century into the future.

Every manager has his own ideas as to how a training camp should be run and the best methods to put his players into shape. Tenney told his readers about an innovation Speaker brought to his first camp in charge of the Indians. "The new game of elimination invented by Tris Speaker has been added to the daily training camp stunts, as it made such a big hit when tried out yesterday. The game is played with one player batting and the others in line fielding. Each drops out as he makes an error, and the last man to stick it out wins, just like the man who stays last in the old fashioned spelling bee."[7] Tenney didn't say who the last Tribesman standing was after the first round of "elimination."

Speaker's method seemed to lessen the monotony of spring training. And there would be plenty of monotony as the Indians would play just nine exhibition games, all of them against minor league clubs.

The Indians were plagued by unseasonable weather throughout the first week of camp. They managed to squeeze in their first exhibition game on March 7, defeating the New Orleans Pelicans, Gilbert's former team, 11–6. "The attendance at Sunday's Indians-Pelicans opener, while a little below normal, gave the teams a larger financial take than usual as it was the first game played here under the new Southern League prices, which are 75 cents in the grandstand and 40 cents in the bleachers," reported the *News*. "The crowd numbered about 2,000, which was considered splendid as it was the coldest March Sunday in many years."⁸ It was so cold that the following day's practice was cancelled by snow. "Yes, snow in New Orleans," Edwards told his readers. "Big flakes that turned into rain." Two days later, the temperature soared to a balmy 73 degrees, but the Tribe still couldn't practice because it was still raining.

With training camp in full swing, it was time for the "experts" to weigh in on the club's prospects for the upcoming season. The *Plain Dealer* ran a series of articles written by Philadelphia *Public Ledger* sports editor Robert Maxwell in which he assessed each team's strengths and weaknesses. Maxwell wrote about the Indians in glowing terms:

> The Cleveland ball club will start the season under a handicap. Tris Speaker and his athletes have been hoisted into first place by wise persons, and all they have to do between April 14th and October 3rd is live up to the advance notices. Loyal boosters of the tribe [sic] have won the pennant so often in the winter league they are confident the only thing between Cleveland and the American League flag is six months. That's a tough break for the fans, as six months is a long time to wait. If ever there was a favorite in the American League, Cleveland fills the bill this year. The team is loaded to the water's edge with high class playing talent, and it is difficult to point out the weak spots.

Maxwell went on to warn that "The best pitchers will be saved to be used against the men of Speaker and the opposing players will be on their toes. Nothing can be taken for granted and every game will be a hard one."

Maxwell's opinion of the defending champion White Sox wasn't as optimistic. "After winning a glorious victory in the American League last year and flopping so miserably in the World Series ... the Chicago White Sox are rehearsing [in Waco, Texas] for another shot at the pennant. However, the hose appear to be run down at the heels and out at the toes, and it will take considerable darning to make them presentable." The reason for Chicago's World Series flop wouldn't be known — at least by the public — for several months, although Maxwell alluded to it, apparently without realizing it.

"Chick Gandil, the stellar first baseman, and Swede Risberg, shortstop, are among the missing and not expected to return. Risberg refused to leave a profitable restaurant business on the coast, and Gandil has announced he will manage an independent ball club in Anthony, Idaho."⁹ Gandil and Risberg had been the masterminds behind the Black Sox. Risberg eventually left his profitable restaurant behind and rejoined the White Sox, but Gandil had to be replaced.

Billy Evans, an American League umpire in the summer and syndicated sportswriter in the winter whose daily column was carried by the *Plain Dealer*, disagreed with Maxwell about Chicago's chances of repeating. On April 11, Evans expressed the opinion that the White Sox would be contenders in 1920 as long as manager William (Kid) Gleason could maintain at least a semi-harmonious clubhouse.

"Many critics are giving little or no consideration to the Chicago White Sox," Evans told his readers. "Most of them figure the champions are slipping and will not figure as a contender. I don't agree with such an opinion, provided the proper spirit pervades the athletes. I think Chicago will be a dangerous contender if Kid Gleason is able to create a spirit of contentment on the club." Evans added that "differences over salaries have caused trouble" among the White Sox players. Charles Comiskey's penny-pinching had been responsible for the willingness of some of his players to listen to the overtures from gamblers seeking to fix the previous year's World Series.

Although Evans was aware of ill-feeling in the White Sox clubhouse, he wasn't aware of its true cause, or, like other baseball officials, he chose to ignore it. Asked in January of 1920 by a reader of his column if he placed any stock in rumors that the previous year's World Series had been fixed, Evans replied, "I regard reports that the recent series was not on the square as absurd. Cincinnati won because it played the better ball and deserved the victory. Convincing proofs must be presented to me before I would believe any Chicago player failed to give his best efforts."

Detroit manager Hughie Jennings added his own opinion. The *Press* quoted Jennings as saying, "Well, sir, if the Yankees don't win the pennant this year, I am a very sad guesser and [Yankee co-owner] Cap Huston is even a sadder one. With Ruth and the others, New York looks to have the strongest team in the league. I will say on paper the Yankees look to be a better club than the White Sox, and that right now Cleveland seems to be the only team likely to beat them."[10]

Speaker begged to differ with his Tiger counterpart. "Speaker doesn't agree with the [prognosticators] who pick New York's Yankees as the heaviest rivals of the Indians for the 1920 pennant," reported the *Press*. "Nor does he think the champion White Sox will give the Tribe the hardest battle. He looks for the heaviest opposition to come from either the Detroit Tigers or the St. Louis Browns." The *Press* quoted the Indians' manager directly as saying, "The Tigers and Browns have both the speed and the hitting ability and it looks to me like they ought to get some pretty fair pitching on both those teams."[11] Speaker made the comments before the White Sox had even reported to spring training.

"Kid Gleason figured the White Sox should get the latest start of any big league outfit down south," the *Press* noted. "He didn't set out for Dixie with his men until March 12th, way after every other bunch was into training work up to the neck. Gleason may have delayed the start in order to cover up as much as possible the glaring signs of discontent and dissatisfaction that makes the [prognosticators'] pick the White Sox for a big slump this season."[12] Baseball's powers-that-be may have hidden the fix of the 1919 World Series from the public, but there was no hiding it from the teammates of the perpetrators.

Dunn attended the Tribe's practice on March 19 and liked what he saw. "The squad as a whole is in better shape than I expected in view of the bad weather experienced this spring," he said. "The entire bunch is hustling, and with a hustling manager in charge, they ought to get somewhere. Everyone seemed to be full of pepper and gave me a severe attack of baseball fever. I can't wait now until the season opens, and I see the bunch winning a lot of games from the Browns, White Sox and Tigers."[13] Dunn didn't say how many games he thought his club would win from the Yankees, Red Sox, Athletics and Senators.

The owner had more to say later in the month. On March 29, beneath the *Plain Dealer* headline, "JIM DUNN DECLARES IT IS AN INDIAN YEAR," Sunny Jim gushed that "My recent trip to New Orleans was worthwhile simply for me to see the happy family way in which the boys are working. I never saw a training squad going at its work in such an enthusiastic way, and with such a start, I cannot see anything but success for the Indians. We think that we have the players. We know that we have harmony. Our hope is to bring the American League pennant of 1920 to the shores of Lake Erie."

Edwards polled the players as to which teams they felt would give them the most trouble. To a man, of course, they believed they would win the pennant, but 15 said the stiffest challenge would come from the Yankees, who'd finished third in 1919 and had acquired the game's premier slugger, Babe Ruth, from Boston during the winter. Ten players said that Detroit would give the Indians the most trouble. Four feared Chicago the most, and two were more concerned about St. Louis than the other contenders.

Last but not least, the professional gamblers needed to be heard from. The oddsmakers installed the Indians and Yankees as co-favorites at 5–2, followed closely by the White Sox at 4–1. In the National League, the Reds and New York Giants were prohibitive 2–1 favorites. The Brooklyn Dodgers were 12–1 longshots.

Although they played just six exhibition games against New Orleans, winning five, the Indians did more under the southern sun than work up a sweat taking batting, pitching, and fielding practice. When they weren't beating up on the Southern Association Pelicans, they took part in several spirited intra-squad games, including the annual "Righties versus Lefties" game, won by the right-handed players, 5–1, thanks to the stingy pitching of Stan Coveleskie and "Sarge" Jim Bagby. They would prove to be the club's ace hurlers, combining for 55 victories once the season began. The "Righties versus Lefties" game was apparently something the Indians did once each spring, and the Righties triumphed despite the presence of Speaker in the Lefties line-up. Even though it was just an intra-squad game, Edwards described the action as "not only hotly contested but ... replete with brilliant fielding." It also gave the Tribe's right-handed players bragging rights over their southpaw counterparts until the next spring.

In the meantime, the Gilbert saga dragged on past St. Patrick's Day. Ed Bang continued to insist that Gilbert would put his signature on a Cleveland contract sooner rather than later. He told his readers on March 23 that "Gilbert is sure to sign within a day or two, take a tip from us." Those who took that tip to a bookie, and bettors were known to wager on anything in those days, regretted it.

Three days later, under the headline, "GILBERT REFUSES TO PLAY," Bang mournfully reported Gilbert's decision. "I think the Indians have a wonderful chance to win the pennant and realize that it would mean about $5,000 extra to me," he quoted Gilbert as saying. "I like everybody connected with the club, but I can't see my way clear to join the club and run the risk of losing the business I have here. I have advised Speaker of my decision and hope Mr. Dunn can see his way clear to let me play with the New Orleans team. I believe the Cleveland and New Orleans clubs will be able to get together on the trade. I can protect my business while playing here. I could not do it if forced to move to Cleveland. Mr. Dunn treated me very kindly and I am sorry I could not join the ball club."[14]

Dunn granted Gilbert's wish and allowed him to return to the Pelicans. During that era, many a major leaguer who was unprepared for life after baseball scratched out a living pumping gas when his career was over. Gilbert chose to do it while he was still playing.

Dunn wasn't as charitable toward Harris, who immodestly proclaimed himself the best right-handed hitter in baseball (based on 176 career games) and demanded to be paid accordingly. "Harris arbitrarily put an exorbitant price on his services and refused to listen to reason," Dunn fumed. "If Harris wants to play in Cleveland, it will have to be at my terms. I have been more than fair with him, and he can take it or leave it."[15] Although contract negotiations would continue surreptitiously through mid-season, Harris would ultimately choose to leave it.

"Outside of his hitting," Bang noted, "we don't think the Indians will miss Harris very much. Johnston is a far better all around fielder and thrower." Harris had contributed one home run and 46 runs batted in to the Cleveland offense in 62 games the previous season, after missing part of the year holding out for a better contract, but Dunn and Speaker were satisfied that Doc Johnston could fill his shoes at first base.

As the Indians broke camp and headed north, the *Plain Dealer* declared, "SPOKE IS PLEASED WITH HIS HURLERS." "Spoke" was one of Speaker's nicknames, the other being "The Gray Eagle." The origin of "Spoke" varies according to which of Speaker's biographers is relating the tale, although both are similar. Timothy Gay says the name was hung on Speaker early in his career, when his teammates would taunt the opposition each time Speaker delivered at the plate by chanting, "Speaker spoke! Speaker spoke!"[16] Charles C. Alexander says the nickname may have originated with Speaker's teammates or with one of his managers in Boston, Bill Carrigan, who would exclaim that "Speaker has spoke!" when Tris got a hit in a clutch situation.[17] As for the origins of "The Gray Eagle," Gay says the nickname came about partly because Speaker's hair had turned prematurely gray, but also "in part because it described the aviary brilliance with which he presided over centerfield."[18]

According to Edwards, Speaker's pitchers had "shown him enough to warrant his believing that he will have the best pitching staff Cleveland has had in many years."[19] Coveleskie and Bagby would be counted on to anchor the staff. The 30-year-old Pennsylvania-born Coveleskie had broken into the major leagues with the Phillies in 1912. After winning two of three decisions that season, he didn't resurface until joining the Indians in 1916. Coveleskie had posted a record of 80–52 in a Tribe uniform heading into the 1920 campaign. He was one of the club's two designated spitball pitchers.

Bagby was a native of Georgia. His career paralleled that of Coveleskie in that both men were born in 1889 and had made their major league debuts in the same year. Bagby won two games and lost none in five appearances with Cincinnati in 1912, and then didn't pitch in the majors again until 1916, when he, too, signed with Cleveland. Bagby's record as a Tribesman was 73–56, and his 45 starts led the American League in 1918. Speaker needed big seasons from both Coveleskie and Bagby if the Indians were to hold off the Yankees and White Sox.

The Yankees, the favorite of just about every expert who didn't pick the Indians to grab the pennant, were having a less than spectacular spring. "Those Yankees, plus Babe Ruth, aren't setting anything on fire by their swatting down south," the *Press* noted as March drew to a close. "They have dropped four straight to the Dodgers, who are rated as a second division ball club in the National League. And they have hit very weakly against the Dodger hurlers, who don't compare to those the Yanks must face on the first division clubs in their own league."[20] Those same Dodger pitchers, from whom the *Press* expected so little, would wind up with the lowest team ERA in the major leagues in 1920.

The pitcher that the Indians would face in their home opener had some thoughts on handling Ruth and wasn't shy about sharing them. "I don't think Ruth will get as many homers this year," Allan Sothoron told reporters. "He's getting so much publicity that all the pitchers will be laying for him and he will find the pickings hard. I'll pass him when I can."[21] Discretion was clearly the better part of valor in Sothoron's mind. Ruth couldn't hammer pitches that he couldn't reach over distant walls.

With spring training winding down, anticipation bubbled over in Cleveland not only for the city's first pennant, but also for an all–Ohio World Series. Beneath the headline, "GOOD IDEA, PAT," the *Press* carried this tidbit: "On July 26th, an off day, the Cincinnati Reds will play an exhibition with the Cleveland Indians at Cleveland. [Reds manager] Pat Moran says he wants to get acquainted with the Cleveland ballpark, in preparation for the world series [sic] next fall."[22]

After the Indians won a pair of exhibition games from another Southern Association club, Memphis, and took the measure of Louisville to wrap up the spring schedule, the *Plain Dealer* tallied up the offensive numbers and declared, "TRIBE WEAK AT BAT IN EXHIBITION GAMES." The article expressed dismay that only six Tribesmen had hit .300 or better in the team's nine exhibitions. Joe Evans led the way at an even .500, followed by Speaker (.396); Elmer Smith (.383); Charley Jamieson (.367); Doc Johnston (.351); and Joe Wood (.333). Evans, Jamieson and Wood were all substitutes. Where was Larry Gilbert when the Indians needed him?

With spring training in the Tribe's rear view mirror, it was time for more predictions. No less of an authority than Hugh Fullerton, the Chicago sportswriter who suspected from the first pitch of the 1919 World Series that something was fishy in Cincinnati and worked tirelessly to prove it, thought 1920 would be the Indians' year.

"Cleveland!" Fullerton wrote in his syndicated column that was printed in the *News*. "At last, after five of the most crushing disappointments any team ever suffered, the Cleveland Indians rank high enough in the dope to win the American League pennant, even should ill luck that has followed them since they entered the league, run against them this season." Fullerton's intricate system for "doping" the pennant races forecast a second-place finish for New York, with Boston third. His system saw the White Sox coming in fourth. In the National League, Fullerton predicted a second consecutive pennant for the Reds, with Brooklyn sixth.[23]

One week before the opener, *Press* sportswriter Fred Turbeyville, who spent March making the rounds of major league training camps, made his predictions for the season ahead. "This year's world series [sic] looks like an exclusive buckeye affair. That is, the honor guests at the party probably will be picked from the two big towns in Ohio — Cleveland and Cincinnati. Someone else may horn in before the invitations are printed, but we doubt it."

Turbeyville was emphatic about his choice to win the American League championship. He assured his readers that "Only disaster can keep Cleveland away from a pennant this year."[24] Fullerton and Turbeyville were both right. Neither the "ill luck" that had plagued the Indians throughout their 20-year existence, nor the worst scandal in the sport's history, nor the unprecedented slugging of the man who would revolutionize the game, nor a tragedy of almost unimaginable proportions could keep the Indians from fulfilling their destiny.

3

They're Off!

If there was a bulletin board in the Indians' League Park clubhouse, Tris Speaker might have clipped a paragraph from Henry Edwards' opening day notes column and affixed it there for his charges to read, just in case they missed it during their perusal of the paper over breakfast that morning.

Edwards first noted that it was fortunate the opener had been scheduled for April 14 and not the day before, since an early spring chill most likely would've caused a postponement because "Jim Dunn thinks when the mercury goes below 40 it is too cold for baseball." The mercury didn't edge much above 40 on the day of the opener, but it rose enough to allow the festivities to proceed. Edwards declared that "the Indians are ready. The Browns are on edge. The fans have been training for months and are in the pink of condition." Speaker had chosen Stan Coveleskie, a 24-game winner in 1919, to pitch for the Tribe. Nonetheless, St. Louis manager Jimmy Burke, assessing for Edwards his team's chances in the season's first game, noted that "Sothoron ought to beat you fellows."[1] Allan Sothoron was the Browns' best pitcher and a 20-game winner the previous year. Burke's confidence in his ace was hardly misplaced as Sothoron's career record against the Indians was a sparkling 16–8.

Burke's comments seem odd today since most, if not all, managers would rather cut off their tongues than use them to give the opposition any extra incentive. Burke today would probably have praised both pitchers and told Edwards that the game figured to be a low scoring affair. But political correctness wasn't in vogue in 1920, and Burke told Edwards what was really on his mind. Besides, if the Indians, prohibitive favorites to, in the terminology of the day, "cop the championship," needed Burke to inspire them to win the opener in front of a packed house of pennant-starved fans, then Speaker had a problem.

Speaker didn't.

"BANDS BLARE WHILE FURS AND FIRES KEEP FANS FROM FREEZING," said the *Plain Dealer*'s headline. The Tribe made the discomfort worthwhile, jumping on Sothoron for four second-inning runs that allowed Coveleskie to coast to an easy 5–0 victory as 19,984 happy fans looked on. Sothoron's career record versus the Indians sagged to 16–9.

"Yesterday was the first time Cleveland fans ever have seen Allan Sothoron pitch without the aid of the freak stuff pitchers were allowed to use the past few seasons," the newspaper reported. "When he could doctor the horsehide, Sothoron was one of the greatest puzzles in the league. It was different yesterday. He was not permitted to shine or rough up the ball yesterday."

The new rules against "freak stuff" imposed by the owners after the 1919 season didn't apply to Coveleskie. The edict allowed each club to designate two pitchers who'd be permitted to use "freak" deliveries such as the spitball, which was Covey's stock-in-trade. He was one of the Tribe's designated spitball hurlers.

Sothoron's performance, in the opinion of the *Press*, was likely to have unexpected consequences. "A vigorous campaign to save the spitball in the big leagues for the hurlers who have been using it for years is being predicted," the newspaper reported. "The disappointing showing of Allan Sothoron of the St. Louis Browns, who was hammered to a 5 to 0 defeat by the Indians in the opening game here, is just one sample of the sort of thing that will start the reactionary crusade to amend the pitching code so as to allow existing spitballists to keep it up as long as they're in the big leagues." The newspaper proved to be prescient. Seventeen spitball specialists would be allowed to continue legally throwing the slimy pitch for the remainder of their major league careers beginning with the 1921 season.

For those who thought pitch counts were the invention of modern managers wary of overly exerting the valuable arms of their young hurlers, the News noted, on a sports page loaded with tidbits of information about the opener, that Coveleskie needed 104 pitches to vanquish the Browns, and Sothoron threw 133 pitches while being pounded by the Indians. The paper even broke down the pitch counts by inning:

Coveleskie: 16–12–10–16–14–7–9–8–12 for a total of 104.

Sothoron: 16–26–12–9–27–19–13–11 for a total of 133.

This information wasn't provided after every game. The opener was special.

Given the interest the supposedly pennant-bound Indians were expected to generate, the *Plain Dealer* informed its readers on the front page of its sports section on opening day that "because of the heavy demands on its telephone equipment, it will be impossible for the *Plain Dealer* to give baseball scores over the telephone." Many newspapers, in that era before radio broadcasts, provided scores by telephone to people who had no other way of finding out how their favorite team was faring. The *Press* and the *News* said nothing about making scores, even the score of the Indians' game, available for the price of a phone call.

Elsewhere in the American League, as far as expected contenders were concerned, the White Sox edged the Tigers, 3–2, starting Detroit on a downward spiral from which it wouldn't recover. In Philadelphia, the woeful Athletics posted a 3–1 victory over the Yankees. Connie Mack's pitchers held Babe Ruth in check in his regular season debut for the Yankees.

The Indians and Browns dodged raindrops on April 15 and 16. Both days' games were washed out. Before the scheduled game on the 16, Speaker addressed the "Stick to the Finish Club" at the Hotel Statler. "Blame me if we don't win the pennant," he told the die-hard fans. "I'm the boss of the club in reality as well as in name. President Dunn has placed no strings on my managerial powers. I can buy any player that I want if that player is for sale. I can release any player I desire. It's strictly up to me. If the team fails to come through, blame me. I think the Indians are the best team in baseball and I think they will win the pennant barring accidents. If we aren't on top in July, don't despair. Remember, pennants are won in October."[2]

"SPEAKER LOOKS TO KEEP UP NICE RUN OF VICTORIES," read the *Plain Dealer*'s headline the morning of the season's second game, twice postponed by rain. That "nice run" stood at a single victory, and that was where it ended as the Browns took the second and final game of the series, 5–4, pinning the loss on George Uhle, who couldn't hold an early two-run lead. The Indians tied the game in the seventh and lost the lead for good in the eighth. A ninth inning rally fell a run short. "ELMER SMITH SWATS BALL TO TOP OF FENCE IN NINTH, BUT CHAPPIE DIES AT PLATE," read the newspaper headline. "Chappie" was shortstop Ray Chapman, possibly the team's most popular player even with the presence of

Opposite: The 1920 Cleveland Indians. Several of the players pictured here (Boehling, Cycowski, Neu, Petty, Murchison, Grabfelder and Lambeth) were released or sent to the minors early in the season and contributed little or nothing to the pennant and World Series title.

Speaker. And the headline writer had no idea how chillingly prophetic those words would turn out to be.

Detroit visited League Park for a four-game series that was shortened to three by rain and cold weather. The Indians blasted the Tigers in the opener, 11–4, but needed heroics from reserve catcher Les Nunamaker to edge Detroit in the second contest. Nunamaker was in his second season with Cleveland, backing up Steve O'Neill. He played in only 26 games in 1919, ten of them as a pinch-hitter. O'Neill simply didn't miss many games, but when he did, Nunamaker filled in capably, batting .250 the previous season and .333 in 1920, when he spelled O'Neill only 17 times.

On that cold April afternoon, Speaker called on Nunamaker to bat for Charlie Jamieson in the seventh inning with the bases loaded and the Tribe trailing, 5–2. Nunamaker responded with a double that cleared the sacks and tied the game. It would be Nunamaker's only pinch-hit of the season. Bagby, who wasn't pitching one of his better games, singled Nunamaker home to give the Indians a lead that the pitcher couldn't hold. Detroit tied the score in the top of the ninth, and the Indians prevailed in the bottom half when O'Neill doubled home Nunamaker, who had stayed in the game to play first base, for a 7–6 victory.

The *Plain Dealer* described the third game of the series as a "weird struggle." Edwards noted that "the weather conditions were anything but favorable for baseball, and only a small crowd was present, but Spoke, a firm believer in the adage that it pays to get 'em while the getting is good, decided the game should be played as he preferred tackling the Tigers when their pitchers were not ready, than meeting them later with conditions possibly reversed."

Neither team's pitchers were ready for the cold, raw weather they had to perform in. The two clubs combined for 22 hits (13 by the Tribe), 18 walks, one hit batsman and 21 runs in a marathon that lasted three hours and four minutes. The Indians held a seemingly comfortable 11–5 lead heading into the eighth inning, only to let the Tigers score five runs on just one hit. Tribe pitchers, possibly unable to grip the cold and wet ball, walked six consecutive batters before Guy Morton was summoned from the bullpen to restore order with the bases loaded. Morton needed help himself in the ninth, loading the bases before Uhle got the last out and the Indians staggered to an 11–10 victory.

The last game of the series and the homestand was rained out even though, according to Edwards, the afternoon "was better adapted for baseball than any other day this month." Speaker and club president Ernest (Barney) Barnard called the contest after consulting with the weather bureau, which predicted the morning's rain would continue. Instead, the sky cleared and the angry Tigers accused Speaker of being afraid to face them a fourth time. Speaker dismissed the Detroit complaints as "bunk" and said that had the game been played, the Indians would've won.

The Tigers weren't alone in their dismay over the hasty postponement. "It was 11:00 when it was announced the contest would be postponed," Ed Bang wrote. "At the time the skies were overcast with clouds and it looked very much as if there would be considerable more of the damp stuff that had been falling almost constantly since the wee small hours of the morning. Then, too, the ground was soggy as a result of the heavy rainfall. It looked like all right judgment to call off the game.

"But fifteen minutes after the clouds broke in the west, and in another fifteen minutes Old Sol started to get on the job. It was not only possible to play, but it was a downright shame to think that the game was called off, especially since a contest was staged Tuesday when the weather conditions were a great deal worse. Why wouldn't it be a good plan to have a 'set time' for calling off games, say not earlier than 1:30? In that way, the Cleveland club officials would not only be protecting themselves against criticism and financial loss, but they would strike a responsive chord with local fans."

The Tribe concluded its first homestand of the season with a 4–1 record and three postponements. It was on to St. Louis to help the Browns open their home season. The Browns were convivial hosts and the Tribe cruised to an 11–3 victory. When the second game in St. Louis was postponed due to cold weather, Edwards took advantage of the unexpected day off to write a column praising the Tribe's veteran third baseman, Larry Gardner.

"Gardner is up to his old tricks," Edwards wrote. "He may not make as many hits as some of his fellow Indians, but he has a knack of inserting his safe blows when they will do the most good. It was Gardner who kept Cleveland in the race with his timely hitting a year ago, and it is the same veteran who is turning the trick this season." Gardner had played every inning of the Indians' 139 games in 1919, and through the first six games of 1920, he'd driven in nine runs.

Gardner was no stranger to the pressure of a pennant race, and no stranger to Speaker. The 34-year-old native of Enosburg Falls, Vermont, broke in with Speaker's Red Sox in 1908 and was the starting third baseman on Boston's 1912, 1915 and 1916 World Series champions. Gardner enjoyed a career year in 1920, establishing personal highs in at-bats (597), hits (185), doubles (31) and runs batted in (118) while playing in all 154 games, the second consecutive season in which the durable Gardner didn't miss a game. The Indians had acquired Gardner as much for his glove and his experience as his bat. All of those attributes proved invaluable as the 1920 season progressed.

Larry Gardner had a knack for winning. Gardner played third base for the 1912, 1915 and 1916 world champion Red Sox before coming to Cleveland (by way of the Athletics) to anchor the Indians' infield.

The Indians flattened the Browns, 10–1, in the second game of the series, but Sothoron had his revenge for his rough treatment in the Tribe's home opener, pitching the Browns to a 4–1 win in the final game. It was assumed Sothoron used only a variety of completely legal pitches as he improved his career mark against Cleveland to 17–9.

It was back to Cleveland after winning two of three in St. Louis, and waiting for the Indians at League Park were the league-leading White Sox, who'd won their first six games. "It is pretty nice to be in front with no defeats," Chicago manager Kid Gleason noted. Unlike Jimmy Burke, Gleason was careful not to say anything that might light a fire under the already hot Indians. The Browns weren't expected to contend (except by Speaker), so Burke had nothing to lose. Not so with Gleason.

"But we have not played Cleveland yet," Gleason continued. "It is Cleveland we must beat out to win the pennant again. If Spoke can show us a real lefthander, the Indians are going to be a tough team to down. And there are some other tough teams in the league. It is not going to be any picnic this season."[3] It was quite a diplomatic statement from the man who once pitched (winning 17 and losing nine) and played second base for the Orioles of the 1890s, a team that sneered at its opponents, and umpires, and everyone else.

The opening game of the early first place showdown was a pitchers duel between Coveleskie and Chicago's Urban (Red) Faber, one of the "Clean Sox." The Indians reached Faber for single runs in the sixth, eighth and ninth to win, 3–2, and hand the White Sox their first loss of the season. Chicago's second defeat was administered the next day. Speaker's lunging catch of a drive off the bat of "Shoeless" Joe Jackson, with two runners aboard in the seventh inning, protected the one-run lead the Tribe had taken with two runs in the sixth, and the Indians downed the Sox again, 5–4. Bagby picked up the victory.

Before the concluding game of the series, the *Press* reported that "Those Indians had the Indian sign on [Chicago pitcher] Lefty Williams last year. They knocked him out of the box on several occasions and were the only team that consistently got to him." The newspaper claimed that Williams rarely survived the second inning of his starts against the Tribe the previous year, and that "the Tribesman all figure they'll still have his number this season." Speaker's boys were said to be salivating at the prospect of teeing off against Williams and finishing a series sweep. Williams won 23 games for the White Sox in 1919, and a check of the game-by-game statistics shows that he started six times against the Indians. The two teams split those six games.

The crowd for the final game of the series was "the largest crowd that ever attended a game of baseball in Cleveland in April on any day other than Sunday," according to Edwards, who then neglected to mention the attendance in his game story. Newspaper box scores of the day didn't include attendance figures. However many people were in the League Park stands that day, they left disappointed, unless they were White Sox fans, as Williams notched one of the 22 victories he'd register on the year, holding the Indians to a pair of hits in a 6–1 win. Chicago moved back into second place by percentage points over the Indians. Both teams were one game behind the surprising Red Sox, who stormed out of the starting gate despite the fact they no longer had Ruth in their outfield. Williams, one of the Black Sox, would prove to be a thorn in the Tribe's side all season.

On another front, the editors of the *News* were less than pleased with the conduct of the fans during the series with the defending league champions.

Beneath a headline that read, "for shame, fans," the editors took the paying customers to task for their abominable behavior.

> To the shame of Cleveland fans, it must be said that they have taken up the practice of hooting opposing ball players without any provocation whatsoever. Truth be told, we doubt if there is ever an occasion that warrants the hooting of a rival player, and when the fans take it upon themselves to hoot and use cat calls at such high class players and gentlemen as Eddie Collins, George Weaver and Joe Jackson, it is time to call a halt.
>
> Collins, Weaver and Jackson are paid to give their best services to the Chicago club, and they are to be commended for their efforts in this direction. Instead of hooting them local fans, at least the fair-minded ones, should give them the applause that their excellent work merits. This trio was hooted frequently Tuesday when there was absolutely no call for it.
>
> We want to win the pennant as much as the next one, but we don't want to do it by bulldozing or rowdy tactics. Give the opposing player everything that is due him just as you do for the homeboys. Of course root, and that with all your might, for the Indians but do it in a gentlemanly high class way, one that will not reflect on Clevelanders as fair-minded ball fans. So let's tie the hooting and cat calling and jeering outside, fans. What do you think?

Ed Bang, who, as the paper's sports editor, probably had a hand in the editorial, took up the cause in his column a few days later.

> Cleveland is fast getting the reputation as being "the worst baseball city in the country." By that we do not mean that attendance is poor or that the team isn't coming up to expectations for the patronage is all that could possibly be hoped for when one considers the inclement weather conditions while the club itself is making a noise as if it is going to be in the pennant scramble right to the finish.
>
> It's the fair-minded angle we have in mind, fans! Visiting players regard Cleveland as just a little more unfair to the opponents of the home team than any other city. And umpires voice the same opinion. Instead of looking forward to their visits to this city, the Indians rivals and even the umps dread coming here. Why? Simply because there are a number of unthinking fans who boo, hoot and at times even hiss them. This condition should be remedied, and the issue is up to the fans themselves. Let's taboo the hooting and jeers altogether, fans. Give every player his due whether he is with Chicago, Detroit, Washington or any other city.

3. They're Off!

Bang stopped short of suggesting the "Stick to the Finish Club" should've rolled out the red carpet for visiting teams when their trains arrived in Cleveland and served them breakfast in bed at their hotels.

The loss to Chicago was the Indians' final game in April. On the morning of April 30, the American League standings looked like this:

Boston	9–2	.818	—
Chicago	7–2	.778	1
Cleveland	8–3	.727	1
St. Louis	5–4	.556	3
Washington	5–5	.500	3½
New York	4–6	.400	4½
Philadelphia	2–7	.222	6
Detroit	0–11	.000	9

It was taking the Yankees some time to adjust to the presence of their new star, Ruth. Gleason was managing to keep his team focused despite the animosity in the clubhouse between the Black Sox and "Clean Sox." No one expected Boston to stay in the first division, except the club's manager, Ed Barrow, and Hugh Fullerton. Barrow, who had to be badgered into putting Ruth in the outfield to take full advantage of his powerful bat and who had insisted Ruth would be "down on his knees, begging me to pitch" the first time he encountered a slump, talked to Edwards during spring training.

"Boston will show the league something for we have a great defensive team," Barrow told Edwards. "If our pitchers deliver ... we will win a lot of games because of our ability to nose other fellows out in small score battles."[4] Boston would have to learn how to win low scoring games since five starters from the 1918 World Series champions were gone, most notably Ruth. One month into the campaign, Barrow's assessment of his club had been right on the money. Barrow also had some comments about Ruth, without whose potent bat the Red Sox were learning to cope.

"Ruth smokes altogether too much for a batsman who hopes to continue at the top for a number of years. You know he is only 26 and has his best years before him. He smokes incessantly. He starts puffing when he rises and he will be found with a cigar between his teeth when he falls asleep."[5] Ruth did everything an athlete supposedly shouldn't. He smoked, drank, ate and enjoyed the company of women to excess, and still rewrote baseball's record book. Barrow was right about one thing — the Babe's best years were ahead of him, including the remaining months of 1920. Ruth wasn't fazed by his slow start for his new team and assured his fans in a short column carrying his byline that he'd pick up the pace soon enough. The column was carried in the *Press*.

"I haven't started hitting yet," Ruth admitted. "Last year I hit only .185 for the first two months of the season, but I finished with a satisfactory average, I believe." Ruth batted .322 in 1919. He'd soon emerge from his early season slump and start swinging the bat the way the Yankees expected him to. And that would be bad news for the Indians.

Ruth didn't write the weekly column that carried his name. It was composed by Marshall Hunt, a sportswriter for the New York *Daily News* whose regular assignment was to cover Ruth on a daily basis. Not the Yankees, just Ruth.[6] So fascinated was the public with Ruth that he became the first, and probably only, athlete in history to have a sportswriter assigned to report on his daily activities, at least those that could be printed in a family newspaper.

Completing the analysis of the season's first two weeks, no one foresaw Detroit's mystifying crash and burn (least of all Speaker), while the Indians were just one game out of the position they expected to occupy in early October.

The race was on.

4

All Aboard!

The Indians didn't spend the entire month of May riding Pullman cars from one end of the American League to the other, although it may have seemed that way to the players. Veterans were accustomed to the kind of odyssey the schedule maker arranged for the Indians. It started in Detroit on May 1 and ended in Washington on May 26. It included two single day stops in Cleveland. Five of the 23 scheduled contests were wiped out by rain, making long road trips later in the season even longer.

The journey began on a positive note, as the Indians swamped the Tigers at Navin Field, 9–3. The park at the corner of Michigan and Trumbull avenues had originally been called Bennett Park after Charley Bennett, a catcher for Detroit's National League club in the 1880s. The facility was almost completely rebuilt in 1912, when ballparks throughout the major leagues were being converted from wood to steel and concrete structures, as League Park had been in 1909, and re-christened Navin Field, in honor of the team's owner, Frank Navin. Several expansions and renovations later, the park's name was changed in 1938 to Briggs Stadium to honor Walter Briggs, who'd succeeded Navin as club president. In 1961, the name was changed one last time to Tiger Stadium, which it remained until the ballpark was closed after the 1999 season. The Indians would enjoy their three visits to Navin Field in 1920, particularly the final one.

A crowd of 20,000 was on hand to watch the drubbing, which the *Plain Dealer* praised as "a remarkable demonstration of loyalty to a club that has failed to win a single contest in a dozen starts." The victory was the Tribe's ninth, and among the reasons for the club's quick start was the work of the offense that the *Plain Dealer* had been so concerned about at the end of spring training. Weekly statistics printed in the paper on the first day of the month showed the Indians leading the league with a robust .309 team batting average. Individually, Doc Johnston's blistering .469 average tied him with Chicago's Joe Jackson for the league lead.

The man who'd lead the league in home runs, by a wide margin, slammed his first in a Yankee uniform on May 1 as New York shut out Boston, Ruth's former team, 6–0 at New York's Polo Grounds, the park that the Yanks shared with the Giants. The game account described Ruth's feat. "He drove a ball over the right field roof ... a feat done only twice before." Ruth had done it himself in 1919 as a visiting player, and Jackson had accomplished the feat while with Cleveland in 1913. It had taken Ruth awhile to get accustomed to his new surroundings, but there would be no stopping him now that his first home run was in the books.

The Indians kept Detroit winless on May 2, scoring three runs in the fifth inning to break a 1–1 tie and post a 5–2 victory, the win going to Jim Bagby. The Tigers dropped to 0–13. As all good things must come to an end, so must all bad things, and Detroit's season-opening losing streak finally ended on May 3. Two Tribe errors contributed to a 5–1 loss, charged to Guy Morton.

In the National League on May 3, the Boston Braves topped Brooklyn, 2–1, in 19 innings. It was miraculous that the Dodgers could even stand up, let alone play baseball, since the final inning of that marathon marked the 58th inning of baseball the club had played in 72 hours ... in two cities! In Boston on May 1, the Dodgers and Braves engaged in the longest game in major league history, a 26-inning, 1–1 deadlock in which both pitchers, Joe Oeschger of the Braves and Leon Cadore of the Dodgers, finished what they started. Mother Nature dropped the curtain on the proceedings with the arrival of nightfall.

The next day, the Dodgers lost to the Philadelphia Phillies, 4–3, in half the time they'd needed to tie the Braves, a mere 13 innings. Then, it was back on the train to meet the Braves again, the game ending in the 19th inning. The 58 frames played by the weary Dodgers shattered the previous record of 45 innings over three games set by the Pittsburgh Pirates in 1917. The Dodgers somehow summoned the strength to win the pennant in spite of the ordeal.

"If Elmer Myers remains in the American League the rest of his ball playing life," read the *Plain Dealer*'s account of the final game of the Detroit series, "it is doubtful he will ever lose a tougher game than that of this afternoon, which ended 2 to 1 in favor of the Tigers." Myers limited Detroit to three hits and led, 1–0, going to the bottom of the ninth before an error by Ray Chapman and an infield hit by Ty Cobb scored the tying and winning runs.

4. All Aboard!

The Indians rolled into Chicago looking to build on the success they'd enjoyed against the White Sox at League Park in late April. Henry Edwards didn't make the trip, nor did Ross Tenney or Ed Bang. Cleveland writers rarely traveled with the Indians. The *Plain Dealer* carried game stories written by Irving Vaughan of the Chicago *Tribune*. Describing the first game of a five-game set on May 5, Vaughn wrote that "in everything but fielding the Gleason crew had the best of the argument," but those lapses in fielding by Red Faber and left fielder Oscar (Happy) Felsch gave the Indians two gift runs in a 3–2 victory for Stan Coveleskie. Felsch was one of the Black Sox, and in light of what is known today, his misplays have to raise an eyebrow, considering that he was among the league's best defensive outfielders. Historians have never been able to prove or disprove accusations that the Black Sox continued tanking games during the 1920 season, and every misplay by one of the Black Sox arouses suspicion.

In the game on May 5, Faber's throwing error allowed the Indians to break a 1–1 tie, and Felsch's two-base error on Steve O'Neill's ninth inning single enabled the lead-footed Tribe catcher to motor all the way to third base. He scored an insurance run on Jack Graney's sacrifice fly that turned out to be crucial when the White Sox plated one in the ninth on Chapman's error.

"Helpless at bat and not much better in the field, Gleason's White Sox virtually handed the second game of the series to the Indians," wrote Vaughan of the game on May 6. The game that prompted that glowing assessment was a ten-inning, 3–2 Tribe victory secured when Chapman singled in O'Neill in the top of the tenth and Bagby pitched his way out of a bases loaded jam in the bottom of the inning by inducing Sox third baseman George (Buck) Weaver to bounce into a game-ending force play. The win moved the Indians past Chicago into second place behind Boston, which was still surprising everyone except Ed Barrow. Weaver was another one of the Black Sox. Although he possibly did nothing in the field to contribute to Chicago's World Series loss, and took no money from the gamblers, he knew of the fix but kept the knowledge to himself rather than snitch on his friends. He paid the price by being banned for life along with his seven incriminated Black Sox teammates.

Vaughan wasn't impressed by Bagby's performance. "Jim Bagby went the route against the Sox and got by more because of his support than because of his hurling cunning. The Gleason sluggers hammered any number of balls on the nose, but in most instances, they sailed right into the paws of hostile athletes." Vaughan was describing a typical Bagby outing. In 1920, Bagby led the league in victories (31), games pitched (48), games started (39), complete games (30), innings pitched (339.2) and hits allowed (338). He also walked 79 batters, meaning "the Sarge" was almost always surrounded by base runners. His 2.89 ERA indicates that he didn't let many of them score.

An aversion to retiring the side in order must have run in the Bagby family. Sarge's son, Jim Junior, pitched for the Tribe from 1941 through 1945. While winning 17 games in 1943, Jim Junior led the league with 273 innings pitched and 248 hits permitted. He also walked 80, meaning that there were base runners aplenty when the younger Bagby pitched, but his ERA of 3.10 shows that most of them stayed put. Like father, like son.

Also on May 6, the *Press*'s baseball notes column declared that "Hugh Jennings was so terribly tardy in winning a game for Detroit this season that the old stock rumor of 'Jennings out, Cobb in' is being revived and fanned about. Cobb is not the unanimous choice for Jennings' successor among the dopesters. They say now Cobb is the real manager of the club and that is as close as the players of the club would like him to get to it." Jennings, who would resign at the end of the season and hand the reins to Cobb, wasn't the American League's only beleaguered manager.

"In New York, Miller Huggins is having his troubles with the Yankees," the column continued. "He has the most expensive team in the league and one of the strongest on paper, yet the Yanks in action are a choice bunch of misfits. The colonel owners [Colonels Jacob Ruppert and Tillinghast Huston] aren't saying much but they must be thinking a lot."

The *News* wrote that "it begins to look as if Miller Huggins is going to have his trouble as manager of the New York team. There appear to be several would-be managers with the Yanks. During a recent game at Philadelphia, Huggins picked Sam Vick to bat in the pinch in the ninth, despite a demand on the bench for Lefty O'Doul. As if to bear out Huggins' good judgment, Vick worked the pitcher for a pass. The Yanks can't expect to win the pennant or even finish high in the race if they persist in 'butting in' on their manager. Huggins is paid $12,000 a year to direct the fortunes and decide these very questions for the Yanks. He cannot get very far if the players pull in the opposite direction. But that's what you must expect from a team of stars."[1]

Making Huggins' position shakier was the fact that Huston didn't want him managing the Yankees from the start. Ruppert hired Huggins while Huston was serving in Europe during the war, and Huston was furious when he learned that Ruppert had given Huggins the job. It didn't take long for the free-spirited Ruth, who towered over the 5'6" Huggins, to develop a dislike for the manager, as he did for anyone who tried to discipline him. He never hid his contempt for Huggins, derisively addressing him to his face as "the flea" and "the little boy."[2] Huggins never backed down from Ruth, and Ruth eventually came to respect Huggins, even serving as a pallbearer at his funeral in 1929. As for the Yankees having the American League's heftiest payroll, and a team of stars, some things never change.

Chicago's Lefty Williams, who stymied the Indians in Cleveland, did it again at Comiskey Park on May 7 as the White Sox won, 6–1. Four Chicago runs on five hits and two Tribe errors in the seventh inning led to the departure of Ray (Slim) Caldwell, who took the only loss the Indians suffered in the series.

The Tribe scored nine runs off Chicago starter Dickie Kerr and bounced the Sox, 10–6, on May 8. The 16-hit attack made for an easy afternoon for Myers, who allowed three runs in six and two thirds innings to notch the victory. Of the series finale on May 9, Vaughn wrote, "Careless in their fielding and not at all particular about making their base hits produce something, Gleason's White Sox lost to the Cleveland Indians again today, 4–3, before 28,000 co-horts. The Sox did enough swatting to win two ballgames, but they couldn't bunch their hits sufficiently to offset what the Speaker gang gathered on the strength of safe clouts mixed with the comical fielding of Chicago." One can't help but get the feeling that, in Vaughn's admittedly biased opinion, the Indians weren't winning these games. The White Sox were giving them away. By September, others would be suggesting the same thing.

Coveleskie took a shutout into the ninth inning, only to lose it on his own throwing error that allowed two runs. With the victory, the Indians moved into first place, a half game ahead of Boston and two ahead of Chicago. Nine games were in the books, and the road trip wasn't even half over.

Lee Fohl returned to League Park on May 9. While the team he once managed was in Chicago battling the White Sox, Fohl was calling the shots for Templar Motors of Cleveland's Class AAA amateur league. Templar lost to Young Furniture, 6–5, although the game story in the newspaper indicated that Templar could've won handily if Fohl had stuck with 37-year-old pitcher Glenn Liebhardt, who'd won 36 games for Cleveland from 1906 through 1909 and was still playing on the city's sandlots. Instead, Fohl decided to take a look at three young pitchers, and it cost him in his debut with Templar, just as a pitching decision had cost him in his last game with the Tribe. The account noted that "Judging from the audible signs, most of the 3,000 fans ... were pulling for the Templars, or rather for Fohl, and every decision against the former manager of the Indians was hooted."[3] This was somewhat surprising considering that Fohl had resigned because he was convinced the fans were against him.

Off days were more plentiful in 1920 than today because teams actually scheduled doubleheaders, although the owners usually didn't give the fans two games for the price of one, as they'd do in later years, and then stopped doing since the advent of free agency. Morning-afternoon twin-bills, with separate admissions to each game, were the rule rather than the exception in 1920, and they've returned to vogue in recent years thanks to the explosion in player salaries.

The schedule maker had given the Indians a day off on May 10 to travel from Chicago to Boston. However, since the Browns also weren't scheduled to play that day and found themselves in the general vicinity of Cleveland — well, somewhere in the Midwest, anyway — it was decided that a game washed out during St. Louis's first visit to Cleveland would be made up that afternoon. The one-game homestand gave fans a chance to enjoy a vintage Babgy performance. The Sarge "limited" the Browns to 15 hits as he went the distance in a 7–3 Tribe victory.

In his column May 10, if two and occasionally three short paragraphs can be considered a "column," Ruth revealed that he didn't know what to make of the Indians despite their fast break from the gate.

"I believe the Cleveland club will slip before long," the Babe wrote. "The Indians have to come east some of these days and then we will be able to tell with some accuracy whether the team has the strength it has shown since the season opened. Fans as a whole are looking to the west again this year in the American League, but I believe they are in for a surprise. The eastern teams have been strengthened while the western clubs have not."

Immediately after the victory over the Browns, the Indians lugged their bags, which they doubtless hadn't bothered to unpack, to the train station and departed to continue their road trip. They arrived in Boston at 1:45 on the afternoon of May 11th where they were scheduled to take on the Red Sox at three o'clock. Fortunately, there was no need for a police escort to get them to Fenway Park in time as the game had already been called off due to rain.

Writers for Boston newspapers took advantage of the postponement to interview Speaker and obtain his thoughts about the unfolding pennant chase. "This will be a better, tighter fought race than a year ago," Spoke said. "The players on all teams are in better condition, physically and mentally, to play tip-top ball than a year ago."[4] Speaker added that he expected the Tigers to rebound from their 0–13 start and claw their way back into the race, and that the defending champion White Sox, from whom the Indians had won six of eight meetings so far, would be even tougher than they'd been in 1919.

The rain relented, but only briefly, on May 12. The Tribe answered Boston's five-run fourth inning with a five run fifth and sloshed to a 9–7 victory, which the official scorer credited to the Tribe's starter, Caldwell, even though he was relieved in the fifth inning. Morton kept Boston from doing further damage until the ninth, when a two run rally was too little, too late. Then the skies opened up again and washed out the contests scheduled for May 13th and 14th.

Speaker was dismayed by the postponements of three of the four games in Boston. "Those postponements mean doubleheaders later, and maybe at a time when our pitching department will not be able to stand the extra strain." The inclement weather also caused a more immediate problem. "The trouble with the pitching staff now is that there is not enough work to keep them busy," he said as the Indians headed for New York and four games with the Yankees, "and when they lay off, they are likely to become wild."[5]

Speaker also talked about the pressure of great expectations. "They're figuring us as favorites for this pennant all around the circuit, and ordinarily you'd think that would make it all the harder for us. But I'm not looking at it that way. On the contrary, I'm glad they'll be set to battle us the hardest for they'll all be set for us to trim them and that very feeling will help us win ballgames just as our confidence in our ability to win those ballgames is going to win them for us. The other teams will all be on edge looking for us to break loose somewhere, and the very fact that they are in that state of mind will make them crack."[6] It sounded as if Speaker had added the duties of team psychologist to those of manager and centerfielder.

Coveleskie was sharp in the May 15th opener in New York, but 37-year-old Jack Quinn was sharper. Quinn, who would pitch in the major leagues until he was 49, blanked the Indians and hit an eighth-inning home run that accounted for the game's only runs as the Yankees won, 2–0. Each pitcher allowed four hits.

The largest crowd ever to squeeze into the Polo Grounds, larger than any drawn by the Giants, who'd been playing at the site since 1891, watched the Indians mow down the Yankees, 8–2, in the second game. The gathering of 38,600 eclipsed the previous record attendance of 38,281 for the first game of the 1911 World Series. An estimated 10,000 fans were turned away. The Indians knocked New York ace Carl Mays out of the game in the first inning, and Bagby cruised to a victory. Mays wasn't accustomed to being treated so rudely by the Indians. He'd won 12 of his first 14 career decisions against Cleveland. The first two games of the series had drawn 60,000 spectators, much to the disgust of New York Giants manager John McGraw, whose club had owned New York since McGraw arrived in July of 1902. McGraw chafed as the team that his Giants shared the Polo Grounds with gained rapidly in popularity.

While he and his teammates were getting their first look at the Indians, Ruth dismissed the White Sox as contenders in his May 17 column.

"Anyone who thinks the White Sox have a chance to win the American League pennant this year is entitled to the brown derby," Ruth said derisively. (A brown derby hat in those days was presented to someone who'd made a big mistake.) "They're shot to pieces in several places and haven't but three pitchers who can even come close to being called first string." It was a harsh, and inaccurate, assessment of Chicago's pitching staff.

"Cleveland cannot turn out a crowd of 38,000 such as was on hand Sunday when the Indians trounced the Yankees," Edwards noted in his column on May 18, "but it is expected 25,000 or more will be present at League Park Sunday when the tribe [sic] jumps from the east to play the Athletics. Ordinarily, the Athletics wouldn't draw such a crowd, but Cleveland fans are eager for another sight of the redskins, who have beaten all comers on their road trip. It is unfortunate that the new left field stand will not be completed in time for the game as it would add considerably to the seating capacity."

The Yankees did the trouncing in the third game. Bob Shawkey limited the Indians to three hits and New York won, 11–0. Coveleskie earned a series split in the finale, pitching a six-hit, 5–0 victory. In two starts against the Yankees, Coveleskie pitched 17 innings and allowed just two runs, but won only once.

The final game of the series in the Polo Grounds featured an odd occurrence that spiced up an otherwise dull afternoon for Yankee fans. "With Ruth gone from the line-up and Coveleskie throwing zeros, about the biggest excitement ... came when a lost soul wandered down from the stands and deposited himself in front of the Indians' dugout. Smiling but refusing to leave the field, the stranger left only from a push through the nearest exit by home plate umpire Brick Owens. So who was this mystery visitor? 'Probably a diamond salesman who has read in the papers that

4. All Aboard!

Cleveland is likely to be in the World Series' the *Times* figured. 'He wanted to sign them up.'"[7] Maybe so, but it was much too early for the Indians to be fitted for World Series rings.

According to the game account written by Robert Maxwell, the Philadelphia scribe who thought so highly of Cleveland's team in spring training, "a good time was had by all" at Shibe Park when the Indians opened a series against the Athletics with a 10–4 victory on May 20. Bagby was given some breathing room when the Tribe scored five times in the ninth inning. Maxwell didn't say why Philadelphians enjoyed the outcome. They may have appreciated good baseball on the part of the opposition since they didn't see it from the home teams. The Athletics lost 104 games in 1919 and would lose 106 more in 1920. A few blocks away, the National League Phillies weren't faring much better. The Phillies lost 90 games in 1919 and would lose 91 in 1920.

Caldwell's pitching and a three-run homer from Speaker led the Indians to a 9–4 triumph in the second game. Managing was easier when your center fielder hit home runs and caught every ball that didn't fly over the wall. The Philadelphia portion of the series concluded on May 22, when the Indians topped the Athletics, 4–1, and then came to the aid of besieged umpire George Hildebrand after the game. Outraged by two calls Hildebrand made favoring the Indians, which Maxwell described as "absolutely fair," fans ran onto the field after the final out and tried to block Hildebrand's path to the umpires' dressing room. According to Maxwell, "Tris Speaker jumped in front of the mob and held them back single-handed until the umpires left the field. Doc Johnston grabbed a bat and rushed to his assistance, and was followed by Chapman, Gardner, Wamby, Graney, and Wood. Then some of the Philadelphia players decided to take a hand, but the danger was over."

The fourth and final game of the series was played at League Park since Sunday baseball was prohibited in Pennsylvania in 1920. The Athletics, Phillies and Pirates wouldn't be allowed to play at home on the Sabbath until 1934. It was common practice for those teams to interrupt a homestand to hop on a train and play a Sunday contest on the road, as the Athletics did on May 23.

Much to the dismay of the large crowd that Edwards had predicted, the Athletics notched one of the 48 victories they'd achieve in 1920 on that Sunday afternoon. A rookie pitcher named Pat Martin held the Indians to five hits and bested Coveleskie, 2–1. The game was scoreless until the eighth, when Philadelphia reached Coveleskie for both of its runs. Martin did the rest. It was his only major league victory.

American League batting and pitching statistics printed in that Sunday's edition of the *Plain Dealer* showed that the Indians had dropped to third in the circuit with a .285 team average. Johnston still led individual batters with his .409 mark. None of that had intimidated Martin. His victory was the Athletics' first at League Park since August 1, 1918. Philadelphia failed to win a game in Cleveland in 1919. The Athletics didn't win many games anywhere in 1919, posting just 36 victories.

The Detroit to Chicago to Cleveland to Boston to New York to Philadelphia to Cleveland odyssey wasn't over yet. After the disappointing loss to the Athletics, the Indians headed east again for three games with the Washington Senators. It wasn't worth the trip. The first two games of the series were rained out. Washington scored four runs off Caldwell in the first inning of the third game, which was actually the first game, and won a 13–9 slugfest, tagging Caldwell and relievers Dick Niehaus and Morton for 17 hits. The loss, coupled with a Boston victory, dropped the Tribe into second place, a half game behind the Red Sox, who just couldn't be convinced that they weren't contenders. That was the bad news. The good news was this: the road trip, which took the Indians to every American League city except St. Louis, was over. When the Indians arrived in Cleveland, they could unpack their bags and stay awhile.

Before they arrived, however, there was the small matter of playing the Pirates in Pittsburgh on May 27. Unheard of today, exhibition games during the regular season, sometimes against minor league clubs and often against teams in the other league, were common in the early years of baseball. Club owners were more than willing to sacrifice off days in order to make a few extra dollars. The Pirates, who finished fourth in the National League in 1920, beat the Tribe, 4–2. One must wonder how much effort either team's players expended on these meaningless contests.

Joe Harris made the trip from nearby Franklin, Pennsylvania, to Pittsburgh to visit his former teammates. Ed Bang speculated that it may have meant Harris was ready to accept the Tribe's contract terms. Harris was not.

On the same day the Tribe tangled with the Pirates, Edwards opened his notes column thusly: "What's wrong with [second baseman Bill Wambsganss] Cleveland fans are asking? This is provoked by the frequency with which Wamby's name appears in the box score as having committed an error. As a usual thing, Wamby's errors are few and the fans scarcely can reconcile themselves to present conditions. Wamby's trouble is that he is not batting with his customary success at this time of the year. He generally is hitting around .300 and driving in his share of runs. This season he scarcely is hitting his weight and is not among the big men of the team. But once he hits his stride at the bat, his fielding will pick up as the two slumps go together."

Wambsganss, who celebrated his 26th birthday in spring training, was a native Clevelander who made his Indians debut during the 1914 season, when the club lost 102 games and was auditioning players to find someone, anyone, able to play at the big league level. Wambsganss played 36 games at shortstop, filling in for Chapman, who'd suffered an ankle injury, and four games at second base, in the absence of the man he'd replace on a full-time basis the following year, future Hall of Famer Napoleon Lajoie. It's never easy to succeed a legend, but Wambsganss acquitted himself well. He did so well, in fact, that Chapman reportedly once told him, "Bill, you're the only second baseman I'll ever play next to."[8] Wambsganss and Chapman formed the Tribe's keystone combination for the next six seasons. He was also a newspaper typesetter's worst nightmare, his name often appearing in box scores as "W'mb'g'ss," or some derivative thereof, or simply as "Wamby."

Bill Wambsganss was a product of Cleveland's sandlots who endured a sub-par season in 1920. He atoned for it with the only unassisted triple play in World Series history in game five.

Although Edwards claimed that Wambsganss' batting average was usually flirting with the .300 mark by Memorial Day, the statistics tell a different story. Wambsganss' career average was .259, and he exceeded .300 just once, when he batted a robust .352 for the Athletics in 1926, his final season, playing in just 54 games and coming to bat only 54 times.

Wambsganss was far from an automatic out, however, collecting 1,359 hits and driving in 519 runs during his 13 major league seasons. The 1920 campaign would be one of his least productive offensively.

If it seems like the Indians saw a lot of the White Sox early in the 1920 season, it's because they did. The Sox provided the opposition when the Tribe opened a homestand on May 28, and Cleveland won, 13–6. Chicago did manage to knock out Bagby in the fifth inning, after the Sarge was a little too generous with the base runners for Speaker's liking. In Bagby's defense, he hadn't been scheduled to pitch that afternoon. He took the mound amid a tragedy in the Tribe family.

"The flag at League Park flew at half mast in respect to Mrs. Stanley Coveleskie, who died at her home in Shamokin, Pennsylvania, yesterday morning," Edwards wrote in his game notes.* "Stanley, the Tribe's star pitcher, received the notice at noon. He had expected to pitch yesterday, but upon receiving the news made preparations to leave for home. Mrs. Coveleskie, who had been ill for nearly three years, was not thought to be in a critical condition and her death came as a great surprise to her husband. Covey expects to return to Cleveland later next week." Coveleskie either had nothing to say to reporters, or the reporters respected his situation and didn't burden him with questions, as there were no comments from him in any of Cleveland's newspapers.

Ever the pragmatist, Speaker was concerned about how the loss of his best pitcher would affect his club on the field. "It is a tough blow to lose Covey for a week just now, but it will give our pitchers the chance they have been looking for. Some of them have been sighing because they had few opportunities to work. They will have all the chance they want with Covey gone and two doubleheaders on our schedule a few days apart."9

The first of those doubleheaders was on May 29, and the Indians should have won both games. The Tribe led the opener, 7–3, after eight innings but allowed five ninth-inning runs, three scoring on bases loaded walks issued by Bagby, pitching in relief, as the White Sox squeezed out an 8–7 victory. Using starters in relief was common in that era, and Bagby was no stranger to that role. He pitched in nine games as a reliever in 1920, winning six and losing one. Caldwell salvaged the nightcap, scattering ten hits in an 8–1 victory and stroking three hits of his own.

The Indians won the series finale, 8–6, exploding for five runs in the seventh and two in the eighth after being held in check by Chicago's Eddie

---

*All of the game notes referenced are from the Cleveland *Plain Dealer*. Likewise, stories and statistics attributed to a wire service are from the *Associated Press*, which supplied the *Plain Dealer* with their news and sports wires.

Cicotte, another of the Black Sox, through six innings. The Indians had taken three of four from the White Sox in the latest encounter and nine of 12 during the season's first month and a half. The two teams would meet just ten more times over the remaining four months of the campaign.

On the morning of May 31, with the traditional Memorial Day doubleheaders on tap, the American League standings looked like this:

Cleveland	24–11	.686	—
Boston	21–13	.618	2½
New York	21–15	.583	3½
Washington	19–16	.543	5
Chicago	19–17	.528	5½
St. Louis	13–21	.382	10½
Philadelphia	12–24	.333	12½
Detroit	11–23	.324	12½

The Red Sox were hanging in, the Yankees were coming on, and the White Sox were fading after their fast start. For what it was worth, the White Sox were 3–9 versus the Indians and 16–8 against the rest of the league.

The Indians were just where they, and their fans, expected them to be, with Detroit in town for a holiday twinbill. With the pitching situation in disarray due to Coveleskie's absence, the *Plain Dealer* reported that "there is no telling whom Speaker will select for pitching duties. Chances are he will put three or four names in a hat and draw one in the morning and one in the afternoon."

If that was the method Spoke used to choose his starters, it worked. The Indians took a pair from the Tigers, who showed no signs of climbing back in the race as the Tribe manager had suggested they would, 9–5 and 7–3. The sweep gave the Indians a record of 18–8 for the month of May.

June, the club's perennial nemesis, awaited.

5

Summertime Blues

The poet T.S. Eliot referred to April as "the cruelest month." Eliot must not have been a baseball fan. At least not a fan of the Indians.

One of the enduring charms of all sports is that each new season begins with fans of every team hoping that the season about to unfold will bring a championship. In baseball, every team is a contender before the first pitch is thrown in April. Dashed hopes are always painful, but there's something inherently humane about a team crashing and burning right out of the starting gate, as the Tigers did in 1920. Detroit's atrocious 0–13 start told its fans that "1920 is going to be one of those years." False hope was extinguished early.

The Indians have experienced similar starts. Who among my generation of Tribe fans will ever forget the 1–15 disaster of 1969? And every team has teased its fans with a quick burst from the post, only to fall back to, and often behind, the pack long before the home stretch is reached, such as the Tribe's 14–1 break from the gate in 1966, or the 16–4 start of 1988. That's the kind of thing Clevelanders became accustomed to, particularly in the 1930s, when the Tribe would start fast and lead the league through April and May, only to fall victim to the dreaded "June swoon." Once all was said and done, the Indians were exposed as a good, but not great, team. They were good enough to win 80 to 85 games and finish far behind the accursed Yankees.

Though most of the Indians' June swoons were ahead of them in 1920, Robert Maxwell's allusion to the number of times the Tribe had won pennants during the off-season indicates it wasn't a completely unknown phenomenon. If the Indians were the best the American League had to offer, as the experts claimed, they could go a long way toward proving it by avoiding a June collapse, or even a slight stumble.

The Tribe opened the month by continuing the series it began so promisingly with a doubleheader sweep of Detroit on Memorial Day. The Tigers won the third game, hammering George Uhle with six second-inning runs. The Indians responded with seven in the sixth to close the gap to one run, but couldn't get any closer. The Tigers won, 11–10. Uhle's performance was quickly becoming a source of concern.

On June 1, Ruth started his first game as a pitcher for the Yankees. Displaying the kind of stuff that made him a star in Boston, Ruth held Washington in check until manager Huggins dismissed him for the day with New York holding a 12–2 lead in a game the Yankees eventually won, 14–7. It was New York's ninth straight victory. It had taken the Yankees a couple of weeks to get their act together, but they were now just 2½ games in back of the first-place Indians and closing fast.

Also on June 1, presidents Ban Johnson of the American League and John Heydler of the National League announced that major league players who had jumped their contracts to play for independent teams outside the umbrella of "organized" baseball would be permanently barred if they didn't return to their teams within five days. The ruling pertained specifically to players who'd joined the Franklin and Oil City, Pennsylvania, clubs in the Oil League.[1] Among them was Joe Harris, who was still holding out for more money than the Indians were willing to pay. With the Indians in first place and leading the league in hitting, Harris's bargaining position had weakened considerably. This was the era of the reserve clause, meaning, in the opinion of the owners, whose opinion was the only one that mattered, Harris was still considered to be Cleveland's property even though his contract had expired. The reserve clause bound Harris to the Indians for the 1920 season, if they still wanted him, which they did, though not badly enough to meet his demands, particularly with Doc Johnston hitting better than .300. Harris ignored Johnson's ultimatum and sat out the 1920 season. But he returned to the major leagues in 1922 with the Red Sox. So much for a lifetime ban.

While the Indians were beating Detroit, 8–5, on June 2, Ruth was swatting three homers in a doubleheader split with Washington. The roundtrippers gave the Babe 15 for the season. He hadn't hit a home run in April, yet was already more than half way to breaking the record of 29 he'd set in 1919 with four months left in the campaign.

Detroit won the finale of the five game set, 6–3, on June 3. In the following day's baseball notes column, the *Plain Dealer* expressed the opinion that "the Tigers are stepping along some for a team that dropped the first thirteen games of the season. On this trip they have won ten and lost nine, which is .526 ball. A team playing at that rate won't stick in the cellar position long." And the road trip wasn't over yet. The Tigers moved on to Chicago after leaving Cleveland. The newspaper would prove to be right about Detroit not being long for the American League basement, but only because Connie Mack had assembled another truly rotten club in Philadelphia.

The Browns followed Detroit to League Park and handed the Tribe a 7–6 loss on June 4, pinning the defeat on Bagby in front of a small gathering. "Cleveland fans, particularly the women, opined that yesterday's weather was too chilly and one of the smallest crowds of the season was present," observed the *Plain Dealer*. The fans who stayed home didn't miss much.

The Browns won the next day, 6–0, but there was one positive development. "Stanley Coveleskie has returned from Shamokin, Pennsylvania, whither he was called a week ago by the death of his wife. He worked out yesterday and will pitch one of this afternoon's games against the Browns," the *Plain Dealer* reported. Coveleskie understandably wasn't on top of his game and surrendered six runs in seven innings as St. Louis made it three straight over the Tribe, 6–2. Bagby prevailed in the nightcap, 2–1, to prevent a sweep.

The Browns left town with more than just three victories over the first-place Tribe. "Lee Fohl, former manager of the Indians and more recently manager of the Templar Motors class AAA team will leave here tomorrow night to join the St. Louis Browns as coach and possibly scout, manager Burke completing the deal yesterday," the *Plain Dealer* reported. "Fohl had intended to retire from the big show and liked his position with the Templar Motor Company, but Burke made him such a good offer that Lee felt he could not turn it down." Burke may have regretted that offer. Fohl took over as St. Louis's manager at the end of the 1920 season and guided the club to third-and second-place finishes the next two years. Fohl's 1922 St. Louis squad finished 93–61, a game out of first place and the only Browns team to post a .600 or better winning percentage.

Pittsburgh came to Cleveland for an exhibition game on June 7, and Speaker took advantage of the chance to get a look at a hotshot high school pitcher named Ted Odenwald. Speaker took a good long look at the fireballer, allowing him to pitch a complete game against the Pirates as the Indians won, 5–3. Odenwald allowed eight hits but disappointed the crowd by failing to live up to his reputation as a strikeout king. Not a single Pittsburgh player whiffed. In his final game for Hudson, Wisconsin, Odenwald had fanned 22 batters and swatted a pair of triples in a 2–1 victory. Nonetheless, Edwards was impressed. "Ted Odenwald, the eighteen year old high school pitcher of the Indians, has the makings. He is likely to be a real big league pitcher within a year or so. He has speed and a good curve ball." Edwards had more to say on the topic of pitching, particularly the rule banning the doctoring of the ball that took effect with the 1920 season. He wrote the following on June 8:

> The average baseball fan has to laugh when he recalls the drastic measures to reform baseball adopted at the February meeting of the big leagues, and how the powers that regulate the national game since put forth their efforts to modify those rules. A limit was placed on the number of spitball pitchers a team could carry. In the American League, each club was restricted to two and it was specified a club must name its spitters ten days before the season opened. Nothing was said about substituting one pitcher for another in mid-season or making a belated nomination. Yet we find Sothoron of St. Louis using the spitter today despite the fact St. Louis' original nominees were [Bert] Gallia and [Urban] Shocker. Gallia was later released, but the original rule had nothing in it that would allow Sothoron to be his successor.
>
> It is believed that before the season is over, the big leagues will withdraw the rule regarding freak deliveries that was supposed to do away with the shine ball and its brothers. The rule makers decreed no player would be allowed to rub on his clothing or even his gloved hand. During the St. Louis series just ended, Sothoron rubbed the ball with his glove while [Carl] Weilman persistently spat on his hand just before a new ball was thrown to him. Dutch Leonard repeatedly rubbed the ball on the leg of his trousers. In every instance, manager Speaker drew the attention of the umpires to the violation of the rule and received answers to lead him to think this particular rule ... was becoming a dead letter.

The rule against freak deliveries was not withdrawn, but would be amended to make allowances for the spitball after the 1920 season. Other freak deliveries such as the shine ball, a favorite of Chicago hurler Eddie Cicotte, would remain banned. As far as substitutions on the pitching menu were concerned, Edwards must have missed the memo from the league office. Some six weeks earlier, on April 21, the *Press* had noted that "president Ban Johnson announces that American League managers may substitute others for the two spitballers now permitted each team, provided they give five days notice of the change. The ruling grew out of the wish of the St. Louis Browns to substitute Allan Sothoron for Bert Gallia as their spitballer."

Ruth had a few thoughts for fans as the Yankees packed their bags and headed west. "The trip of the Yankees west naturally has brought up the question of whether I will be able to keep up the bombardment that has already given me 15 home runs. I believe I will. It isn't much of a shot over Cleveland's right field wall. Chicago is a hard place to hit home runs in, but I have done it and probably will again. St. Louis offers something a little easier again. When you're hitting them as hard as I have been, you get confident, and it's pretty hard to stop a man who steps to the plate believing he can smack one out of the park."[2]

The first western trip by the league's eastern clubs brought Philadelphia to Cleveland on June 8. The Athletics were just what the Indians, reeling after losing three of four to St. Louis, needed to cure what ailed them. The Tribe won the first game, 7–5, and the second, 6–1. Uhle's complete game victory over the visitors prompted Edwards to conclude that the native Clevelander's slump was over.

Edwards wrote the following in his game summary:

> He displayed the brand of pitching that caused him to win ten games in the American League last season. His work indicated he stands an excellent chance of holding down one of the regular berths along with Coveleskie, Bagby and Caldwell. Until yesterday, the big Cleveland boy had been a disappointment to manager Speaker. He had failed to win either of the games he started and had shown but little in most cases where he had been used as a relief hurler. He looked like a different hurler yesterday and his trial can be considered a good test as no matter what the faults of the Athletics may be, no one ever accused them of being weak with the stick.

If that was the case, someone wasn't paying attention. The A's would finish last in the league in scoring and team batting average. But a victory was a victory, and Uhle wasn't about to throw it back.

In that simpler era, Uhle wasn't the first Cleveland pitcher to make good after being discovered on a local sandlot diamond. In early August of 1902, Cleveland manager Bill Armour was so desperate for pitching that he asked the very same Henry Edwards to sound the call in his column for aspiring pitchers to show up for a tryout at League Park the next day. On consecutive days, August 5 and 6, Otto Hess (who showed up for the tryout) and Charlie Smith (who paid for a ticket to watch a game and was literally plucked out of the bleachers) pitched and won games for Cleveland. Hess survived a flurry of bunts from Washington batters looking to unnerve the raw rookie and won, 7–6. The next day, Smith, who signed a professional contract just minutes before taking the mound, held the eventual league champion Athletics to four runs and picked up the victory when the Bronchos scratched out a ninth inning run against future Hall of Famer Rube Waddell to win, 5–4.

Uhle's success far exceeded that of Hess and Smith, although Hess won 70 games (while losing 90) in the major leagues and Smith won 66 (against 87 defeats). Uhle won 200 games in his major league career, including records of 26–16 and 27–11 for the Indians in 1923 and 1926, respectively. After his performance against Philadelphia, Edwards was convinced he had the right stuff to be the Tribe's fourth starter.

On the same day Edwards wrote his glowing review of Uhle's work, a story from Cincinnati appeared on the front page of the *Plain Dealer*'s sports section. "The jury in the trial of Lee Magee, Cincinnati ballplayer, in his suit against the Chicago National League club for $9,500; returned a verdict for the defense. The jury deliberated about an hour.

George Uhle was signed off Cleveland's sandlots and won five games in 1920. Uhle posted 200 career victories, most of them in an Indians uniform.

"Magee, who formerly played with the Cincinnati, Brooklyn and Chicago Nationals and other major league clubs, charged he was released by the Chicago Nationals without just cause last February, thereby being deprived of earning a livelihood as a professional baseball player." When he took the stand in his own behalf, Magee told the jury that he'd bet on the Reds when he played for them in the first game of a doubleheader against the Braves on July 25, 1918. Magee claimed teammate Hal Chase, a notorious game fixer that baseball's establishment somehow never managed to get the goods on, largely because it barely tried, assured him the Braves' starting pitcher had been bribed and would throw the game to Cincinnati. The fix was foiled when Braves manager George Stallings switched starters.[3] The Magee court case wouldn't be the last time the word "fix" was heard in baseball in 1920.

The six runs the Indians scored in the fifth inning were more than Coveleskie needed to win the third game of the Philadelphia series, 7–2, and Bagby completed the sweep with a victory that Edwards described as "one of his rare games ... and the Athletics were folded away, 5–2. Bagby allowed the Philadelphians only four hits, and only once did the Mackmen even threaten." That concluded the undercard. Next came the homestand's main event.

"Probably the most crucial series at League Park since the halcyon days of 1908 when Nap Lajoie and his Naps lost the pennant to the Detroit Tigers by a half game, or surely since 1913 when the Naps made a game fight to land the flag," wrote Ed Bang of the visit from the Yankees.

"Babe Ruth and his home run hitting colleagues will be here today, tomorrow, Monday and Tuesday," said the *Plain Dealer* on June 12. "On the result of the four game series depends the possession of first place in the American League, for the time being at any rate. The Yankees come here half a game behind the Indians. They came up from far in the rear, passing St. Louis, Washington, Chicago and Boston. They have made their advance by some of the most wonderful hitting in the history of the game, having bombarded pitchers at Fenway Park, the Polo Grounds and Navin Field with scores of doubles, triples and home runs in the last three weeks."

The *Press* had a warning for its readers. Sounding a lot like the editors of the *News*, under the headline "No Bad Actors," the paper said, "It's hoped there'll be no repetition of ill-bred and uncalled for booing in this series when Babe Ruth steps up to the plate. A few fans did this without any excuse whatever when Joe Jackson was here early this season with the White Sox. Jackson merely answered them by pounding the ball all over the lot and making life miserable for Indian hurlers. So let's shut up anybody who tries to boo or jeer Babe Ruth. He's one of the greatest players in the history of baseball and as such should be greeted with cheers instead of jeers." The civility of Cleveland's sportswriters in 1920 was overwhelming.

Ray Caldwell got the four-game showdown for first place off to a good start, holding Ruth hitless and winning, 5–4. "On their toes every second, the redskins battled harder than at any previous time this year," Edwards wrote, adding "the crowd numbered but 20,000." The Indians led New York by 1½ games.

The weekly major league statistics published on Sunday, June 13, showed the Indians on top of the league with a .304 team batting average. The two best offensive clubs in the circuit would be on display at League Park that afternoon.

"What Wellington did to Napoleon at the well-known Waterloo, what the allies did to the Germans at the Argonne, what Jack Dempsey did to Jess Willard at Toledo — that's what the Yankees did to the Indians at League Park yesterday when they routed the redskins, 14 to 0," began Edwards' mournful game summary. "Fourteen to nothing. That's correct. Some walloping the runners-up handed the league leaders, and to make it worse, it was in front of the largest crowd that ever paid to witness a ball game in our bustling city."

A crowd of 29,266 watched as New York torched Uhle, who retired just one batter in the first inning. Apparently shutting down the woebegone Athletics hadn't been such a big deal after all. It was the kind of game that Yankee owner Jacob Ruppert enjoyed, as the Yanks scored six in the first and then steadily pulled away. Ruppert admitted to enjoying ten-run first-inning outbursts, but he probably wasn't inclined to be greedy on that particular afternoon. Ruth put an exclamation point on the mauling, hammering his 17th homer in the sixth inning, a blast off Elmer Myers described as "clearing the right field screen, the ball crossing the street and dropping behind a house on the opposite side."[4] Ruth didn't hit many cheapies.

The Indians failed to score despite stroking a dozen hits. Their lead over New York was again down to a slim half game.

That night, Tribe catcher Steve O'Neill was recovering from the debacle at the home of boxer Johnny Kilbane. Two days earlier, O'Neill's wife, May, had given birth to twins. Today, athletes are expected to leave their clubs to be at the side of their wives for such events, but not in 1920. O'Neill had been assured that mother and children were doing just fine. However, a telegram arrived at Kilbane's home with the message "May worse. Nothing serious but come at once."[5] Undoubtedly recalling that Coveleskie's wife wasn't believed to be seriously ill, O'Neill left for his home in Pennsylvania without even packing a suitcase. The problem proved to be, as the telegram said, nothing serious. O'Neill was back behind the plate within days.

O'Neill was a Tribe veteran, having played his first game in a Cleveland uniform in 1911. He'd suffered through the miserable 1914 and 1915 seasons when the Indians lost a combined 197 games. When Dunn purchased the club and began the rebuilding process in 1916, he, Speaker, and

Steve O'Neill enjoyed a career year in 1920. He was behind the plate in all but five of Cleveland's 154 games.

Fohl quickly determined O'Neill to be a keeper and one of the players they'd build around. O'Neill enjoyed his best season in 1920, catching in 149 games and setting career highs in batting average (.321), at-bats (489), hits (157), doubles (39) and runs batted in (55). With O'Neill behind the plate, Wambsganss and Chapman in the middle of the infield, and Speaker patrolling center field, the Tribe's up-the-middle defense was the envy of the league.

The Indians were nothing if not resilient. Shaking off the previous day's shellacking, they turned to Coveleskie to restore order. He limited the Yankees to five hits and the Tribe won, 7–1. The lead was again 1½ games. It expanded to 2½ the next day.

"Our own little June World Series came to an end yesterday when the Indians made it three out of four from the Yankees by winning 10 to 2," Edwards wrote on June 16. "It was a cinch for the redskins as Jim Bagby was in "splendid form" and Cleveland fans know what that means." In this case, splendid form meant a complete game seven-hitter with five strikeouts. The Tribe made things easy for the Sarge with a five-spot in the fifth inning. After the game, Bagby praised Les Nunamaker, who was filling in for O'Neill, and Nunamaker praised Bagby.

"Jim had wonderful control and could put every ball just where I wanted him to," Nunamaker said. "Les called a beautiful game," Bagby commented.

The series result was typical and magnified the Tribe's one weakness. The three victories were achieved by Coveleskie, Bagby and Caldwell, who would rack up 75 wins among them. The fourth starter, Uhle, had been hammered. Speaker needed someone to step up and pitch well on the days Coveleskie, Bagby and Caldwell were resting. The likely candidates were Uhle and Elmer Myers, but both had been remarkably inconsistent. Since it was 1920 and not 1902, Speaker wasn't going to drag any amateurs out of the stands or ask Edwards to run an advertisement for pitchers in his notes column.

The sun shone brightly on the afternoon of June 16, when the Indians were scheduled to continue their homestand against Washington. However, a morning downpour had left the League Park diamond unplayable, and the game was postponed. So was the game scheduled for June 17, when the rains came again. That meant that four of the five scheduled games between the Tribe and Senators had been washed out thus far, and "that means doubleheaders when the tribe goes east and when Washington returns here. No doubleheaders are played on a club's first trip to a city," according to the *Plain Dealer.* Like any manager, Speaker hated the prospect of a weary pitching staff being overextended by doubleheaders in the second half of the season, especially when the pennant race figured to be nip and tuck all the way. While the Indians were at the mercy of the weather, the Yankees were beating the White Sox twice in Chicago, reducing Cleveland's lead to one game.

When the skies cleared and League Park dried out, the Indians dusted the Senators and their ace pitcher, Walter Johnson, on June 18. "Even Walter Johnson was unable to stop the Indians yesterday," wrote Edwards. "The tribe knocked the speed king from the box and won, 9–2. Cleveland has driven the speed king from the box before, but that was years ago." Caldwell allowed Washington seven hits in picking up his eighth win.

The Senators jumped on Coveleskie for three early runs and won the second and final game of the abbreviated series, 5–1. Washington pitcher Olaf Erickson walked six Indians and hit a batter but surrendered just four hits.

As part of their pitching plan, the Indians sent their rookie phenom, Odenwald, to the Des Moines, Iowa, minor league club on June 20. "Tris expects that Odenwald will be back, for the Wisconsin high school boy did so well in the game with Pittsburg [Pittsburgh was spelled without the "h" on the end in those days] that Spoke believes he will be able to deliver in the big show after he has had some minor league experience," said the *Plain Dealer*. Odenwald did return to Cleveland, in 1921. He delivered exactly one victory in "the big show."

On offense, the weekly statistics published on Sunday, June 20, showed the Indians still leading the league with a .308 team batting mark. However, the two rainouts cost them the league lead in runs scored. The Yankees held first place in that category.

"To avoid disappointing some 4,000 fans who preferred visiting League Park, despite the rain and cold, to remaining inside where it was warm and dry, the Indians played an alleged game of ball with Boston yesterday," Edwards wrote of the first game of the series with the Red Sox that would close out a homestand of almost a month's duration.

"They lost it, 10 to 9. It may have been June 20th, but there was no other excuse for playing unless the management thought Boston would be easy picking." That was a possibility, since the Red Sox had begun performing as they'd been expected to perform and had fallen from first place after their surprising start. On this day, however, Bagby couldn't hold a 6–1 lead and proved himself, in the opinion of the *Plain Dealer*'s sports headline writer, not to be "a winter pitcher." That must've been a very cold June afternoon, made colder by the loss of a game that should've been won handily.

Game two of the set with Boston was the Tribe's first of the 1920 season to require extra innings. "It was one of those rare birds in the American League," said Edwards' game summary. "A pitcher's battle. In view of recent contests in which the opposing teams scored anywhere from fifteen to twenty runs, Cleveland fans had acquired a belief that the model for such a game had been thrown away." The Indians prevailed, 3–2, when O'Neill led off the 12th inning with a double, was sacrificed to third by George Burns, who was batting for Guy Morton, and scored on a single by Charlie Jamieson. Uhle redeemed himself after his miserable outing against New York by pitching the first ten innings and holding the Red Sox to a pair of runs.

The third game was one of those contests where the opposing team scored in droves from 15 to 20 runs. Eighteen runs to be exact, with the Indians coming out on top, 13–5. Caldwell benefited from a five-run fourth inning and a four-run fifth inning. He won his ninth game despite allowing 12 hits.

"Today's contest," noted the *Plain Dealer* on June 23, "will be the last game for the Indians at home until July 26th when the Cincinnati Reds, the world's champions, play an exhibition contest here. In the meantime, the Indians will visit every other city in the league once and Chicago twice." That was only fair since every team in the league had visited Cleveland during the Tribe's homestand.

Edwards raved about the game that was played at League Park on that June afternoon. "As a game replete with thrills, it has had few equals this season," said the scribe's game story. "There have been many better games, but none that could provide more excitement and keep fans on the anxious seat for so long. It was won by Cleveland because the Tribe played the same desperate nervy game it has displayed all season, fighting it out every inning when the outlook was gloomiest." Boston reached Bagby for three runs in the ninth inning to take a 6–3 lead. The Indians tied the game in their half of the ninth and won it in the 14th on consecutive singles by Chapman, Speaker and Elmer Smith. Bagby righted himself after his rocky ninth inning and picked up the victory.

The Indians had prevailed in 18 of the 27 games on their homestand. They left on a road odyssey, which would take them to every city in the American League, with 1½ game lead on the Yankees. Coming up steadily behind New York were the resurgent White Sox. As fate would have it, the first stop on the Tribe's trip was Comiskey Park.

The first game was a landmark occasion. "When Ray Chapman, the Indians' up and doing shortstop, lined up in Chicago with his teammates Friday for the first game of the series with the White Sox, it was Chappie's 1,000th game as a member of the local American League team," noted the *News*. "This makes him the veteran of all the Cleveland players in point of service. Few and far between are the players who have participated in 1,000 games as a member of the Cleveland team." To be precise, only infielder Terry Turner (1,645 games from 1904–18), Nap Lajoie (1,615 games from 1902–14), and third baseman Bill Bradley (1,231 games from 1901–10) had played more games in a Cleveland uniform than Chapman.

Despite having their ace ... and Coveleskie was the staff's ace even though Bagby would win more games — on the mound in the first game, the Tribe lost, 6–3. The Sox grabbed the second game, 12–7, chasing Caldwell with a seven-run third inning uprising. The wire service dispatch sent to the *Plain Dealer* noted that "five of the Cleveland runs were made in the last two innings when the Sox were so far ahead there was no chance of Cleveland winning." The Yankees clobbered Boston, 14-0, that day to inch to within a half game of first place. The White Sox were four games back with a chance to cut the deficit to three before the Indians moved on to St. Louis.

On June 25, the *Press* noted that "the Oil City team has cancelled its remaining schedule of eight games with the Franklin team, claiming the fans were too abusive in their language." The Oil League brethren were only about ten miles apart and had apparently developed a rivalry every bit as heated as that of the Dodgers and Giants in the National League. It was too heated for Oil City's liking. Among Franklin's players was former Tribe first baseman Joe Harris, who'd visit Cleveland twice in July. The second visit would be another strange chapter in a season filled with such developments.

On the final Sunday of the month, the weekly statistics showed that the Indians had raised their league-leading team batting average to a healthy .310, but they'd have gladly traded that honor for raising their lead in the standings. They escaped Chicago with one victory as Bagby held off the White Sox, 4-1, on June 27. The Sarge kept Chicago off the scoreboard until the ninth inning. The Yankees won again, but the White Sox had slipped five games behind.

The local scribes hadn't made the trip west, so Clevelanders were forced to make do with wire service reports of their club's exploits on the road, such as this one, filed by an imaginative correspondent after the Tribe beat the Browns on June 28. "Cleveland's dynamo, Tris Speaker, Stanley Coveleskie and Elmer Smith generated enough force and resisting power to charge the Indians' motor with one more victorious whirl toward Pennantville, the 7 to 4 victory over the Browns sending the Fifth City boys another half game ahead of the Yankee machine." A few days earlier, figures from the U.S. Census Bureau gave Cleveland a population of just over 796,000, making it the fifth most populous city in the nation, hence the "Fifth City boys" reference.

On that same afternoon, Philadelphia snapped a monumental 18-game losing streak with a 6-2 win over Washington. The Athletics were already 25 games out of first place, and July was still a few days away. When Connie Mack fielded a loser, he didn't fool around.

The Indians extended their winning streak to four on June 29, sweeping a twinbill from the Browns, 9-6 and 5-4. Caldwell won the first game and Morton the second.

On the morning of June 30, with just one day and one game remaining in the month that had often been, and would again be many times in the future, the Tribe's downfall, the American League standings looked like this:

Cleveland	43–21	.672	—
New York	42–23	.646	1½
Chicago	37–26	.587	5½
Washington	31–27	.534	9
Boston	29–30	.492	11½
St. Louis	30–34	.469	13
Detroit	21–42	.333	21½
Philadelphia	17–47	.266	26

The Tribe lost to the Browns, 10–8, to close out the month but maintained its tenuous hold on first place. The Indians hadn't run away and hidden from the rest of the league, but there had been no June swoon. Their 17–11 record had kept them ahead of the competition, if only barely. Barely was all that was required.

6

And Then There Were Three

The Indians enjoyed an off day on July 1, their enforced idleness costing them sole possession of first place. While the Tribe rested and prepared for three games with the Tigers at Navin Field, the Yankees beat Philadelphia to move into a first-place deadlock with Cleveland. The two clubs had different records but identical .662 winning percentages.

They remained tied after the activities of July 2. With Stan Coveleskie on the mound, the Indians trounced Detroit, 10–3. The newspaper dispatch indicated that Tris Speaker was the recipient of several rousing ovations during the contest. "Speaker was cheered every time he came to bat," the *Plain Dealer* reported. "Detroit fans would like to see Tris lead a pennant winner."

The Tigers did their part to make that happen, dropping all three games to the Tribe. The middle contest, a 6–3 Cleveland victory, featured a dazzling catch by Speaker on a ball hit by Tiger outfielder Bobby Veach. According to the game story in the *Plain Dealer*, "with one down in the sixth, Robert laid his club against the ball with great force. No one in the stands believed it possible for Speaker to get near the ball, to say nothing of making the catch. But Tris ran like a deer, wheeled around, threw out his gloved hand and hauled the horsehide down." Bagby did the rest, but it wasn't enough to keep the Indians from slipping into second place as the Yankees took two games from Philadelphia. The Tribe trailed New York by four percentage points.

The Indians completed the series sweep with an 11–3 win on the Fourth of July, scoring four runs in the eighth and four more in the ninth after the game had been knotted at three apiece. Coveleskie replaced Guy Morton in the seventh and was the beneficiary of the late inning offensive explosion. Coveleskie himself was a contributor, hammering a triple in the ninth inning that drove in Larry Gardner with an unnecessary insurance run. "Coveleskie would have made a home run if he had not loafed on his long drive to the center field bleachers," reported the newspaper game notes. "Stanley figured there was nothing at stake and jogged around to third." Speaker undoubtedly was more concerned about Coveleskie retiring the Tigers in the home half of the ninth than legging out an inside the park home run in a game that had degenerated into a rout. The victory, coupled with Washington's win over the Yankees, put the Indians back in first place by percentage points. The two teams (and eventually the White Sox, once they clawed their way back into contention) would often be separated by such a slim margin as the season wore on.

A quirk in the schedule had the Indians returning to Chicago, where they'd started their trip, for a three-game series that opened with a doubleheader on July 5. They had less luck during their second visit to Comiskey Park. The White Sox took both ends of the twinbill, 5–3 and 6–5. The nightcap loss was a particularly bitter pill for Speaker's boys to swallow. After their nemesis, Lefty Williams, out-pitched Caldwell in the first game, Coveleskie matched up with Dickie Kerr in the second and took a 5–0 lead into the eighth inning. According to the *Plain Dealer*'s game story, picked up from a wire service, "Coveleskie looked absolutely unbeatable and the 21,000 patrons saw little to celebrate. Then the Gleasonites unloosed the pyrotechnics. Falling desperately on Covey, who had suppressed them with an allowance of two blows in the first seven stanzas while facing only twenty-three batters, the Sox unbuckled a tremendous rally. Eleven White Hose hitters paraded to the plate and eight delivered resounding drives, six runners crossing the plate. The last tally put the Gleasonites on top. Spoke had four flingers toiling in the bullpen throughout the slaughter of his mighty spitball pitcher but for some mysterious reason declined to summon a relief slabbist."

The stunned Indians didn't rally in the ninth. Fortunately, the Yankees lost a doubleheader to Washington the same day. The second game of the morning-afternoon twinbill drew the largest crowd ever to watch a baseball game at Washington's Griffith Stadium. Ruth had quickly become baseball's biggest drawing card.

The day after the Indians doubled their displeasure in Chicago, Henry Edwards used his notes column to laud the work done by Tribe outfielder Joe Evans.

> It was lucky for Cleveland that Tris Speaker knew of Joe Evans' playing ability and declined to let him go to Detroit

when the Tiger management was willing to make what appeared to be an advantageous trade. Spoke, however, turned a deaf ear to any trade that included Evans.

That Spoke is a wise old bird is shown by the fact that Evans has played a capable sun garden and has batted better than .300 ever since he broke in as a regular. Because of the injury to Jamieson, Evans has been playing left field most of the time on this western road trip, hitting against right-handed pitchers as well as southpaws. Nevertheless, he has made seventeen hits, including five triples and two doubles, up to yesterday afternoon's game for an average of .362.

The Indians played their last game at Comiskey Park for the year on July 6, and they were undoubtedly glad to leave town, having lost five of their last six contests in Chicago. The final loss was a 5–4, 11-inning heartbreaker charged to Bagby, who couldn't hold a one-run lead in the ninth and surrendered Happy Felsch's game-winning home run in the 11th. Instead of winning two out of three, as they should have, the Indians were swept by a Chicago team playing as it had when it won the pennant the year before.

"The series was a heavy blow to Speaker's crew," the *Plain Dealer* noted, "for his three ablest right-handers, Caldwell, Coveleskie and Bagby were taken over the jumps." While the Indians were losing to Chicago, the Yankees were crushing Washington, 17–0, to strengthen their hold on first place. And the rejuvenated White Sox were just two and ½ games behind the stumbling Tribe. Perhaps the June swoon was a month late.

The Indians took advantage of an open date on July 7 to stop in Cleveland and regroup before resuming their road trip in Washington, where the two earlier weather postponements had necessitated a six-game series over four days. Speaker had words of reassurance for anxious Tribe fans jittery after the flop in Comiskey Park.

> We're in great shape right now, Our pitching staff is looking better and we're hitting the ball like mad. Those White Sox are every bit as dangerous contenders as the Yankees to my way of thinking. Hence there is nothing that should surprise anybody in finding them right at our heels. It's a three-cornered pennant race right now, and I fully believe the Indians are the best team and have the best chance to cop of the three contenders. Chicago had all the breaks in cleaning up on that series, but we're ahead of them and in first class condition. Let the faint-hearted folks worry over our beating in Chicago. I refuse to share in their worry. We'll show them a thing or two on this trip east.[1]

Ruth begged to differ with his former Red Sox teammate. Continuing to dismiss Chicago as a contender, Ruth wrote that "the race has narrowed itself to the Cleveland and New York clubs. The fact that the White Sox have been coming along nicely is due to a Yankee slump while the Sox were driving hard. The Chicagoans took a few from Cleveland, which meant a great deal to them. But remember that the Sox cannot beat New York, *and neither can Cleveland* (italics by the author). And New York can defeat the other clubs. That means a pennant."[2] Ruth was getting some early experience at calling his shots — through his ghostwriter, Marshall Hunt.

The debacle in Chicago hadn't caused at least one writer to leap off the Cleveland bandwagon. In a dispatch to the *Plain Dealer* from Washington, J.V. Fitzgerald wrote that "the Indians started their second invasion of the east today as befits a probable pennant winner. They slugged their way to a double victory over the Nationals, and it pushed them once more to the van in the American League scramble." Fitzgerald was particularly impressed with Morton's performance in the Tribe's 4–2 win in the opener.

"Morton's showing, if it means he can duplicate his performance in turn from now on, should spell a pennant for the Indians," predicted Fitzgerald. Morton went the distance, holding the Senators, or Nationals, to five hits. Dick Niehaus started the second game and wasn't nearly as effective. George Uhle replaced Niehaus in the third inning and held Washington to a pair of runs the rest of the way as the Indians won, 9–6. Detroit beat New York, moving the Tribe back into first place, and Chicago lost half a game in the standings despite defeating St. Louis.

Caldwell, Niehaus and Bagby combined to top Washington, 8–4, on July 9. The Indians scored four runs in the seventh and four more in the eighth to wipe out a 3–0 Senators lead. The Yankees kept pace by topping Detroit while the White Sox fell a game further behind with a loss to Philadelphia. Chicago was suddenly four back.

From his office in Cleveland, Edwards offered some insight into the Tribe's trip. "The eastern trip of the Indians may not prove such tough sledding after all. Captain Harry Hooper of the Red Sox is said to be out for the season while Allen Russell, the hardest pitcher Boston has for the Indians to hit, is suffering from an injury that may prevent his pitching for two or three weeks. With the Indians scheduled to play five games at Boston, Speaker and his Indians are probably not shedding any tears because Hooper and Russell will be unable to play against them."

On the topic of being unable to play, the Indians dodged a bullet in Caldwell's victory over the Senators. "It appeared for a few minutes in the seventh inning yesterday that manager Speaker's services might be lost to the Indians for quite a lengthy spell," the game notes in the *News* said.

"In reaching second when forced by Wood on the double play that ended the round, Speaker's spikes caught the bag and he fell heavily on his left leg. It was feared his ankle had been sprained. It was some minutes before he was able to limp to his position and resume play. He retired in favor of Jamieson after the Tribe piled up a safe lead in the eighth. The ankle had been tightly strapped and Spoke said this morning he intends to carry on as usual." Speaker hadn't missed a game to that point, and he'd play in all but four of the Indians' games in 1920. But his absence in those four contests would be keenly felt. The loss of a .388 hitter always is.

Tribe pitching held Washington to four runs in 17 innings on July 10, but that was only good enough to earn a split of a doubleheader. Coveleskie pitched the Indians to a 7–2 win in the opener, but Bagby was a tough luck 2–1 loser in the second game. The Yankees edged Detroit to move back into a virtual first-place tie with Cleveland, with the Indians on top by four percentage points. Chicago shut out Philadelphia to move within 3½ games of the lead.

The weekly statistics in the *Plain Dealer*'s edition of Sunday, July 11, showed the Indians still leading the league in hitting with a .312 mark, 13 points ahead of Washington. And Washington didn't do much hitting in the final game of its series with the Tribe. Facing Morton for the second time in three days, the Senators were blanked by the right-hander, 4–0. "Morton was in no more danger of being beaten than in the first game Thursday," Fitzgerald wrote. "He had everything in the line of a change of pace, control and a sharp-breaking curve. Unless he has an unexpected slump, he should be the final link in the pennant chain for the Indians."

Few gave the right-hander from Alabama much chance of sticking with the Indians after he had posted a 1–13 record in his rookie season of 1914, setting an American League record that stood until 1982 by losing his first 13 decisions. Morton's 3.02 ERA indicated that he pitched far better than the record showed, and he proved to be big league material by winning 16 games the next season, his high water mark in the majors. Morton spent his entire 11-year career in a Cleveland uniform, winning 98 games. Among them was a 14-hit complete game shutout, the club record for most hits permitted while holding the opposition scoreless. As for being the reliable fourth starter the Indians needed in 1920, Fitzgerald's optimism had been misplaced. Morton's two victories over the Senators represented 25 percent of his season total.

Morton's shutout of Washington was the Tribe's 77th game, marking the halfway point of the season. Cleveland's record of 51–26 put it on a pace to win 102 games. Whether the Indians could maintain that pace, and whether 102 victories would win the pennant, remained to be determined. No American League team had won 100 or more games without capturing a pennant. For the moment, after winning five of six in Washington, the Indians were still clinging to first place by percentage points over the Yankees, who beat Detroit. The idle White Sox dropped to 4½ games behind.

Edwards made this assessment on July 11:

> If the Indians are in first place, or in a position to win the pennant on August 15th it is the intention of the Cleveland baseball club to make tentative arrangements for the world's series [sic]. The championship may not be decided until the very last day of the season, but Jim Dunn and business manager E.S. Barnard feel it would be unwise to wait until late in the season to make such preparations as will be necessitated in the event of lightning striking the redskins. It may be time and money wasted, but Dunn does not want to take a chance on putting off some of the details until September. Such action practically is forced by Cleveland fans who, for several weeks have been writing the club to make world's series reservations. Hundreds of such letters have been received.

Guy Morton spent his entire career in a Cleveland uniform. He won eight of his 98 career victories in 1920 as a spot starter and long reliever.

Edwards noted that each inquiry had been responded to, with the Indians telling anxious fans it was far too early to begin taking reservations for World Series tickets. But Dunn had no intention of making those anxious fans wait until the last minute, and he was convinced he'd have World Series tickets to sell.

"You know there's no chance of any deals now under the rules that prevent strengthening up after July 1st with any players from other big league clubs," Dunn told the *Press*. Did the owner feel that club needed any tinkering? "I don't see how they can beat us now," he continued. "We have no weak spots and have plenty of great substitute material to fill up any holes due to accidents."[3] The Indians would need that substitute material come September.

Assuming that "great substitute material" included pitchers, the Indians nearly found themselves dipping into their reserve supply in July. In mid-month, Ross Tenney broke an intriguing story:

> A few weeks ago, a determined effort was afoot to induce ... Morton to jump to the outlaws [the renegade Oil League in neighboring Pennsylvania]. Joe Harris was the prime mover. The secret of the gumshoe visit to Cleveland by the former slugging first sacker of the Tribe has just been revealed. Said visit happened about two weeks after ... Harris had been here in an unsuccessful effort to get together with Tris Speaker on terms by which he'd return to the Tribe.
> At that time, Harris said "nothing doing in Cleveland for me. I've got too good a thing in the pool room that folks presented me with to persuade me to play independent ball in Franklin, Pennsylvania." And he went on his way. But he slipped back to Cleveland with a wad of coin to try to get Morton to join the Franklin team. He sought to keep his visit a secret from the Cleveland ball club. But the tempter fell down. Guy stuck to his post tho [sic] things in a pitching way were going none too good for him.[4]

On the day Tenney revealed Harris's skullduggery, Morton's record was 5–1. Pitching statistics printed in newspapers each week didn't include ERAs or the information necessary to calculate them.

The fact that Morton was under contract to the Indians for 1920 ... and beyond, due to the infamous "reserve clause," didn't matter to Harris or the owners of the Franklin team. The Oil League operated outside of so-called "Organized Baseball" and didn't recognize the contracts players signed with major league teams. A legal fight over Morton's services would've been just about the last thing the Indians needed as the pennant race heated up, although it's difficult to imagine a court ruling in Franklin's favor since Morton would have broken a valid contract to pitch in the Oil

League. His loyalty to the Indians made it a moot point; it was an interesting sidelight in a season filled with them.

From their successful engagement in the nation's capitol, the Indians moved on to Philadelphia to tangle with the last-place Athletics. Caldwell made Chapman's sixth-inning home run stand up for a 4–3 victory in the series opener at Shibe Park. The wire service account of the game laid the blame for the loss squarely on Connie Mack for his choice of starting pitchers. Mack sent Dave Keefe to the hill, "and before the first inning was over, [Keefe] was enjoying a cool shower bath in the clubhouse and was a spectator in the shade for the remainder of the afternoon. When he quit pitching, the Clevelands, except for one chap, quit hitting the ball." But Keefe was far from the worst pitcher on Mack's staff. His 6–7 record and 2.97 ERA were quite respectable on a club that would lose 58 more games than it would win in 1920.

Keefe was replaced by Ed Rommel, and the wire story went on to say that "Edwin pitched such ball as he could not be recognized as an Athletic hurler. All he did was hold the Indians, except for the aforementioned exception, hitless for the rest of the route." The knuckleball Rommel threw to Chapman that wound up in the left field seats enabled the Indians to stay even with New York, which split a doubleheader with St. Louis. The White Sox, who were on an eastern excursion of their own and followed the Indians into Washington, disposed of the Senators and remained 3½ games back.

The Indians took the second game from the Athletics, 5–4, as Coveleskie overcame a slow start in which he allowed three runs on four hits in the first inning. He limited Philadelphia to four additional hits over the next eight frames while the Tribe scored single runs in the seventh, eighth and ninth innings to wipe out what was left of Philadelphia's lead. The Indians added another win at Philadelphia's expense, 5–1, on July 15th. Bagby picked up the victory in a contest shortened to six innings by rain. The day's big news was made in New York, where the Yankees out scored St. Louis, 13–10. Ruth provided the winning blow with a three-run homer, his 29th, tying the major league record for round-trippers he'd set the previous season before.

"Ruth took but little more than half the season to equal his previous record," said the game story. "He failed to pound out a circuit smash in April but made an even dozen in May and June." Only one of Ruth's blasts had come at the expense of the Indians, that being his smash over the 40-foot high right field wall at League Park against Elmer Myers during New York's 14–0 drubbing of the Tribe in front of a record crowd on June 13. The Yankees had paid a staggering price for Ruth's contract ($100,000 plus a $350,000 loan to Boston owner Harry Frazee, with Fenway Park as collateral) but the investment was paying the desired dividend. The win over the Browns kept New York 1½ behind the Indians. Chicago's game at Washington was postponed due to wet grounds, leaving the White Sox five in arrears.

Philadelphia denied the Tribe a sweep on July 16. Robert Maxwell described the 5–4 defeat as "a tough game to lose when victories mean so much. An opportunity to gain a full game on the Yankees was lost, but the defeat came after a hard battle." Errors by Wambsganss, Gardner and Johnston sank the Tribe, with Uhle taking the loss after failing to protect a 4–3 eighth inning lead.

Baseball players have always been the most superstitious of professional athletes, and Speaker was no exception, as evidenced by his explanation for not allowing Morton to pitch against the Athletics despite his success in Washington. "Philadelphia is Morton's jinx town, and that is why I am not using him today," the manager said before the final game at Shibe Park. "No matter how good Guy is going, he always runs into hard luck here. He is more fortunate in Boston."[5] Imagine a manager today not starting a hot pitcher because of a belief that the pitcher is "jinxed" in a certain ballpark.

Speaker did start Morton at Fenway Park, and Guy responded with a complete game, nine-hit, 5–2 victory that followed a complete game, seven-hit 5–2 victory by Caldwell in the first game of a doubleheader necessitated by one of the three rainouts during Cleveland's first visit to Boston in May. Meanwhile, the Tribe's closest pursuers met at the Polo Grounds, and the Yankees pounded the White Sox, 20–5.

"MAKE 22 HITS, THREE OF THEM BEING HOME RUNS, BUT NOT BY RUTH," blared the headline above the newspaper's game story. That gave New York two 14-run outbursts, a 17-run explosion, and a 20-run detonation, all within a month's time. The acquisition of Ruth had transformed the already powerful New Yorkers into the most fearsome offensive club baseball had seen since the 1911 American League champion Athletics, whose 861 runs scored were a modern (since 1901) major league record. The A's plated all those runs while hitting just 35 homers. Ruth and the Yankees were redefining how baseball was played. How could the Indians hold them off?

In actuality, the Indians were more than holding their own against the Yankees. The weekly statistics printed on Sunday, July 18, showed the Indians still on top of the American League with a .311 team batting average. In the all-important runs scored category, the Tribe was running neck-and-neck with Ruth and Company, having plated 460 runs to the Yankees' 466. The pennant would boil down, as it usually does in baseball, to pitching.

In his "Comment on Sports" column that same Sunday, Edwards noted how baseball had changed over the past few seasons.

> It has been years since any Cleveland baseball club has stole as few bases as the Indians have this season. A few years ago, Ray Chapman and Bobby Roth each stole as many bases in the campaign as the entire Tribe has to date this season. Yet the Tribe's failure to purloin sacks is no indication that Tris Speaker is mustering a slow-footed bunch of Indians. The reason the Indians are not stealing is that Speaker has discarded that system of play. He found early in the season that his men could hit with men on bases, and he elected to work the hit and run rather than to take chances on being thrown out in efforts to steal bases. The out-and-out steal has been resorted to as a rule only when there were two out and a runner on first.
>
> Because of the practical elimination of base running tactics, the Indians have fared but poorly in their few efforts to steal their way along. They have been turned back more often than they have succeeded. Larry Gardner, for instance, has stolen but twice in eleven attempts. Wamby has lost nine times out of fourteen. Speaker has found the ball waiting for him seven times while stealing five bases. The successful bandits have been Evans, who has stolen five bases and not been turned back once; Chapman, who has been successful in twelve out of eighteen tries; and Johnston, who has stolen six bases in seven attempts.

For the season, the Indians would swipe 73 bases. Chapman and Johnston tied for the club lead with 13. The Indians would become the first American League pennant-winner to steal fewer than 101 bases. In the National League, the Dodgers would swipe just 70 bases, making them the first league champion of the modern era to fail to steal at least 100 sacks. The age of so-called "scientific" baseball was rapidly coming to an end as the sport was being transformed into a game of brute strength, with a certain New York outfielder leading the charge.

Edwards made another observation in that Sunday column. "For the first time in his big league career, Tris Speaker has landed at the halfway mark with a batting average better than .400. And last year, when he finished the season with an average of only .296, they said it was the old, old story of managerial duties getting the better of a star batsman and causing him to lose his batting eye."

Edwards noted that Speaker had led the American League in batting in 1916, his first season in Cleveland,

> But the Indians faced a rather small number of left-handed pitchers in 1916. Such a statement cannot be made this year, as

Cleveland is heavy with left-hand hitters and has been called upon to face a big bunch of left-hand pitchers. Spoke, though, has hit them as hard as right-handers.

Should Spoke be able to finish the season with .400 or better, he will be acquiring membership in the class made famous by such hitters as Pop Anson, Dan Brouthers, Ross Barnes, Pete Browning, Jess Burkett, Fred Clarke, Ty Cobb, Ed Delahanty, Hugh Duffy, Joe Jackson, Willie Keeler, Tip O'Neill, Dave Orr, Jake Stenzel and Sam Thompson.

Edwards' history was a bit faulty. According to *The Baseball Encyclopedia*, neither Orr, Clarke nor Stenzel ever hit .400. Of the others, Anson, Brouthers, Barnes, Browning, Delahanty, Duffy, Keeler, O'Neill and Thompson had all cracked the .400 barrier prior to the turn of the 20th century. O'Neill and Browning both topped .400 in 1887, when baseball's rule makers had decreed that walks would be counted as hits, a one-season experiment that was quickly abandoned. Burkett had batted over .400 twice for the Cleveland Spiders in 1895 and 1896. Curiously, Edwards omitted from his list Napoleon Lajoie, who holds the American League record for highest batting average with .422 (or .426, depending on your source) for Philadelphia in 1901. Lajoie played for Cleveland from 1902 through 1914 and was the franchise's biggest star before Speaker's arrival. Edwards also forgot Joe Jackson, who established Cleveland's team record with a .408 average in 1911, yet didn't lead the league, finishing well behind Cobb's .420 mark. Speaker couldn't maintain the blistering pace he set in the first half of the season, but still batted a nifty .388. He was clearly leading by example.

Tribe fans were hitting the road to watch their heroes in action. "Several hundred Clevelanders, probably between 400 and 500, are discovering all of a sudden that they have important business in New York this week," the *News* reported on July 19. "And strangely enough the majority declare that it will be necessary for them to be there by Wednesday morning. Railroad officials say they are swamped with requests for reservations leaving here for the metropolis Tuesday night. The business reason — our Indians play the New York Yankees four games at the Polo grounds [sic] starting Wednesday."

The Indians divided a twinbill in Boston on July 19, while the 400 to 500 faithful were packing their suitcases and double-checking their reservations. Bagby won the opener in relief of Coveleskie after Stan was driven from the mound by a three-run rally that tied the score at six. Bagby benefited from a four-run uprising in the ninth that gave the Tribe a 10–6 win.

Fully warmed up, the Sarge started the second game and held a 4–3 lead heading into the bottom of the ninth. After allowing the first two Boston batters to reach base, Bagby was replaced by Uhle, who almost pitched out of the jam. Uhle retired the first batter on a force play. He then induced what appeared to be a game-ending double play ball, but Johnston couldn't scoop up Wambsganss's low throw to first as the tying run scored. A hit batter, a stolen base and a single produced the winning run for the Red Sox in the tenth. At the Polo Grounds, the Yankees and White Sox also split two. The Tribe's lead over New York was still 1½ games. The lead over Chicago was a seemingly comfortable 5½ games.

In his notes column of July 20, Edwards compared the arrival of the Indians in each of the cities on their road trip to the miraculous healing powers of Lourdes.

> Well, they cannot accuse the Indians of fattening their percentage by jumping on cripples, for all the cripples get well when the Tribe appears in sight. Washington had three regulars out of the game before the Nats came to Cleveland last month. [Joe] Judge and [Clyde] Milan, though, got back in the game when the Nats hit the Fifth City, while [Bucky] Harris, the third hospital resident, was in the line-up when the redskins played at Washington.
>
> When the tribe reached Philadelphia, it found [Whitey] Witt and [Joe] Dugan back on the job, and that pair was responsible for the Athletics' only victory over the Clevelanders. Harry Hooper, captain of the Red Sox, was out of the game when Boston was playing the other eastern teams but got back in when Cleveland hit town. The New York cripples, [Roger] Peckinpaugh, [Bob] Shawkey, and [George] Mogridge have cast aside their crutches and are ready to aid in entertaining the Indians in the series that starts tomorrow. Well, if Cleveland licks 'em, they will not have any alibis.

In his column of July 20, Ruth re-iterated his belief that the White Sox couldn't possibly remain in a three-team race with his Yankees and the Indians. "The White Sox are not in the American League race at all. They are as high as third place because most of the other clubs have not played against them as they have against the Yankees and Indians. They do not match the Cleveland club in the slightest sense as a contender with the Yankees. The Chicago club cannot hope to battle us for the pennant. They haven't the pitching." It was a curious analysis of a team that would produce four 20-game winners.

Before the Indians departed for New York, they had one more game to play in Boston, and it turned into a typical Fenway Park slugfest. The Indians scored seven runs in the first three innings, but Morton, making his second start of the series, couldn't hold the big lead and Niehaus and Uhle provided no relief. Boston's relievers kept Cleveland off the scoreboard until the 11th, when the Indians pushed across two runs. They needed both. Bagby allowed a run in the home half of the inning but held on for the 9–8 win, giving the Tribe four out of five in Beantown. In the Polo Grounds, where the Indians would be the next day, the Yankees split another doubleheader with the White Sox. The Tribe would arrive for a the season's second showdown in the Big Apple with a two-game lead.

The end of the season's longest road trip was in sight, and before the first of four games at the Polo Grounds, the *Plain Dealer's* sports editor, James Lanyon, looked ahead to the upcoming homestand. "Cleveland fans will be given a chance to compare the abilities of the world's champions and the Ohio contenders next Monday, for the Indians play the Cincinnati Reds here. It should furnish a good contest if the managers insert their regular line-ups for the fans who are looking for a world series [sic] between the two clubs this fall." Cincinnati was second in the National League, trailing Brooklyn by three games, so an all–Ohio World Series was a possibility.

Ruth and his friends would have plenty to say about that, however, and spoke loudly with a 4–3 victory over Cleveland in the first game of the series between the team that was in first place and the team that wanted to be. The *Plain Dealer's* sports headline writer summed up the contest's nail-biting ending this way: "WITH BAGS OCCUPIED, CLEVELAND ONE RUN BEHIND AND TWO OUT, SHORTSTOP PULLS A CASEY." The reference was to Ernest L. Thayer's classic poem *Casey at the Bat*, in which the mighty Casey disappoints the fans of Mudville by striking out in the bottom of the ninth inning with two runners on base and Mudville trailing its arch rival, 4–2. Chapman didn't disappoint many in the crowd at the Polo Grounds when he whiffed for the final out with the bases loaded and the Indians down by a run, with the exception of the 400 to 500 fans who had departed Cleveland by train the night before in hopes of watching the Indians defeat Ruth and friends. The Indians had rallied from a 4–0 deficit as the ninth inning started and seemed poised to tie the game, if not take the lead, had Chapman been able to connect.

"The Indians put on a ninth inning rally that taxed the nerves of 25,000 rooters who turned out for a titanic struggle and saw one," wrote W.J. Slocum in the game summary picked up off the sports wire by the *Plain Dealer.*

"Caldwell had the satisfaction of holding Babe Ruth hitless yesterday," Edwards wrote, "but that was poor satisfaction. He would have rather had a hit in the ninth score a runner." The loss reduced the Indians' lead to 1½ games.

The second game was played in an intermittent rain, perfect conditions for a spitball pitcher, or so one would think. The Yankees weren't bothered by the moisture falling from the clouds or the moisture on Coveleskie's pitches. Stan was gone in the second inning and New York cruised to an 11–3 victory shortened to 6½ innings by the inclement weather. The first two rounds of the heavyweight fight had gone to the home team, and the Indians' lead had been reduced to seven percentage points. The White Sox beat Boston and moved to within five games of first place.

"The sight of Coveleskie being taken from the box was something which the Yankees have enjoyed infrequently," wrote the *Plain Dealer*. "Covey usually can make the Hugmen jump through a hoop, but this was not his day." The next day wasn't the Tribe's day, either, as the Yankees made it three in a row with a 6–3 victory that dropped Cleveland out of first place by percentage points. A prosperous eastern swing was quickly becoming disastrous.

It would be up to Bagby to salvage one game of the series, and the Sarge was up to the task. "A crowd that was limited only by the size of the Polo Grounds turned out for the battle," wrote Slocum. "The attendance was close to the 37,000 mark, and would have been higher except for the fact that club officials declined to let fans on the field in center directly in line of the pitcher and batsman. About 1,000 fans might have utilized the space, but the players complained."

It took 11 innings, but the Indians escaped with a 4–2 victory. Gardner drove in the winning runs with a triple and Bagby limited the Yankees to six hits. Both New York runs were the results of solo home runs, including Ruth's 34th blast of the season. Each homer the Babe would hit for the rest of the year would establish a new single season record. More importantly, first place had been reclaimed, if only by the skin of the Indians' teeth. The victory made the train trip home for the players, and those of the 400 to 500 faithful who stayed for the entire series in New York, a bit more enjoyable.

Edwards rolled out the welcome mat for Cleveland's road warriors in his column on the morning after the final game in New York.

> The Indians return home today after being away since June 24th. While on their travels, they visited Chicago twice and

each other city in the league once. They went away in first place with a percentage of .672. They returned in first place also, but their percentage shrunk to .656, seven points ahead of New York and forty-five points ahead of Chicago.

They encountered a severe setback at the start when they lost five out of six games to the White Sox in their two trips to Chicago. But from then on, or until they invaded New York, it was a triumphal tour for the redskins. They took four out of five from St. Louis, three straight from Detroit, five out of six from Washington, three out of four from Philadelphia and four out of five from Boston. Twenty-one games were won and eleven were lost on the trip, a showing of which the Tribe can well be proud.

The homestand started with a make-up game against the White Sox, who sent Lefty Williams to the mound in search of his fourth victory of the season over the Indians. He didn't get it. The Tribe broke open a close game with three runs in the seventh and another in the eighth to spank the White Sox, 7–2. Coveleskie earned some revenge for his last performance against Chicago, when he'd blown sky high after seven innings and squandered a 5–0 lead. The White Sox left Cleveland five games behind the Indians. The Yankees beat Boston and stayed percentage points back.

Tenney wrote in his game account that "while the Indians were playing perfect ball behind Stan Coveleskie, the Kid Gleason delegation broke sadly behind Lefty Williams at critical moments and the Tribe took advantage of every break." Two of those miscues involved shortstop Swede Risberg, who made a wild throw on a double play pivot and played, in Tenney's words, "Alphonse and Gaston" with second baseman Eddie Collins on a pop fly by Joe Wood. Neither man caught the ball. Risberg, like Williams, was one of the Black Sox. No one will ever know if gaffes such as the two committed by Risberg in the Indians' seventh inning uprising, which put the game out of Chicago's reach, were genuine or not.

Speaking with reporters after the game, Collins offered his assessment of the pennant race. It was the polar opposite of Ruth's. "Tisn't the Yankees who'll give us trouble," said Collins. "It's the Indians we have to worry about."[6] The White Sox had just three games remaining with the Tribe, in late September at League Park. They'd won five of their last seven meetings with Cleveland.

In his column of July 26, Edwards offered an analysis in the form of a prediction. "The Yankees troubles begin this week," he told his readers.

"Miller Huggins will be called upon to take his pennant chasers away from the Polo Grounds. They play at home today and then take the train for St. Louis where they are scheduled to play five games in four days. New York has seventeen games to play in the west and two at Washington before they return home for a two weeks stay. Not having the advantage of playing at the Polo Grounds with its trick boundaries, the Yankees should strike a slump. It would be no surprise if they go back home in third place with Cleveland leading them by three or four games." New York failed to take advantage of its final game at the Polo Grounds, getting waxed by the Red Sox, 9–0.

The Indians weren't idle on that July afternoon. They played the much anticipated exhibition with the defending world champion Reds and lost, 4–3. With Ted Odenwald, who had pitched the Tribe's last exhibition game, toiling in Des Moines, Speaker used the occasion to check out two other young prospects, collegians George Ellison and Bob Clark. Ellison had prepared for the start by hurling batting practice at Cleveland batters during the just concluded road trip. His pitches were easy pickings for the Reds, who reached him for four runs and seven hits in five innings. Clark finished up and dazzled the Reds, holding them scoreless on one hit over the final four frames. Both pitchers showed enough to stick around briefly. Ellison pitched one inning for the Tribe in 1920, walking two, striking out one, and not allowing a run. It would be his only major league appearance. Clark would pitch in 11 games, starting two and notching one victory against two defeats.

The fans didn't beat down the doors to League Park to watch the battle of Ohio. The *News* estimated the crowd at between 7,000 and 8,000. An exhibition game was still an exhibition game, even when the world champions were providing the opposition and the game had the potential to be a World Series preview. If the Indians and Reds were to meet in October, Ellison and Clark wouldn't be pitching, and there wouldn't be more than 10,000 empty seats in League Park.

It was back to work on July 27, with the Senators in town for a make-up doubleheader. Morton, who'd pitched so well when the Indians were in Washington, started the opener and carried a 4–1 lead into the ninth inning despite being "hit fiercely," according to Edwards. The Senators rallied to tie the game but the Indians won it in the home half of the ninth on a single by Chapman.

Washington put on a clinic in fierce hitting in the second game, scoring three off Caldwell in the first inning and tacking on nine more in the second. When it stopped raining hits at League Park, the Indians had been pummeled, 19–6. Meanwhile, the Yankees had the day off to make the long trip from New York to St. Louis but inched back to within percentage points of first place. The White Sox beat Detroit and were four games behind.

July 28 was a day for shutouts involving the American League's contenders. One day after the Tribe's pitching staff had coughed up 23 runs to Washington, Bagby blanked Boston, 8–0, in the opener of a four-game series. The Sarge allowed six hits and didn't walk a batter. In St. Louis, the Browns edged New York, 1–0, and in Chicago, the White Sox whitewashed the Athletics, 3–0. The Indians now led the Yankees by a 1½ and the White Sox by four.

The Indians took the second game of the series from Boston, 9–3. A seven-run eighth inning explosion made a winner of Coveleskie. The other contenders were playing doubleheaders on July 29, and both the Yankees and White Sox split. The Tribe's lead over New York was two games. Chicago trailed by 4½.

Game three of the Boston series was a 13–4 laugher in Cleveland's favor. "Caldwell was at his best," noted Edwards. "He held the Red Sox to one run and three hits for seven innings and then hoisted the 'what care I' sign and just easing the ball over and giving his support a chance to get some action." Boston reached Caldwell for three runs and six hits over the final two innings, when "Slim" was just trying to end the game quickly and adjourn to his favorite watering hole.

A man who enjoyed a drink or three, or more, Caldwell's contract with the Indians was probably the most unique in baseball. On the verge of drinking himself out of the game, Caldwell was picked up off the scrap heap by Speaker in 1919, after being cut loose by the Red Sox despite a 7–4 record. Tris was convinced that Caldwell could help the Tribe win a pennant, and Caldwell was grateful for one last chance to pitch in the major leagues. The 32-year-old Pennsylvania native had broken into the major leagues with the Yankees in 1910. His high water mark for victories had been 19 in 1915, but he posted losing records the following two seasons for run-of-the-mill ball clubs and found himself with the Red Sox by 1919. Ed Barrow had his hands full dealing with the rambunctious Ruth and quickly tired of Caldwell's shenanigans, placing him on waivers despite his winning record. Slim won five of six decisions after the Indians picked him up, including a no-hitter against his former Yankee teammates. He brought a pedestrian 107–104 record into the 1920 campaign.

According to Franklin Lewis, Caldwell's contract negotiations with Speaker went like this: Caldwell promised Speaker he'd swear off the booze.

Speaker, having heard that before, was skeptical. He also wasn't certain that he wanted Caldwell if the pitcher stopped drinking. In fact, the contract Speaker slid in front of Caldwell contained the following clause: "After each game he pitches, Ray Caldwell must get drunk. He is not to report to the clubhouse the next day. The second day he is to report to manager Speaker and run around the ballpark as many times as manager

Ray Caldwell, pictured here with the Yankees in 1918, joined the Indians the following season and won 20 games in 1920. Caldwell's one-third of an inning pitched in game three of the World Series is still the shortest stint ever by a starting pitcher.

Speaker stipulates. The third day he is to pitch batting practice, and the fourth day he is to pitch in a championship game."[7] Speaker assured a confused Caldwell that the contract language was correct. Speaker wanted him to get drunk after each game that he pitched.

Caldwell signed. It isn't known where he spent the night of July 30, but assuming he lived up to the terms of his contract, and since that contract called for more money than he'd been paid by either the Yankees or Red Sox, the drinks might well have been on Slim.

In his notes column of July 30, Edwards expressed the following opinion:

> If there is one quality the Indians possess, it is that of being able to come back after having sustained more or less of a losing streak. Three times they have turned that trick and brought the fans rallying to their support when the same fans were almost of the opinion the tribe was due to take a long slide on the toboggan.
>
> Early in the year, the Browns came to town and took three out of four from Cleveland. The pessimists feared it was the old, old story and prepared for the worst, whereupon the redskins proceeded to clean up the four eastern clubs. The eastern teams out of town again, the Indians went to Chicago and lost five out of six. Did they lose their fight? Not a bit of it! They went east and fattened their percentage at the expense of Washington, Philadelphia and Boston. Then they hit New York and lost three out of four, causing the New York writers to declare the Indians' machine had broken and that the tribe would soon be in third place.
>
> What happened? The Indians came home after winning twenty and losing twelve games on the road and whipped Chicago, broke even with Washington, and have won three straight from Boston. No other club in the league has shown such comeback qualities, with the possible exception of Chicago.

Unwittingly, Edwards had pointed out a disturbing trend. After handling Chicago and New York with relative ease early in the season, the Indians had lost eight of the 11 games they'd played against the other contenders on the grueling road trip. The White Sox and Yankees knew they could beat the heavy favorites. The Indians had only three games left against the White Sox in Cleveland, but they had three series remaining with the Yankees, including one more trip to New York. With the Indians flattening the also-rans, those games figured to decide the pennant.

The American League standings on the morning of July 31st looked like this:

Cleveland	64–32	.667	—
New York	64–36	.640	2
Chicago	60–37	.619	4½
Washington	44–46	.489	17
St. Louis	44–49	.473	18½
Boston	40–51	.440	21½
Detroit	34–58	.370	28
Philadelphia	28–69	.289	36½

The Indians closed the month on a high note with Morton's one-hit, 2–1 victory over Boston. The newspaper game story provided the details:

> Defeating Boston, 2 to 1, thus making it four straight for Cleveland from the Red Sox, Guy Morton all but engraved his name in the hall of fame [sic] by pitching a no-hit game. Unfortunately for the Alabama squirrel hunter, it was not a no-hit contest as Boston made one hit. True, it was not a clean hit, but it was a hit just the same, and it kept Morton from having his name recorded among those who have set their adversaries down without a safe blow. [Stuffy] McInnis, Boston first sacker, was the batsman who spoiled a perfect afternoon for the Alabamian.
>
> McInnis was the first up in the second inning and he caught one of Morton's fast ones squarely on his bat and having taken a toe hold, hit a fierce bounder toward left field. It struck the ground a few feet in front of Gardner, Indian third sacker, and had that player absolutely handcuffed. Larry threw up his hands as the ball came to him on a terrific bound but it shot through on its way to left field. From then on, not a semblance of a hit was made by Boston.

The un-attributed game summary added that "the crowd was sadly disappointed that Morton was not credited with a no-hit game, and thousands of fans thronged the space about the plate below the press box and begged the scorers to change their verdict and charge Gardner with an error. This, of course, could not be done as scorers have specific orders from President Johnson that no such changes shall be made to the scoring of hits."[8]

No one asked Gardner how he felt about this assault on his fielding average, nor did anyone ask Morton if he felt he'd been done an injustice by the official scorer.

Chicago lost its final game of the month, 5–1 to Philadelphia. New York was outscored by St. Louis, 13–8. As the sun set on July 31, the Indians held first place by three games over the Yankees and 5½ over the White Sox.

As singer Al Jolson used to say to his vaudeville audiences during the roaring twenties, "You ain't seen nothin' yet!"

7

Come a Little Bit Closer

There are two schools of thought pertaining to what a team must do to win a championship.

School #1: to be the best, one must beat the best. This is the kind of inspirational message managers and coaches like to write in bold letters above the locker room door to encourage their players.

School #2: beat up on the bums and break even with the contenders. This philosophy has been attributed to Indians Hall of Fame shortstop Lou Boudreau, who played and managed the club to its second World Series championship. It isn't known which belief Tris Speaker subscribed to, but based on the Indians' performance against Chicago and New York in July, August and September of 1920, it appears to have been the latter. Actually, Speaker would've been happy to break even with the White Sox and Yankees during the season's final three months. If the Tribe had split its games with its pursuers, winning the first pennant in franchise history would've been much easier.

The Indians kicked off the month of August by losing to one of the bums. Washington topped the Tribe, 8–5, scoring two in the second and two more in the third against Sarge Bagby. "It was a game in which the Nationals drew all the breaks and Cleveland drew nothing but chunks of hard luck," according to Henry Edwards' game account in the *Plain Dealer*. The Tribe threatened to tie the game in the late innings, and if it had, reserve outfielder Joe Wood would've pitched the 10th inning since using Dick Niehaus and Bob Clark in relief of Bagby had depleted Speaker's bullpen. Wood was sent to the pen in the eighth inning to warm up, just in case he was needed. "The fans were eager for a drawn battle if for no other reason than to see Smoky Joe perform once more," reported the newspaper.

Wood, unfortunately, was no longer the pitcher who dazzled American League batters with his speed while winning 34 games and losing only five with a 1.91 ERA in 344 innings for the 1912 World Series champion Red Sox, whose star centerfielder was a fellow named Speaker. That workload placed such a strain on Wood's arm that he won just 35 games over the next three seasons and was finished as a pitcher by 1916. Not ready to give up the game, Wood, who'd always been a capable batter, signed with the Indians in 1917 (upon Speaker's recommendation) and earned a roster spot as a part-time outfielder and occasional pitcher. He was only a very occasional pitcher. Wood hit .296 in 119 games in 1918, and would contribute a .270 average, one home run and 30 runs batted in to the Cleveland cause in 1920. The 30-year-old Kansas City, Missouri, native made one appearance on the mound that season, though not in the afore-

Smoky Joe Wood had lost his "smoke" when he was signed by the Indians at the urging of his friend and former teammate, Tris Speaker, in 1917. Wood stayed in Cleveland through 1922, contributing 30 runs batted in as a part-time outfielder (plus his final pitching appearance) in 1920.

mentioned game. For the fans who clamored to see the former fireballer, it would be a classic case of being careful what one wishes for since one may get it. And the fans who wanted to watch Wood pitch that afternoon against the Senators didn't have to wait long for that wish to be granted.

The White Sox and Yankees began a series at Comiskey Park on August 1 with Chicago taking the opener, 3–0. New York was still three games back. Chicago moved a game closer to the Tribe at 4½ out.

"Two predictions made in this column a week ago have come to pass," Edwards wrote on August 2. "The Yankees struck a slump and Babe Ruth found it more difficult to get home runs on the road than he did at the Polo Grounds, where he was averaging almost one a day his last two weeks at home. The Yanks had a tough week of it, the worst of the season, losing five games and winning only two."

Tenney echoed the sentiments of his fellow scribe, but in greater detail. Both Edwards and Tenney seemed to revel in any misfortune suffered by the New Yorkers. Tenney wrote the following the day after New York opened its series at Comiskey Park.

> That long-delayed slump has hit the Yankees at last, I have never figured them to be the team that the Indians must beat out when it comes to the September stretch in the dash for the flag. In fact, they really have upset the dope by hanging around as long as they have. The White Sox are the team, if any, that'll give the Tribe (the *Press* spelled "Tribe" with a capital "T," the *Plain Dealer* didn't) the big fight for the pennant, and just how strong the White Sox will fight depends on how well their pitching staff comes along as the race nears the finish.
>
> They did none too well in dropping two games to the lowly Mackmen, which is more than Connie's pets have been able to take from the Speakerites in any series this season. But just look how the Yankees have been slipping. It looks as if they overreached themselves when they edged the Tribe out of first place for 24 hours in that third game in New York a week ago. For they haven't done a thing worthwhile since then. The Indians got first place back by winning the final game of the New York series. Then the Yankees were walloped by the Red Sox, 9 to 0, just before they started west. They dropped three out of five in St. Louis while the Tribe was cleaning up the Red Sox four straight. And now they've opened up in Chicago by being whitewashed on Sunday.
>
> If that isn't slipping up, what is? And furthermore, those Yanks have lots more chance to slip during this trip west, for seven of their remaining games are with the White Sox and Indians.

Ruth acknowledged the obvious in his column. "We Yanks have done better, can do better and mighty well have to do better than we did this week to pull down the Indians before the end of the season."[1]

The Indians evened their series against Washington with a 2–0 victory on August 2. Stan Coveleskie provided the shutout pitching and George Burns generated the offense. The Indians had purchased Burns's contract from the Athletics on May 29, and he divided his time between the outfield, first base, and pinch-hitting. Sent to the plate to bat for Elmer Smith in the eighth inning, Burns provided "an excellent illustration of what a pinch-hitter should be," in the opinion of Edwards, by stroking a double to drive home Speaker and Gardner with the game's only runs. Doubles were nothing new to Burns. He'd lead the American League with 64 two-baggers in 1926.

In Chicago, more than 30,000 fans watched Ruth connect for his 38th home run as the Yankees pounded the White Sox, 7–0. The loss dropped them 5½ games behind the Indians.

The *Press* noted that Speaker was catching some heat from Cincinnati fans liv-

George Burns didn't see much action in 1920 but produced when he played. Burns' double scored the only run of game six of the World Series. Burns would accumulate 64 doubles in 1926, when he was named the American League's Most Valuable Player.

ing in northeastern Ohio who had eagerly anticipated the late July exhibition with the Reds and counted on the Indians pulling out all the stops to win, which didn't include turning the pitching duties over to a pair of non-descript rookies. "Cincinnati fans here are criticizing Tris Speaker for presenting a patched-up line-up in the recent exhibition game between the Reds and the Tribe at Cleveland. But Tris should worry — it won't be patched up if Cleveland and Cincy meet in the world series." (World Series was spelled without capital letters in 1920.) With New York and Chicago breathing down the Indians' necks, Speaker had better things to do than concern himself with winning an exhibition game, even if the defending world champions were the opponents.

Cleveland's search for that elusive fourth starter to bolster the rotation of Coveleskie, Bagby and Caldwell continued in early August. The Tribe gave up on one of the candidates. "Elmer Myers, the tall pitcher, will leave in a day or so to join the Boston Red Sox, which club claimed him via the waiver route," the *Plain Dealer* reported. "Elmer proved to be a great disappointment this year. He showed so much stuff last year that Speaker had counted on him for regular work this season. Elmer has suffered considerably with a sore arm and also with a stitch in his neck. His weakness was a lack of control. No pitcher in the league has a better curveball than Elmer, but without control he was of little value to the club." Myers proved to be of significant value to Boston, posting a 9–1 record for his new employer.

As one pitcher departed, another emerged. Edwards wrote about the situation on August 3:

> When the Indians were training at New Orleans in the spring, manager Speaker had a very large squad of pitchers. As the time grew near for the team to leave New Orleans, the younger pitchers naturally began to wonder who would be kept and who would be chased to the minors. One of those who indulged in such speculation was Bob Clark. Bob had been pestered with boils at training camp and had but little chance to show whether or not he had any pitching ability.
>
> But Tris Speaker, a hustler himself, likes players around him who hustle also. For that reason, he liked Bob Clark and decided if it were possible without exceeding the player limit, Bob would be the one to be kept. The fact that Bob was cheerful and always willing to work appealed to him. He also knew that Bob was a youngster who did his best to heed the instructions given him and overcome his mistakes.
>
> Day after day, Bob was sent to the box in batting practice. He did so willingly, for he felt that some day the time would come when he could do something beside mere rookie's work. That day came Sunday when he made his real American League debut in front of a crowd of 28,000 and acquitted himself with such credit that yesterday when it was necessary for Speaker to send a pitcher to the rubber to relieve Caldwell, the crowd was a unit in calling for Clark.

> It so happened Bob was just a temporary relief pitcher to work while Bagby completed warming up, the Sarge not being ready when Caldwell ran into his tough luck.

Clark retired two of the three batters he faced to retire the side with the Tribe trailing, 5–3, in the fifth inning of a contest Edwards described as "sort of a nightmare characterized by hard hitting, bad pitching and reckless base running." The Indians struck for six runs in their half of the fifth inning and had grabbed a 6–5 lead by the time Speaker sent up a pinch-hitter for Clark who, as the pitcher of record in a game the Tribe would win, 10–5, would qualify for the victory under today's scoring rules. The official scorer instead credited the victory to Bagby, who pitched four scoreless innings of relief. Edwards expressed the hope that the league president might overturn that decision and award the victory to Clark. He didn't. Clark, however, shook off any disappointment to notch one of the season's most important victories in the final game of the homestand.

At Comiskey Park, the White Sox trimmed the Yankees, 3–1. New York's first place deficit was 4 games. Chicago's was 5½.

Morton carried a 3–1 lead over Washington into the sixth inning of the game on August 4 but developed a "kink" in his pitching arm and surrendered four runs before Speaker could get a reliever warmed up. The bullpen was of no help. Clark coughed up a run in the seventh, but the Tribe's deficit was just three when Speaker sent Wood to the mound to start the eighth. That decision may have delighted the fans, but it delighted the Senator batters even more. There wasn't much smoke on Smoky Joe's offerings. Wood was touched for five runs in two innings in the final mound appearance of his career, and the Senators drubbed the Tribe, 11–3.

In Chicago, the White Sox made it three out of four from New York, 10–3. Ruth continued packing them in everywhere the Yankees played as the series drew an estimated 126,000 fans, "the largest on record for a series where single games were played." The Yankees stayed four games behind while the White Sox picked up a game. "The White Sox advance is almost as threatening as the Yankees," the *Plain Dealer* noted. For the moment, however, Cleveland held both of its pursuers at arm's length.

As the Yankees took their road show to Detroit, the *Press* noted that "Babe Ruth has [socked] one or more home runs in every American League city except Washington. He's banged 22 of them at the Polo Grounds." Ruth had connected for 16 homers on the road. The paper also noted that Ruth's clouting was highly profitable for the league.

"It is estimated that Babe Ruth's little stunt of hitting homers will net the American League $400,000 in profits for 1920. He draws equally well on the road as at home."[2] It was little wonder that owners like Dunn hoped Ruth would swat a homer or two when the Yankees played in his ballpark, providing the home team won the game.

With the Indians idle on August 5, both New York and Chicago failed to take advantage. The Yankees were bounced in Detroit, 7–1, and Chicago lost to Boston, 4–2.

Sensing the season that was unfolding could be historic, the *News* (which cost three cents per copy) in an effort to give its readers their money's worth, began running a feature entitled "In the Yesteryear of Baseball," in early August. It could more appropriately have been called "In the Yesteryear of Cleveland Baseball" as it dealt with games of historic importance to the city's long baseball tradition. Among these was a contest played on July 24, 1882, when the Cleveland team was a member of the National League, played its home games at Kennard Street (now East 46th) and Cedar Avenue, and was known as the Forest Citys.

Assuming that Ed Bang, as sports editor, selected the games featured, he may have chosen this 19th century struggle because Forest Citys second baseman/manager Fred (Sure Shot) Dunlap, in an era when players shunned gloves, handled 18 chances at his position. Dunlap's teammates were busy as well on that summer afternoon as the visiting Chicago White Stockings, the forerunner of today's Cubs, pounded out 29 hits, scored in every inning except the second, and ran up the second highest single game run total in major league history, obliterating Cleveland, 35–4. Chicago's 31-run margin of victory remains the largest ever. It took the White Stockings an interminable two hours and 40 minutes to inflict the carnage on the shell-shocked Forest Citys. There was an extenuating circumstance to the embarrassing defeat, however.

The Forest Citys had just two pitchers on their roster, which was common for the era, and neither threw a pitch on that July afternoon. Jim McCormick, who led the league with 36 victories, needed a day off, as did McCormick's understudy, George Bradley. Bradley, a 45-game winner for St. Louis during the National League's inaugural season of 1876, would win just eight games in his two seasons with Cleveland. With his entire pitching staff on the shelf, Dunlap gave the ball to Dave Rowe, his rifle-armed centerfielder. Rowe had exactly one inning of major league pitching under his belt, for Chicago in 1877, in which he'd been touched for two runs. On the July afternoon in question, Rowe hurled a complete game (relief pitching was virtually non-existent in 1882, and with both of his pitchers sidelined, Dunlap had no one to call upon to relieve Rowe). Rowe allowed 29 hits (16 singles, nine doubles, one triple, and three home runs), walking seven and striking out not a single White Stockings batter. Rowe's teammates didn't make his task any easier by committing nine errors (about double their season's average of 4.8 miscues per game). A crowd of 1,500 witnessed the demolition.[3]

"Just to show that defeats like this were not Cleveland's style," the *News* pointed out, "the Forest City men turned around the following day and won a brilliant game, 3 to 2." Cleveland fielded a decent club in 1882, finishing fifth with a 42–40 record. McCormick, who relinquished the manager's job to Dunlap after just four games (all losses), led the league with 68 games pitched, 596 innings, and the 36 victories. With a workload like that, McCormick was understandably too busy to manage the club, too. For the record, the White Stockings, who won the 1882 pennant, outdid themselves in 1897, trouncing Louisville, 36–7.[4] Neither the 36 runs in one game nor the 31-run margin of victory are recognized by those who insist record-keeping begins with the 1901 season.

In spite of the rude treatment Rowe received at the hands of the White Stockings, his strong arm tempted desperate managers to send him to the mound twice more. In 1883, Rowe pitched four innings for Baltimore of the American Association, allowing 12 hits and walking two while not being involved in the decision. In 1884, he picked up a victory, hurling a complete game for St. Louis of the Union Association and permitting just two earned runs (according to The *Baseball Encyclopedia,* which acknowledges that statistics from the Union Association, a "major league" in name only, are unreliable). Rowe's lifetime pitching ledger was 1–2 with 54 hits and 11 walks allowed in 23 innings, three strikeouts and a 9.78 ERA.[5]

The *Plain Dealer*'s James Lanyon wrote the following on August 6.

> Day by day, things happen to make the Cleveland ball club stand out as the real thing in the American League as well as the coming champions of the American League. What if Cleveland should win the pennant? How will Cleveland behave?
>
> Winning the American League pennant will place Cleveland in a position it never held before. It will mean playing at least half the games of the world series [sic] in this city. And for the time being, such a thing would make the city the metropolis of the sport world. It would be a great thing for Cleveland. If the pennant comes here, what will Cleveland do? Cleveland has been clamoring for such an honor for years. It has been hungry for a pennant winner. It has stood for any position in the league with sportsmanlike spirit. It has been second more than once and has "gone through" with the club the following season.
>
> So if Cleveland does win the American League this year and

some of the games of the world series are played here, let us continue to be sports. Let us give the opposing club a run for its money. Let us give the fans an example of sportsmanship that is warranted. If the visiting club wins, give it credit and give the fans who support the National League contender every courtesy. Let the best club win and more power to it.

Will we behave ourselves as the spirit of Cleveland baseball has told us to do? Let us be the sportsmen that the record of the Cleveland club in the American League has told the world we are. If Cleveland wins the American League pennant and games of the world series are played here, let us give credit where credit is due every minute and permit supporters of the National League entry to support their team, regardless of the outcome, and let us show everybody the proper spirit. So, with this spirit in mind, let's plug for the Indians to win the pennant.

First, the *News* had admonished Clevelanders for verbally abusing opposing players. Then the *Press* pleaded with the fans to treat Babe Ruth with the proper respect. Finally, the sports editor of the *Plain Dealer* asked the fans to be nice to the visiting players and fans should the Indians make it to the World Series. Cleveland baseball fans must have been a rowdy bunch in 1920.

The fact that Philadelphia needed a telescope to see seventh-place Detroit didn't stop the Indians from losing to the Athletics, 2–1, on August 6. Edwards blamed Chapman for the loss as charitably as possible. "Shortstop Chapman of the Indians was possibly too careful in his preparations to throw out a batsman in the ninth inning," he wrote. "It was the toughest loss of the season for the Indians, for they had victory practically in their grasp in the ninth round when Chapman made a wild throw that eventually allowed the Athletics to tie the score." Philadelphia scored again in the tenth to pin the loss on Coveleskie.

Though Philadelphia was miles out of first place, Edwards told his readers that "no longer is there any easy picking in the American League. At the outset of the season, the Tigers and Athletics were considered rather soft, but times have changed. The Athletics have been putting a stubborn fight against all comers and ask no favors of anyone. The Tigers also have come to life and even Boston, which went into a long slump, has been putting a game battle of late.

"The reason is all these three have better pitching than they had earlier in the year. Philadelphia appears to have about as good a pitching staff as there is in the circuit. It may not win a lot of games, but when it loses, it is by a margin of just a run or so." It isn't known if manager Connie Mack or his players took any solace in losing tighter games than they'd been losing earlier in the campaign.

While the Indians were dropping a close one to the Athletics, New York outslugged Detroit, 11–7, and Chicago edged Boston, 4–3. The Tribe's lead over the Yankees was 3½. The White Sox were four behind.

Things returned to normal on August 7. Cleveland hammered Philadelphia, 9–1. Bagby allowed ten hits, stranded 11 runners, and, in the words of Edwards, "did not have to exert himself except when a hit meant a run or so." The Indians scored three in the first and Bagby operated on cruise control from there. With New York winning and Chicago losing, the Tribe's lead held at 3½ over the Yankees and increased to five over the White Sox.

The Sunday newspaper statistics of August 8 showed Speaker leading the league with an average of .416 on 161 hits in 387 times at bat. St. Louis first baseman George Sisler was second at .401, and Chicago's Joe Jackson third at an even .400. Speaker didn't fatten his average at the expense of the cellar-dwelling Athletics that afternoon. The Tribe's manager didn't start the contest due to a bout with neuralgia (the *Press* described his malady as an ulcerated tooth) but was barely missed as Caldwell pitched a six-hitter and blanked the visitors, 5–0. Speaker played the game's final inning so as to maintain his perfect attendance record. All three contenders were involved in shutouts on that Sunday. Detroit stopped the Yankees, 1–0, and Chicago beat Boston, 2–0. The Indians led New York by 4½ and the White Sox stayed five back. The next stop on the Yankees' western swing was Cleveland, and Edwards previewed the four-game showdown.

> Another little world's series [sic] starts at League Park tomorrow when the New York Yankees arrive for a series of four games with the Indians. To a certain extent, this series will have a considerable bearing upon the chances of the tribe winning the pennant.
>
> When the Indians last visited New York, they lost three out of four games. Speaker and every last one of the redskins now wants to offset those reverses by taking at least three out of four from the Yankees here. If they but break even, though, the Yankees will not have gained any ground on their greatest rivals and an even break will not aid them to making up the ground they have lost on their present western trip. Cleveland, however, cannot afford to only split even as there is no telling what the White Sox will do with the Nationals at the same time.

As Edwards had predicted, the Yankees struggled on the first three stops of their 19-game road swing in St. Louis, Chicago and Detroit. The loss on August 8 to the Tigers dropped their record to 5–8, with the four games at League Park coming up.

Today's owners in all professional sports could learn a lesson from Indians team president Jim Dunn, who had a chance to enhance his revenue stream with the Yankees coming to Cleveland for a confrontation that figured to draw a lot of paying customers to League Park. But to "Sunny Jim," a promise was a promise.

"Big-hearted Jim Dunn, owner of the Indians, cannot forget he was a boy once," the *Plain Dealer* reported the day before Ruth and company arrived. "During the club president's absence from Cleveland, it was announced that the free school boy tickets for the four New York games starting tomorrow would not be good on those dates but would be honored yesterday, today and next Saturday." The story didn't say which team official decided that the Indians couldn't afford to give away tickets that they could easily sell with baseball's biggest drawing card and his powerful bat in town. The school kids would have to be content to watch their heroes do battle with Philadelphia and St. Louis instead.

"Dunn got back to town yesterday and at once proceeded to revoke that order," the newspaper continued, "announcing the school boys could come to the New York games as originally scheduled."

Said Dunn, "There were no strings attached to those gifts. I want the boys and girls that drew tickets to come to my park next week and see Babe Ruth. I gave those tickets to the school children. I want them to be present and I hope Ruth makes a home run each day, providing, of course, the Indians win each game."[6] By admitting four thousand children to each game free, Dunn was losing a potential 16,000 paid admissions.

Neither of Dunn's wishes came true. Ruth failed to hit a home run against his team, and the Indians didn't sweep the series. They were swept instead. Whatever had been ailing the Yankees away from the Polo Grounds was cured on the shores of Lake Erie.

New York took the opener on August 9, 6–3. Edwards attributed the defeat to "Guy Morton's wildness in the first inning and redskin errors throughout the contest. Accumulating five errors, they crowded more misplays into the one contest than they had in the previous eleven games." The game notes expressed the opinion, or hope, that "the Indians must have got all the errors out of their system yesterday and should give the Yankees an even more strenuous battle today."

While the Indians were losing, the White Sox were sweeping a doubleheader from Washington. They were 3½ games behind and virtually tied with New York for second place. Rain washed out the second game of the set in the second inning, disappointing a Tuesday afternoon crowd of better than 21,000 described as "the largest crowd for a Tuesday that wasn't a holiday."

Edwards asked the follow-up question on the morning of what became a day off caused by the weather.

> Have the Yankees lost their punch that characterized their playing earlier in the year? There are more than a few who believe so. It cannot be denied the New Yorkers are not hitting as hard as they did prior to this western trip.
>
> True, the Yankees downed the Indians Monday, but that was because of Indian errors and pitching wildness. The Yankees did nothing at bat to entitle them to the victory, and, according to the newspapermen with the team, the Huggins aggregation has not batted like the real Yankees except in two or three games upon their trip.
>
> Babe Ruth is in hitting form, but his teammates are not, and the club as a whole does not display the same confident spirit it did earlier. Should the slump continue much longer it will be no surprise if Huggins tries out a bunch of recruits he has headed toward the Polo Grounds when the club comes west again. New York has several players out among the minors on options and those players, it is said, have orders to report this fall for further trials.
>
> Nothing like that is in Tris Speaker's plans. The Indians will go through the season composed as present. Only a few players are eligible to call for this year and it is doubtful if Speaker will ask any to report before next March.

Tenney called on an expert to verify his belief that the Yankees weren't serious contenders: Frank Chance, the "Peerless Leader" who played first base and managed the Chicago Cubs to four pennants and two world championships from 1906 to 1910. Chance hadn't fared nearly as well when hired to manage the Yankees in 1913, finishing seventh. The team was floundering in seventh place in 1914 when Chance resigned with 20 games remaining. By 1920, Chance was a club owner in the Pacific Coast League and, while visiting Cleveland, gave Tenney his take on the pennant race.

"The Yanks should land in about third place if my dope's correct," Tenney quoted Chance as saying. "They're a slugging team, and when you say that you've said it all. A team has to be more than just a bunch of big hard hitters to cop the flag. Just now my pick for the pennant would be the Indians, tho [sic] I don't know how I'd be picking if the White Sox were even with the Indians. Anyhow, it's the White Sox that the Indians must beat out to win."[7]

Just as Ruth (or his ghostwriter) continually insisted that the White Sox weren't serious contenders for the pennant, Edwards and Tenney probed for any chink in the Yankees' armor. New York would spend its extended visit to Cleveland proving rumors of its demise to be exaggerated.

The game on August 11, played before a crowd of more than 27,000, the largest to witness a Wednesday game in club history, started promisingly. Elmer Smith brought the gathering to its feet with a third-inning grand slam off Carl Mays that gave the Indians a 4–0 lead. Smith led the Tribe with 12 homers, and his slam off Mays wouldn't be the last grand slam he'd hit against a team from New York City in 1920. Unfortunately, it was all the offense the Tribe could muster for the afternoon, and it wasn't enough for Bagby. The Yankees tied the score with three runs in the fifth and one in the sixth. They won it with three more runs in the tenth inning, 7–4. And they won it without Ruth, who stayed on the bench with a knee injury. The Indians' lead over New York was reduced to a 1½ games. The White Sox defeated Washington to creep within 2½ games.

The *Plain Dealer* provided an update on the health of the Yankees' top player.

> Babe Ruth may be able to play in the third game of the series today. He says he will, but his physician may say he cannot and what the doctor says goes. It all depends upon how Babe feels this noon. The physician's report last night was that either there was a slight sprain or a ligament displaced. Heretofore it always has been Babe's left knee that has caused him trouble, this being the first time his right knee has been at fault. Babe suffered considerable pain at the time, but later said he felt much better.
>
> Thousands of fans who had come to Cleveland from all over northern Ohio and even surrounding states were disappointed because of the accident that took the wonderful batsman out of the game. It was to see him that many of them came to Cleveland. If their prayers turn the trick, Babe will be back in the game today.

Before it was known whether Ruth would play in that game, Edwards asked for patience for the suddenly beleaguered Indians.

> Let's stick to the finish. Let's trail with the best ball club Cleveland has had in many a day. Let's give the best we have in the way of encouragement to a club that has been leading the league practically all year. Let's not be discouraged because the

Indians lost two games to the Yankees and now have a lead of only two games over Chicago.

They lost yesterday because they were a trifle overanxious, not because they loafed on the job. There always is a strain in trying to maintain a small lead in the race and the redskins yesterday demonstrated that the pace had affected them to a certain extent. They tried too hard.

The tribe is still two games in the lead of Chicago and has even a greater lead over New York. Victories in the next two games will set the Indians just right and they are far from being a beaten ball club. The Yankees have won two, but there are two yet to be played. Cleveland has the better ball club of the two and will be out to prove it today and tomorrow.

The Yankees contributed the to heartache the next afternoon, winning the third game from Coveleskie, 5–1. New York scored four times in the first inning and the game could have ended there. "Outside of the first inning," Edwards wrote in his game account, "Coveleskie and his successor, George Uhle, out-pitched the New Yorker, but the American League rules call for an accounting of all nine rounds." Threatening weather held the crowd to about 12,000, or roughly half the size anticipated.

The game was viewed by three former Cleveland managers. Jim McAleer had been the franchise's first manager in 1901; Napoleon Lajoie was the club's star second baseman and skipper when it lost the 1908 pennant by half a game; and Lee Fohl was in town scouting the Tribe for his new employer, and Cleveland's next opponent, the Browns. McAleer and Fohl watched from Dunn's private box.[8]

Chicago finished off a four-game sweep of Washington with a 7–2 victory. At this point, the significant disparity in the number of games played by the three contenders makes it tricky computing how far the White Sox and Yankees were behind the Indians. The Tribe had played 107 games, Chicago 111, and New York 112. The Indians had one fewer victory than both the White Sox and Yankees, but Chicago had lost three more games than Cleveland and New York had lost four more. Standings printed in newspapers of the day didn't include the number of games by which a team trailed the league leader.

The Yankees completed their demolition of the Indians with a 4–3 victory over Caldwell on August 13 to end the western part of their trip on a high note. Included in the game notes were these tidbits:

"Babe Ruth drew seven passes in the series. He made but two hits in seven legal times at bat but scored five runs as the result of gifts given him by Indian hurlers.

"Tris Speaker's batting average suffered a severe slump during the series as he made but two hits in sixteen times at bat. Both were doubles and were made off Mays in Wednesday's game.

"The Browns will be here for a series of two games prior to departing for the east tomorrow night. They have been going splendidly of late and are likely to cause the Indians a lot of trouble unless the tribe strikes its gait again."

There was slight consolation in the fact that the final loss to New York cost the Indians only a half game of their lead over the White Sox as Chicago battled Detroit to a tie in a game called by rain. Unfortunately, Cleveland's lead over Chicago had been just a single game when the day began. The Tribe led the Yankees by just percentage points.

The results of the games played on Saturday, August 14, tightened the race even further. St. Louis extended the Indians' losing streak to five with a 5–3 victory at Morton's expense. Morton gave up four runs and Uhle surrendered one in relief.

"It seemed queer to see Lee Fohl in a St. Louis uniform on the coaching lines trying to beat the team he managed for four years," the *Plain Dealer* noted. The newspaper's game notes also reported that "there were six new ushers in the upper first base pavilion at League Park when yesterday's game began. During batting practice, one of the old crew saw fit to knock a certain Indian. Secretary [Walter] McNichols sought to find out the guilty one, and when his investigations were unsuccessful, he discharged the entire squad in that section of the stands." It seems the Tribe's skid had made just about everyone associated with the team a little testy.

While the Indians were losing, New York defeated Washington and Chicago split a doubleheader with Detroit. Five percentage points now separated the three clubs vying for the American League pennant, with the Indians still clinging to first place, the Yankees exactly one point behind, and the White Sox in third.

For what it was worth, the weekly statistics printed on Sunday, August 15, showed the Indians holding on to the top batting average in the league at .308 but trailing the Yankees in runs scored, 638–612. A loss on that day may well have meant they'd be trailing the Yankees ... and the White Sox, in the standings, too.

Speaking of statistics, in an effort to give nervous Tribe fans something to feel good about despite the current losing streak, the *News* noted that August 15 was a magical date in the American League.

"If you are in first place on August 15th, you are destined to win the American League pennant," said the newspaper. And the Indians were in first place as the day's activities began, if only by a tiny margin. The paper provided a chart showing that each of the last ten pennant winners had occupied first place on August 15. If history repeated itself, Speaker's boys had nothing to worry about. The pennant was assured.

"The Indians will play their last home game until Friday, September 3, when the Tigers make their last appearance of the year in Cleveland," the *Plain Dealer* said. The time of the season had already arrived when such notes columns began mentioning "last appearances" of the year. And the homestand that would begin on September 3, would be the Tribe's last, at least of the regular season.

The Indians made their final game at League Park until September, and the final game ever for one of their players, a memorable one. If, as Edwards had written, Bob Clark had toiled dutifully, pitching batting practice and performing whatever other chores Speaker assigned to him in the hope he'd eventually be given something other than a rookie's task, he would receive that opportunity on the last day of the homestand. Speaker turned to Clark to end the Tribe's losing streak and Clark responded with a four-hit, 5–0 victory over the Browns. The rookie pitched out of trouble twice with the game on the line. With the Indians leading, 2–0, two runners on base and two out in the sixth inning, Clark retired George Sisler on a fly ball to Smith. In the eighth, with the score still 2–0 and the bases loaded, Sisler grounded out to Wambsganss to end the St. Louis threat. The Indians scored three insurance runs in their half of the eighth to make Clark's task easier in the ninth inning.

"Clark has as much stuff as any pitcher on my staff," Speaker said after the game. "I did not feel as if I were experimenting."[9]

It would be the only game Clark would win in the major leagues, but he did it in style. "That was a big win for us," may be the most overused cliché in sports, but Clark's victory was truly a "big win" for the Tribe. Had they embarked on a three-week eastern road trip, starting with three games in New York, on a six-game losing streak and in second place, there's no telling how the rest of the season might have unfolded, particularly given the tragedy that would befall the team the next afternoon in the Polo Grounds.

The reason that Speaker started Clark may have been the unavailability of Uhle, who wouldn't be with the club when it departed that night. "The ex-sandlotter has developed a rather severe case of water on the knee as a result of his tumble near third base in Saturday's game," read the newspaper report. "Dr. M.H. Castle, the club physician, says Uhle may be able to rejoin the club in five or six days, but that his recovery may be delayed longer. The accident is a blow to the Indians as Uhle, when injured, was pitching his best ball of the season."

While the Indians were winning for the first time in six days, Chicago defeated Detroit, and New York ended its road trip with a win in Washington. The Indians would be waiting for the Yankees when they returned to the Polo Grounds the next day, still leading by four percentage points (.636 to .632). The White Sox, having won two more games than the Tribe but also having lost three more, were half a game behind with a winning percentage of .626.

As summed up the Sunday *Plain Dealer*:

> The last eastern trip of the western clubs of the American League starts tomorrow. Upon this trip much depends. If Cleveland or Chicago makes as good a record as the last time they swung around the eastern half of the circuit, New York is going to have a tough time winning the pennant, as neither of the two western contenders will have many games away from home when it returns.
>
> On the other hand, if New York puts up such a stand at home as Chicago did while entertaining the eastern clubs, we will be unable to count the Yankees out of it. The three teams now are bunched so closely that it resolves itself into a question of which of the three can stand the strain down the stretch the best.

The article didn't include a by-line, but whoever wrote it had no idea how accurate that assessment would prove to be.

8

Chappie

Had the decision been left to Martin Daly, Ray Chapman wouldn't have been on the train that pulled out of Cleveland carrying the Indians eastward on the evening of Sunday, August 15.

Chapman wouldn't have been in New York City the following morning. Had the decision been up to Daly, Chapman would've been at his desk at the Pioneer Alloys Company, engaged in his duties as the firm's secretary-treasurer. That was Chapman's off-season job, secured for him through Daly's considerable influence as president of the East Ohio Gas Company.

On October 29, 1919, Daly had become Chapman's father-in-law. In his excellent dual biography of Chapman and Carl Mays, *The Pitch That Killed*, author Mike Sowell described Daly, a native of near by Sandusky, as "a self-made millionaire and one of Cleveland's most prominent citizens." Daly had begun his career in the energy business with John D. Rockefeller's Standard Oil Company and taken the reins of East Ohio Gas in 1901. In the words of Sowell, "with his experience and his clout in the community, Daly had the ability to pave the way for his son-in-law when he left baseball to begin his career as a businessman, and that was exactly what the elder gentleman planned to do."[1]

Martin Daly was a baseball fan, as was his daughter, Kathleen. In an era when few women attended baseball games, Katy Daly was a League Park regular and even learned how to keep score. Her interest in the home team's bachelor shortstop led to an introduction, and soon Katy and Ray were an item. Chapman was frequently invited to dine with the Dalys after a game, and those dinners often expanded into lengthy evenings that included sing-alongs around the piano in the family's Euclid Avenue mansion, led by Chapman. Among the many functions Chapman provided for the Indians, aside from scooping up ground balls, turning double plays and stealing bases, was keeping the club loose with practical jokes and leading his teammates in crooning popular tunes of the day.

Chapman had been the Indians' regular shortstop since 1912. When Tris Speaker arrived in 1916, he and Chapman quickly became almost inseparable companions. "The two men had been teammates for the past four seasons," wrote Sowell, "and in that time a strong bond had developed between them. They had become best friends, as close as any two brothers. During the season they shared a seven room apartment in the Hotel Winton. In the off season, they often hunted together, either near Speaker's home in Texas or in the woods around Chapman's home in the state of Kentucky. Their friendship even extended to their social lives. Speaker went with Jane McMahon, who was first cousin and best friend of Chapman's fiancée. At the wedding, Miss McMahon would serve as Kathleen's bridesmaid, Speaker as Ray's best man."[2]

Despite his and his daughter's fondness for baseball, Daly wanted Chapman to hang up his spikes after the 1919 season. He used his influence with William Smith, the president of Pioneer Alloys, to obtain his son-in-law the secretary-treasurer's position. Daly wanted Chapman to learn how a business was operated so that he could run his own company someday. Daly wanted Chapman to be a full-time businessman, husband and father. In Daly's opinion, traveling all over the eastern half of the country playing baseball wasn't the proper way for a family man, especially the man who would be the father of his grandchildren, the first of which Katy was expecting in August of 1920, to earn a living. Chapman promised to think about retiring.

Rumors that Chapman was doing more than thinking of ending his career picked up steam in the fall of 1919, when Boston shortstop Everett Scott, who was in the midst of a consecutive games played streak that would reach 1,307 contests, expressed a desire to bolt the Red Sox and rejoin former teammates Speaker and Joe Wood in Cleveland. As much as Chapman wanted to please his wife and father-in-law, he had an unfulfilled goal for himself and the long-suffering fans of his adopted hometown. He wanted to win a World Series, and the Tribe's relatively near-miss in 1919 convinced him that 1920 would be the year. He quickly put to rest any talk of immediate retirement.

"I'll play next year, for I want to help give Tris Speaker and the Cleveland fans the first pennant Cleveland has ever won. Then I will talk quitting."[3] Chapman talked about quitting with Ed Bang during the winter of 1919–20, saying "well, I guess I'll be a real businessman. But, gee, it will be hard to pull away from Spoke and the boys."[4] According to Sowell, Chapman told his family shortly before he headed for spring training in New Orleans that 1920 would be his last season. Daly would've preferred retirement sooner rather than later, but he didn't want to be known as the business tycoon who convinced Cleveland's star shortstop to retire at the age of 29. After all, Chapman was a key member of a team picked by almost all the experts to capture the American League pennant that had eluded the franchise for so long.

The temperature approached 80 degrees while humidity engulfed the Polo Grounds on that mid–August Monday afternoon. The Indians built a 3–0 lead against Carl Mays, who had beaten them at League Park just five days earlier. Mays was as unpopular as Chapman was popular, his dour disposition earning him the disdain of opponents and teammates alike. He'd come to the Yankees the season before amid a swirl of controversy.

After winning 61 games for the Red Sox from 1916 to 1918, plus two more in the 1918 World Series, Mays was saddled with a 5–11 record in 1919, when he quit the team after deciding his teammates weren't putting forth on his behalf the same yeoman effort he gave them each time he took the mound. It was another reason why he wasn't the most liked player in the clubhouse. Red Sox manager Ed Barrow immediately suspended Mays, and owner Harry Frazee worked out a deal sending him to the Yankees, a deal that was quickly quashed by American League President Ban Johnson, who felt it set a dangerous precedent. Johnson didn't want unhappy players getting the idea that they could force management to trade them by jumping their clubs, as Mays had done. Frazee and Yankee owners Jacob Ruppert and Tillinghast Huston took Johnson to court and obtained an order restraining Johnson from interfering with the transaction. The skirmish proved to be the beginning of the end of Johnson's vice-like grip on the league he'd founded and presided over for two decades.

Mays won nine of 12 decisions for New York in 1919. He'd win 20 or more games three more times in his career. Mays' lifetime record of 208 victories against 126 defeats, 2.92 ERA and 29 shutouts would probably have earned him enshrinement in the Hall of Fame were it not for the pitch he threw to Chapman leading off the fifth inning for the Indians.

Mays threw with an unorthodox, submarine style motion that made his pitches difficult for batters to see. Chapman crowded the plate, and Mays had thrown two inside pitches in Chapman's first at-bat in an effort to back him away. Like most pitchers, especially during that era, Mays regarded the inside corner of the plate as part of his territory. Whether or not Chapman even saw the first pitch Mays threw in the fifth inning won't ever be known. His reaction, or lack of a reaction, would seem to indicate that he didn't. Or he may have frozen at its approach.

"The ball sailed directly toward Chapman's head, but he made no effort to move," wrote Sowell. Major league batters wouldn't wear helmets for more than 30 years. The idea had been advanced before 1920 and sneered at by players who considered it cowardly. "He remained poised in his crouch, apparently transfixed as the ball flew in and crashed against his left temple with a resounding crack that was audible throughout the ballpark."

Mays, thinking the ball had hit Chapman's bat, picked it up as it dribbled toward the mound and threw to first baseman Wally Pipp, who stepped on the bag for what he thought was a putout. But Pipp quickly realized something was terribly wrong when he saw Chapman on the ground at home plate. Blood was gushing from the shortstop's left ear, yet he tried gamely to stagger to his feet. Umpire Tommy Connolly immediately turned to the stands and screamed, "We need a doctor! Is there a doctor in the house?"[5]

While Connolly tried to secure medical assistance for Chapman, Mays rushed the umpire and did some screaming of his own, insisting the ball had struck the knob of Chapman's bat and that Chapman was faking his injury. It's unknown how Mays thought Chapman could be, given the blood pouring from his ear. According to Sowell, Pipp grabbed Mays and forcibly removed him from the scene, telling him to shut his mouth.

Miraculously, Chapman got to his feet briefly, only to collapse again. He was given a warm round of applause by the gathering in the Polo Grounds as he was assisted by teammates to the clubhouse. No one yet had any idea how serious Chapman's injury was. Harry Lunte, who would replace Chapman in the field, also replaced him on the bases. The Indians added a run to increase their lead to 4–0. Stan Coveleskie blanked the Yankees until the ninth, when they rallied for three runs. Speaker considered lifting Coveleskie with two out and the winning run on base but elected to let him pitch to an unknown pinch-hitter named Lefty O'Doul. Though O'Doul would go on to compile an impressive .349 lifetime average in just under 1,000 major league games, Coveleskie induced him to hit a sharp ground ball to Lunte that ended the contest. The Tribe had maintained its fingertip hold on first place.

Within minutes, baseball would be rendered unimportant.

In the clubhouse, the still-conscious Chapman repeated the words,

"Katy's ring, Katy's ring," to trainer Percy Smallwood. Chapman had given his wedding ring to Smallwood for safe-keeping before the game. Smallwood slipped the band on Chapman's finger. Perhaps he had an idea of what awaited him, and he wanted to be sure he was wearing it when the end came.

John Henry, a former catcher with Boston and Washington and a friend of Chapman's who'd made the trip from Boston to watch the game, rushed to the clubhouse immediately after the incident. Henry did his best to comfort his friend while officials scrambled to get help. "John, for God's sake, don't call Kate," Chapman requested of his friend. Possibly knowing that it was a request Henry couldn't and wouldn't honor, Chapman added, "but if you do, tell her I'm all right."[6] Those were Ray Chapman's last words.

At 9:30 that night, doctors informed Speaker, who was keeping vigil at the hospital, that Chapman's condition was steadily worsening. They warned that it would be unwise to wait until Katy, who was by then on a train bound for New York and not reachable by phone, to arrive in the morning and grant permission for surgery. Speaker gave the doctors permission to proceed. The operation took an hour and 15 minutes, and the doctors emerged guardedly optimistic. Chapman's condition improved, but only slightly and only briefly. He died at 4:40 on the morning of August 17.

Speaker could only look at Katy Chapman when she opened the door to his hotel room later that morning. No words were necessary.

"He's dead, isn't he?" she asked. Speaker could only nod. Katy fainted. Tuesday afternoon's game was postponed. Major league baseball had endured its first, and, to date, its only, fatal injury.

On August 18, the *Plain Dealer*'s sports editor, James Lanyon, summed up his feelings about Chapman's death.

> When that sharp breaking curve ball thrown by Carl Mays at the Polo Grounds Monday afternoon cracked against the skull of Raymond Chapman, shortstop for the Cleveland Indians, ended then and there the baseball career, and twelve hours later the life, of one of the best and cleanest ball players the major leagues have ever known.
>
> Ever since August, 1912, Ray Chapman played shortstop for the Cleveland American League baseball club, except for the periods when out because of injuries. And ever since that August he has been, season after season, the shining light of the Cleveland infield. Baseball fans knew him as a great player. His friends knew him as a man — a real man. Chapman played the

game and played it well. He was far and above the average big leaguer. Yet none has heard of his boasting of any accomplishment. His remarks after games were only of regret of some miscue he had made or praise for some good play made by teammates.

It was a pleasure to talk baseball to Chapman. It was a pleasure to see how big he really was when he could so well subordinate his own sparkling accomplishments and give the credit to the other fellow. Major league baseball produces but few of the real character of Ray Chapman.

Among those who give much consideration now to the chance of the Cleveland club's winning the 1920 American League pennant, there is discussion of how the club will get along without its great shortstop. The blow has been severe to the whole team. But if the members of the club are of the right kind, when they recover from the shock, if they can, they will go out and play championship baseball again for the spirit of Chapman will be with them. Memory of him and how eager he was to attain the championship will ever be with the club. With the spirit of Chapman among them, the Cleveland players cannot fall down.

But the pennant is not all to be considered. Rather had the Indians finished in eighth place than Chapman should have died. Worth more than all the pennants ever offered in any league was the great shortstop. In the death of Chapman, baseball loses one of the cleanest players it ever produced, but the saddest of all, the world loses A MAN.

Beneath Lanyon's column was another story with the headline, "RAY CHAPMAN WAS LIFE OF CLEVELAND INDIANS, IN VICTORY AND DEFEAT." The Indians hadn't lost their best player, but they had lost their heart and soul.

Ed Bang paid tribute to Chapman on the front page of the *News:*

He was clean-cut, high-minded, honest and straight forward. He had a personality that contagious, for once you met Ray Chapman you were glad to list him among your friends. Chappie was just as much at home in the ballroom in the highest society as he was among his diamond associates on the field, on the bench or in the clubhouse. He was 100 percent self all the time, no frills ... and that is the trait that won him fast friends among the heads of manufacturing, industrial and mercantile concerns as well as among the newsies on the street corners. All of them will mourn the passing not only of Chappie, the great shortstop, but Ray Chapman, the man and their friend.

If the Indians should win the world's championship — and

there is not one of the players who would not willingly pass up
the honor if it would only bring Chappie back — everybody will
realize the achievement could not have been accomplished without the aid given by the great little shortstop in the past, who
has been called to his reward.

From his Chicago office, league president Johnson issued a statement. "The American League suffered an irreparable loss in the death of Ray Chapman. In all his years as a member of the Cleveland ball club, he never gave the club officials, umpires or the league trouble of any sort. He was a high-minded young man of exemplary habits and I regret his death more than I can express in words."[7]

Underneath the headline, "BANISH THE BEANBALL," Tenney demanded the abolition of the potentially deadly weapon pitchers used liberally in that rough and tumble era, and still use today.

> There is no charge that Carl Mays intentionally hit Ray
> Chapman. Players exonerate him. But Chappie is dead.
> Whether the ball was thrown intentionally or unintentionally,
> the result is the same. And there is the feeling that Chappie
> would be alive and at short today if there had been a heavy
> penalty against throwing the kind of ball that killed him.
>
> The writer believes that with the facts of Chapman's death
> before them, baseball's lawmakers should meet in a special midseason session and adopt a rule that would banish the beanball,
> intentional or unintentional, from the game forever. Penalize the
> ball thrown at the head of the batsman, whether by design or
> otherwise, by giving the batsman and all base runners two bases
> each — and you will see the last of the beanball. The beanball
> has never contributed to the science of baseball. And when the
> beanball costs games, pitchers will not throw them.

Players on the Boston club, many of them former teammates of Mays who were none too fond of him to begin with, circulated a petition seeking his permanent banishment from baseball. The petition was largely ignored, but the question of whether or not Mays should be permitted to continue pitching was not. Within days of the Chapman incident, Johnson decided that there was no logical reason to suspend or banish Mays. There was no evidence that his pitch had been intended to harm Chapman. Being struck in the head by a pitched ball was, then as now, an occupational hazard accepted by men who chose to play professional baseball, as Chapman had done.

Mays, understandably, was shaken by the death. However, those who felt certain he would never find the courage to take the mound again —

Ray Chapman was the "heart and soul" of the Indians who was, arguably, in the midst of a Hall of Fame career when he was fatally beaned by Carl Mays of the Yankees on August 16th. The Indians stumbled badly without him.

and there were many who were convinced Mays had thrown his last pitch — underestimated him. Among them were many of his Yankee teammates, who feared Mays would be useless for the rest of the season, and Tenney, who expressed the opinion that "it's unbelievable that he could get up there again and pitch with the same cool precision that has been winning him so many ball games. He can't help being nervous every time one of his shoots comes uncomfortably close to a batsman. The passing of Mays from the game needn't surprise anyone if it comes in the near future."

In his next start, at the Polo Grounds in front of a sympathetic crowd that greeted him warmly, Mays calmly threw a shutout at the Tigers. The fact that one of his pitches had killed a man never seemed to bother Mays, at least while he was working.

No one on either side felt like playing baseball on August 18, but, the season continued. "Some brilliant pitching by Bagby carried along a dejected ball team for eight innings at the Polo Grounds this afternoon," read W.J. Slocum's game account, "but the Cleveland boxman succumbed in the ninth to the strain under which he labored and the Yankees won, 4 to 3. A single by [Duffy] Lewis and a home run drive to the right field gate by Pipp gave the Yankees two runs and pulled out a victory that seemed destined for the Indians." Slocum noted that "depression hung over the Polo Grounds all afternoon, affecting players of both teams and the crowd." That crowd was in the vicinity of 38,000. Philadelphia shut out Chicago that afternoon, so the Indians stayed a half game ahead of the White Sox. Their lead over the Yankees was reduced to the same margin.

The Indians won the last game they were scheduled to play in New York for the season, 3–2, on August 19. Elmer Smith homered for the Tribe to back the five-hit pitching of Caldwell. One of those five hits was a homer by Ruth. The Indians and Yankees had seen quite enough of each other, having played seven times in ten days. Three more meetings would take place at League Park in September. Chicago's game in Philadelphia was postponed by wet grounds, so the Indians left New York with a one-game lead on the White Sox and 1½ on the Yankees. The next day's scheduled game in Boston had already been postponed to allow the team to return to Cleveland and attend Chapman's funeral.

On August 20, Henry Edwards assessed the situation:

> Statements of pessimistic critics that there is no sentiment in baseball has [sic] been exploded by the action of big-hearted Jim Dunn, owner of the Cleveland baseball club. The funeral of Ray Chapman, killed on his field of action, was set for this morning. The Indians played in New York yesterday and were to play in Boston today.
>
> Dunn knew the hearts of his players would not be in any game they were to play on the day their pal was laid to his final rest. He knew every one of them wanted to be in Cleveland, where his thoughts would be. What does he do but arrange for the postponement of the game at Boston and bring the boys home from New York at his own expense — no small item.
>
> It was only what could have been expected of Dunn, though, for it is conceded that the Indians, from Jim Dunn on down, compose the happiest family in major leaguedom. Jim Dunn does not regard his players as employees. They are his 'boys,' his 'pals.' Neither do the players regard Dunn as merely an employer. To them he is Jim, their colleague, their pal.
>
> When Dunn asked that the game in Boston scheduled for today be postponed, Harry Frazee, the owner of the Red Sox, arose to the occasion gracefully. Don't let them tell you there is no sentiment in baseball. If that were the case, would Tris Speaker leave his baseball club when it was dashing down the stretch in a pennant race that means so much to him? Would he lay aside all thoughts of a pennant, the world's series and the commercial end of the game if there were no sentiment in baseball?

Though Chapman had been Speaker's closest friend on the club, Spoke couldn't attend the funeral. Newspaper reports said that he was bedridden in the Daly family mansion, under a physician's care, suffering from a "nervous breakdown." Speaker's biographer, Timothy Gay, tells a different story.

Speaker was appalled by Katy Chapman's claim that her husband planned to convert to Catholicism, an announcement that also, according to Gay, "came as a harsh jolt ... to Ray's parents."[8] As if the strain of a tight pennant race and Chapman's death weren't enough to fray the players' nerves, the Indians were on the verge of becoming a team ripped apart by dissension over where their beloved teammate's funeral service would be held and where he'd be laid to rest. The Daly family wanted the service in a Catholic cathedral and the burial in the family plot in Cleveland's Calvary Cemetery. The Tribe's Catholic players agreed. Speaker, and the Protestant players, wouldn't hear of it.

"Speaker was a very bigoted man at the time," Gay quoted Wambsganss as saying when interviewed in the 1960s. "He was a 32nd degree Mason of the south and he couldn't see the idea of Chapman being buried in the cathedral."[9]

Tempers reached the breaking point and resulted in a knock-down, drag-out brawl between Speaker, O'Neill and Graney. Just as the writers who covered the Yankees never wrote a word about Ruth's various transgressions, nothing of the fisticuffs was ever reported in the Cleveland newspapers. When Edwards told his readers that Speaker was bedridden in the Daly mansion battling a nervous breakdown, he was actually recovering from the wounds inflicted by O'Neill, who himself was badly beaten by Speaker and Graney.

"They [Speaker and Graney] really knocked the hell out of [O'Neill]," Gay quoted Wambsganss as saying. Years later, Wamby asked Graney for the truth, and Graney insisted the incident never happened. "But I know damn well it did," said Wambsganss.[10]

In the end, Speaker had his way. Chapman was buried in a Protestant section of Cleveland's Lakeview Cemetery. Joe Wood was appointed the Tribe's interim manager until Speaker could pull himself together.[11] And that took some time.

While the Indians were paying their final respects to their fallen friend and teammate, Chicago was winning two games from Philadelphia, the second of which was a forfeit declared when the playing field at Shibe Park couldn't be cleared of rowdy fans. The Indians led the White Sox by five percentage points when they boarded their train for Boston.

It may seem crass, but on the very day Chapman died, Tenney, in addition to venting his rage at the use of the beanball, had the presence of mind to consider pragmatically the Indians' immediate problem. "This is Harry Lunte's big chance. The young infielder possesses one of the greatest pairs of hands in the game today, bigger and roomier than the mitts of any other ball player on the team. But he hasn't had the chance to stick in the game regularly on the great combination of Gardner, Chapman, Wamby and Johnston. But Spoke has always had the greatest faith in Lunte's ability to deliver the goods if ever the opportunity presented itself. On defense, there seems to be little question of his making good, but on the offense, he'll have to go some to fill Chappie's shoes."

The mention of replacing Chapman leads to the question of, had he played long enough to qualify, his fitness for induction into baseball's Hall of Fame, which didn't even exist in 1920. In Jim Bresnahan's intriguing book, *Baseball Experts on What Might Have Been: Play It Again,* Bill James puts forth a case on behalf of a Chapman candidacy. "Ray Chapman would have been a Hall of Famer if he had not been killed," James says, noting that Chapman was one of four major league shortstops born in 1891. "If you compare Chapman with those three players [Dave (Beauty) Bancroft, Walter (Rabbit) Maranville, and Cleveland native Roger Peckinpaugh] up through 1920, Chapman was clearly the best of the group. Since two of those three [Bancroft and Maranville] made it to the Hall, I think you would have to say Chapman would have made the Hall of Fame as well."[12]

In the book, *Total Baseball,* John B. Holway and Bob Carroll include Chapman in the chapter entitled "The 400 Greatest." Holway and Carroll describe Chapman as "the AL's leading shortstop" at the time of his death.[13]

As for the requirement that a player participate in a minimum of ten major league seasons to be eligible for Hall of Fame enshrinement, Sowell believes Chapman would've put his retirement plans on hold after winning the 1920 World Series and suited up again the following season, ignoring the wishes of his wife and father-in-law.[14] Had he done so, 1921 would've been Chapman's tenth season in the big leagues. His career numbers of 1,050 games played, .278 batting average, 1,053 hits, 233 stolen bases and .939 fielding average compare favorably to Maranville's .258 average, 2,605 hits and .956 fielding percentage (in 19 full seasons and parts of four others) and Bancroft's .279 average, 2,004 hits and .944 fielding average over 16 seasons.

Chapman did receive one Hall of Fame vote in 1938, before the ten-year requirement was adopted. Chapman's candidacy has never been seriously considered by the Veterans' Committee, appointed by the Hall of Fame to re-open the cases of old-timers passed over by the Baseball Writers Association of America. It was the Veterans' Committee which enshrined

Cleveland Naps pitcher Addie Joss, who won 160 games against 97 defeats and posted the second-lowest career ERA in modern baseball history (1.88) from 1902 to 1910. Joss died of tubercular meningitis days before the 1911 season began, and his accomplishments inspired the Veterans' Committee to waive the 10-year rule. It would have to do the same for Chapman.

"The Cleveland Indians, physically weary from the long night trip from Cleveland, mentally tired because of the strain and worry of the past few days and lacking the capable leadership of Tris Speaker, were unable to score a run in the doubleheader with the Red Sox this afternoon," read Burt Whitman's game story in the *Plain Dealer,* "trailing 12 to 0 and 4 to 0 with Waite Hoyt and Herb Pennock allowing only three hits in each engagement. In addition, the Indians, after setting the pace practically all season, were forced to see the White Sox slip into first place. It was far from a happy matinee."

Morton took the shellacking in the first game and Coveleskie was the loser in the second. With Chicago beating Washington, Cleveland fell into second place as Whitman noted, 1½ games behind the White Sox. The Yankees lost to Detroit and were 2½ out, a game behind the Indians.

The Indians had the day off after the double pasting in Fenway Park. Edwards took advantage of the off day, August 22, to assure his readers that Chapman's death hadn't squeezed all the fight out of the team.

> The Indians will fight harder than ever. They will not quit because Chapman is gone. They will battle more fiercely than before in memory of their departed colleague.
>
> "Carry on as your departed brother would have you do" was the advice given the Indians by the Rev. Dr. William A. Scullen in the funeral oration Friday morning, and every Indian took the advice to heart and decided it would not be his fault if Cleveland lost the pennant. "Chappie had his heart and soul in the fight for the pennant," said Chester Thomas of the Indians. "And we shall fight as we would were he here with us with this difference — we shall fight just enough harder to make up for his absence."
>
> With such a spirit actuating the tribe, Chicago and New York will have to extend themselves to wrest first place from the Indians despite the fact the Cleveland team is still torn by the shock. It was a wonderful spirit displayed by Tris Speaker. For four days he was so grief stricken by the death of his friend he could not eat. He kept up solely on his nerve and aided the bereaved family in its days of trial. But when the morning of the funeral arrived, nature could stand the punishment no longer. His spirit was willing but his body rebelled.

The time had come for Speaker to go back to work. He needed his team, and his team needed its leader, and its leader's bat and glove. While the Indians rested on August 23, Chicago beat Washington and Detroit topped New York. The Indians were now two games behind the White Sox.

"The Indians are gradually returning to normal as they played a little closer to the ground in gaining a 2 to 1 decision in the first game of a doubleheader today," read the wire service account of the games played on August 24, "and then forced the hose to thirteen innings in the second encounter before the men of Barrow gained the 4 to 3 edge." It was an indication of how far the Indians had fallen that they were being applauded for battling a team that they had dominated the past two seasons into extra innings before succumbing.

Having missed four games, Speaker arrived at Fenway Park in time to pinch-hit for O'Neill in the first game. He started in center field in the nightcap and went hitless in three at-bats. With the White Sox idle, the Indians stayed two games out of first. The Yankees beat Detroit, drawing them to within three games of first place, and within one game of second.

Boston won the series finale, 7–2, besting Bob Clark. The *Plain Dealer*'s headline above its game story read, "CLEVELAND CLUB LOOKS LESS LIKE CHAMPION THAN RED SOX." The Red Sox were in fifth place at the time but had taken four out of five from the Indians. Both Chicago and New York lost, so Cleveland surrendered no ground in the pennant race.

Speaker wasn't worried about the understandable slide in the wake of an unforeseeable tragedy. At least he professed not to be. "We've lost a bit of ground to Chicago in the past few days, but we are still right on the heels of the White Sox and can make it up. In the past few years, the Indians have been the greatest September club in either league, and there's no reason why this year should prove an exception. We're in a fine position to cop with that driving finish in September to go on."[15] Speaker might have added, but didn't, that it wouldn't hurt to be spending most of September at home, as the Indians would.

The Indians fortunes didn't change when they headed south to Philadelphia. The suddenly silent bats were limited to three hits in a 2–1 loss on August 25. "The tribe lost to the Athletics today," read the newspaper story, "but they looked like anything except a ball club that is losing its grip. There was more fight in the tribe's make-up than there was in Jack Dempsey when he hung it on J. Willard." Most of the fight was exhibited by Speaker, who disagreed vehemently with a call made by umpire George Hildebrand, the same umpire that Speaker had defended from angry fans the first time the Indians visited Philadelphia. The game story indicated that Hildebrand took more venom from Speaker than he normally would have, aware of the pressure Speaker had been under. Neither Chicago nor New York was scheduled to play that day, so the Indians lost only half a game to the team they were trying to catch, and half a game to the team they were trying to fend off. Those teams would open a series in the Polo Grounds the next day.

The Tribe's offensive woes continued on August 26. A solid effort by Caldwell was wasted as the Athletics triumphed again, 3–2. The once rampaging Cleveland bats had now accounted for just sixteen runs in the nine games since the Chapman incident. The White Sox scored the same number of runs in dismantling New York, 16–4, to increase their lead over the Tribe to 3½ games and their lead over the Yankees to four.

"Over in Chicago, they're already counting the 1920 pennant as copped by the White Sox," wrote Tenney, who begged to differ with that conclusion. "Chicagoans are predicting the coming series will see the same rival teams going against each other as last year. And they're saying that the White Sox will get good and even for the trimming the Reds gave 'em last year — that they'll incidentally go so good that those rumors about the White Sox throwing the last series will be rammed down the throats of all who repeat them." Those prematurely giddy White Sox fans would prove to be off base on all counts.

"Well, it looks as if the Cleveland ball club has returned to its old form," began the cheery game story in the *Plain Dealer* the morning after the Indians pounded Philadelphia, 15–3, on August 27. "After getting a lot of wild, wooly and woozy baseball out of its system, a massacre was staged at Shibe Park this afternoon with the Athletics taking the short end. The final count was 15 to 3, which is a big enough margin to win a flock of ball games. Up 'til today, the Indians had won four of sixteen contests." The newspaper's game notes said that "Walter Mails, the new Indians pitcher, has not arrived from the coast. This is causing no annoyance. All the mails are slow these days."

Six days had passed since the Indians purchased the contract of Mails, a left-handed pitcher who modestly referred to himself as "The Great Mails," (others called him "Duster") from Portland of the Pacific Coast League. The price was $10,000 in cash and "players to be named later." Mails had plenty to be modest about, despite his nickname. He'd pitched in 13 games with Brooklyn in 1915 and '16, winning none and losing two. But Speaker needed another starting pitcher — Clark wasn't the answer — and he preferred a left-hander. The Indians' scouting reports on Mails

Without Walter (Duster) Mails, the Indians probably wouldn't have won anything in 1920. Mails joined the team in late August and won seven decisions without a loss, including a crucial shutout of the White Sox in late September. Mails added a whitewash of the Dodgers in the World Series.

were positive, so Dunn opened his checkbook and hoped that Mails would be the last piece to the Tribe's championship puzzle. He wouldn't be, through no fault of his own.

The newspaper's joke about Mails being late to report did not indicate that Cleveland's sense of humor was returning after the Chapman incident. As Whitey Lewis wrote in his history of the team, "The Chapman tragedy had left the manager and his players with a very limited sense of humor. There was scant bantering, and jokes were relayed only in the comparative hush of private rooms."[16] The players would soon come to realize that the pall hanging over the team was part of the reason it was in danger of falling out of a pennant race it had led most of the season. Keeping the club loose had been Chapman's specialty. The players knew the gloom and doom wasn't what Chappie would've wanted, and they eventually did something about it.

While the Indians were drubbing the Athletics, the Yankees beat Chicago. The Indians' first-place deficit was reduced to 2½ games. It dropped by another half game on August 28, when the Tribe's game was rained out while the Yankees blanked the White Sox. The Indians arrived in Washington, the last stop on their eastern tour, trailing by two games.

Whatever momentum the Indians may have gained in Philadelphia must've been washed away by the previous day's rain. The Senators scored in the bottom of the ninth to hand Coveleskie a 3–2 loss as the offense was again missing. Caldwell lthen evened the series with an 8–2 victory on August 30. The same day, Tenney offered the Tribe's front office a suggestion as to where it could find a shortstop if Lunte was found to be wanting.

"The Indians don't have to go outside their own town of Cleveland to grab off a topnotcher to help fill the gap caused by Chappie's tragic fate. They could do a whole lot worse by going further away and overlooking Petie Johns, the manager-shortstop who is right now making Templar Motors the most feared team in Class AAA on the sandlots. Petie's one of the brainiest ball players in the business. He's a hard hitter and a great infielder. He'd be on the St. Louis Browns right now if he hadn't said he wanted to get out of pro baseball and stick around his hometown of Cleveland. But undoubtedly he could be persuaded to jump into the breach for the Tribe."

Johns' major league career consisted of 28 games with the White Sox in 1915 and 46 games with the Browns in 1918. His combined batting average was an underwhelming .196 with five extra base hits and 22 runs batted in. The Browns' shortstop in 1920, Wally Gerber, hit .279 and drove in 60 runs while playing in every game, so it seems likely that had Johns made the St. Louis roster, it would've been as a substitute for a player who didn't need one. Although a player jumping from the sandlots to the major leagues wasn't unprecedented (Uhle had done it, and he had no previous big league experience, unlike Johns) the Indians ignored Tenney's well-intentioned scouting report.

On the morning of August 31, for the first time at the end of a month since April, the name "Cleveland" wasn't found at the top of the American League standings. The numbers stacked up like this:

Chicago	77–47	.621	—
New York	77–49	.611	1
Cleveland	75–48	.610	1½
St. Louis	61–58	.513	13½
Boston	58–64	.475	18
Washington	52–65	.444	22½
Detroit	48–73	.397	27½
Philadelphia	39–83	.320	37

The Indians wrapped up the month with a 7–1 victory over the Senators, but no one was sorry to see August end. The Indians had won 11 games and lost 16. They'd fallen from first to third place. They'd endured the tragic death of their starting shortstop, beloved teammate and friend. They'd watched their manager punch out their catcher and the team divide along religious lines. They'd stopped singing and laughing. They still needed a fourth starting pitcher to fill out the rotation behind Coveleskie,

Bagby and Caldwell. The now departed Elmer Myers had, somewhere between League Park and Fenway Park, located the control that had eluded him with the Indians and was racking up victory after victory for Boston, making the inconsistency of Morton and Uhle even more maddening. Could anything else go wrong?

You bet it could.

9

Thank You, Miss Jamieson

From Myers to Uhle to Morton to Mails.

The latest candidate to fill the fourth spot in the Indians' starting rotation, Duster Mails, took the mound in the home half of the first inning at Washington's Griffith Stadium on September 1 and proceeded to lay an egg. The Senators nicked a nervous Mails for two runs on two hits and a walk in the first inning. When Mails walked the lead off batter in the second, Speaker had seen enough. Mails was dismissed and Guy Morton was summoned. Morton, who had pitched well the last time the Indians visited Washington, winning twice, continued his success against the Senators. He allowed the runner he inherited to score, but then limited Washington to a run on five hits over eight innings as the Tribe rallied for a 9–5 victory.

Mails' Cleveland debut hadn't been horrid. Had he been Coveleskie, Bagby or Caldwell, Speaker undoubtedly would've given him a chance to work through his early difficulties. But Speaker was in no mood, or position, to be patient with a new arrival seeking his first major league victory and applied the quick hook. Mails, however, had come highly recommended. No less an authority than Frank Chance, fresh off his prediction that the Tribe would cop the pennant if it could hold off the White Sox, had assured the Indians that Mails was the best left-handed pitcher in the Pacific Coast League. Having cost the Indians $10,000 in cash and players valued at $25,000 more, he'd get another opportunity to prove Chance correct.

The two "players to be named later" sent to Portland by the Indians were Tony Faeth and Dick Niehaus, both of whom tried and failed to be the reliable left-handed reliever Speaker needed. Faeth had no decisions in 13 appearances with a 4.32 ERA. He would not return to the major leagues. Niehaus had a 1–2 record in 19 appearances, including three starts, with a 3.60 ERA. He, too, would never again pitch in the majors.

As the Indians wrapped up their road trip with the win in Washington, Boston beat Chicago and New York shut out St. Louis. Seven percentage points separated the top three teams in the American League as the Indians headed for home and their final League Park homestand of the regular season.

"Jim Dunn, president of the Indians, is as confident as he was a month ago that the Indians will win the pennant," wrote Henry Edwards in the *Plain Dealer* on September 2. "Dunn, who came to town yesterday to go over plans for seating fans at League Park in case the tribe wins the championship, said, 'We have had our slump and are going along nicely now while the White Sox have just started to go through what we went through the last two weeks. I am not worrying about my boys. They have recovered from the disaster that hit them and I expect them to come through nicely for the Cleveland baseball public during the next few weeks.'

According to the Edwards article, the owner had more to say. "'The news from the east was discouraging for a time, but I never gave up hope, for I have too much faith in Tris Speaker and the other men who compose one of the best teams Cleveland ever had. Through all the trouble, we had strong pitching, and that was what we needed more than anything else. We all know the Indians can hit. Give us such pitching as we have had the last few weeks and we are going to be a hard team to beat.'"[1]

The Indians added a pitcher in early September, but not one they could use during the heat of a pennant chase. Ted Odenwald, who had opened some eyes at Des Moines, sustained an injury and was sent back to Cleveland, with the owner of the Des Moines club "preferring that Dunn should pay his salary while he is getting back in shape," according to a newspaper report.

When vying for a pennant, a team can always benefit from some help from an old friend. Elmer Myers, who had apparently found the control of his curveball that had eluded him in Cleveland earlier in the season, pitched the Red Sox past the Yankees, 6–2, on September 2 while the Indians weren't scheduled. The Tribe's lead on Chicago remained a half game. The Yankees trailed by 11 percentage points.

James Lanyon rolled out the red carpet for the Indians on the morning of the day before the season's final homestand opened.

> The welcome sign is hung out today for the Cleveland Indians. They are home, tomahawks in their hands, for the final

stretch down the pennant path. They went away in first place, and they returned in first place, although at one stage of the game they gave way, weakened and slipped into second position for a short period. But no one can blame them.

Now that the boys are home to show the home fans from now until September 26th that they are the fighting ball club they were earlier in the season, let the hammers be buried and the boosters get busy. Be a plugger for the ball club instead of a kicker. Let the grandstand managers turn the managing job over to Tris Speaker in its entirety. Jim Dunn did, and he is as much interested in the success of the club as anybody.

The club is in the lead. It has the advantage of playing most of its remaining games on its home diamond. It should wind up in the position it now holds. So let's go along with the team. The schedule of the league is such that the Cleveland club finds itself in an advantageous a position this early September as it ever did. Cheer up, you chaps who were down in the dumps a week ago and who said "they always get along this far and then break. That's the best we can get." The race is not over. The Indians have the pole. There is a good chance the pennant will come to Cleveland. For the sake of the indomitable manager, Tris Speaker; for the club's great owner, Jim Dunn; and, as the ball players and others say, "for Chappie," let's plug along for the ball club and do not give up or whine from now until the season ends. Be of good cheer.

More than 15,000 fans were in League Park to welcome the Indians home and participate in a memorial service honoring Chapman on September 3. The newspaper account provided details:

> The services were short and impressive. A [bugler] from the Cleveland Naval Reserves, of which Chapman was a member during the war, first appeared near the score board and sounded "Colors" and "Retreat" as the stars and stripes were raised and then lowered. As this was done, the two teams and the spectators stood at attention with bared heads. A choir led by Harper Garcia Smyth sang "Lead Kindly Light" accompanied by an orchestra led by Walter Logan. In came the [bugler] to take a stand near the position filled for eight years by the deceased ball player. There he sounded "Taps." That was all, but there was a suspicious lump in the throat of many a fan as the last notes of the bugle call faded away and the game began.[2]

The ceremony was followed by a classic pitcher's duel between Coveleskie and Detroit's Hubert (Dutch) Leonard. The Tigers were held to five hits but scored the game's only run in the ninth inning.

All was not solemnity at the corner of Lexington Avenue and East 66th that late summer day. "Waivers were asked on many a straw hat at yesterday's game," the *Plain Dealer* reported, "the head gear being torn up and thrown upon the field." This wasn't done in anguish over the loss of Chapman or anger over the Indians' failure to dent home plate even once, but because fashion dictated that straw hats weren't to be worn after Labor Day, which was just three days away. "Jim Dunn was one of the sufferers," the newspaper noted, "the Indians showing no respect to their employer when he walked into the club house wearing his straw lid prior to the game." Such treatment was expected since Dunn was, after all, "one of the boys." And such hijinks were just the sort of thing Chapman would've approved of. The black cloud over the Indians was lifting.

Elsewhere on that Friday afternoon, St. Louis defeated Chicago and New York topped Boston. The three contenders were separated by a measly five percentage points. Things were tight in the National League as well. Three teams were vying for the right to meet either the Indians, White Sox or Yankees in the World Series. The defending world champion Reds led Brooklyn by half a game and the Giants by two. Yet, it wouldn't stay close for long.

"Defeating the Tigers, 12 to 3, at League Park yesterday," wrote an almost giddy Edwards in the *Plain Dealer* in describing the September 4 game, "the Indians displayed all their old ginger, taking all kinds of chances in the field and upon the bases and getting away with them. No fielding chance was too difficult for them to attempt, no chance on the bases too daring. They ran the paths like scared deer, hustled about the greensward like veritable ball hawks and let nothing escape them. Against such a slap-dash article of baseball, Detroit never had a chance, even though it batted practically as hard as the tribe."

Caldwell was touched for ten hits and two first-inning runs. The Indians responded with six runs in the second, and Slim cruised for the rest of the afternoon. The other contenders were playing doubleheaders on that Saturday. Chicago split with St. Louis and New York did the same with Boston. The Indians now led the Yankees by a half game and the White Sox by a full game.

The weekly Sunday baseball statistics printed on September 5 showed that the Indians had fallen into a tie with St. Louis for highest team batting average, both clubs hitting an even .300. Individually, Speaker led George Sisler of the Browns by a point, .395 to .394.

The Indians scored two eighth-inning runs to break a 2–2 deadlock that afternoon, and the insurance tally was needed as Bagby gave one of the runs back in the ninth before hanging on for a 4–3 victory. The contest was briskly played and gave the patrons plenty of time to enjoy other Sunday afternoon activities. "The game at League Park yesterday was one of the shortest ever played in Cleveland, taking only one hour and eleven minutes," reported the newspaper game notes. "Some watches in the press box recorded an hour and twelve minutes while others had it at an hour and ten minutes.

"It was rapid fire work to finish a contest in such a short time, especially as it was showering half the period, thus rendering the ball hard for the pitchers to handle. The quickest inning was the third, when ["Hooks"] Dauss fanned on three pitched balls and [Ralph] Young and ["Donie"] Bush was retired [sic] on the first ball pitched."[3] It was far from a typical Bagby inning.

Joe Evans, normally an outfielder, made his first appearance as an infielder, taking over for Harry Lunte at shortstop in the eighth inning after Lunte (and his .196 batting average) had given way to pinch-hitter Graney in the seventh. Little did anyone know that Evans was about to become the club's regular shortstop, if only temporarily.

Mails made his second start as an Indian in the first game of the Labor Day twinbill against St. Louis on September 6 and calmed any fears that Dunn and Speaker may have had about the wisdom of his acquisition. Mails restricted St. Louis to seven hits in a 7–2 victory. The afternoon game was a different story.

Joe Evans played well wherever the Indians needed him in 1920, until they asked him to play shortstop. Evans' real value to the club was at the plate.

"With St. Louis leading by one run in the last half of the ninth inning of yesterday's battle at League Park," wrote Edwards in his game account, "the Indians staged one of the greatest rallies in the recent history of baseball in Cleveland, winning the contest, 6 to 5." The great rally consisted of a one out triple by Graney, pinch-hitting for Bill Wambsganss, whose bat never caught fire as Edwards had predicted it would, against Dixie Davis, an 18-game winner for the Browns who couldn't close the deal on that Labor Day afternoon. Speaker singled Graney home to tie the game, and Elmer Smith's double put runners on second and third. Larry Gardner, "who cares little for hits when none of the bases is occupied," according to Edwards, "came through with a drive to right center that would have been good for two or three bases had the Vermonter elected to run it out." Gardner settled for a single and the Indians had a sweep. According to Edwards, many men in the crowd of 23,000 who hadn't yet discarded their straw hats celebrated the victory by flinging them onto the field.

That ninth-inning rally proved crucial as all three contenders swept their Labor Day doubleheaders. Eleven percentage points separated the Indians, White Sox and Yankees. Just two points separated Chicago and New York.

Lost in the euphoria of the rally was an injury suffered by Lunte, who had filled in ably (at least defensively) for Chapman, in the first game. Tenney described the injury as a "charley horse," but it was serious enough to render Lunte ineffective for the rest of the season and send the Indians searching yet again for a shortstop.

Neither of the first-place teams was scheduled to play on September 7, and it cost them in the standings. "The major league pennant races became closer today when the leads of the Cincinnati Nationals and the Cleveland Americans were cut to the hair breadth margin of one game," noted the *Plain Dealer*. "While both leaders were resting, the Brooklyn Nationals won twice from Philadelphia. The New York Americans victory over the Athletics put them in second place, a full game ahead of Chicago, which lost to Detroit. The New York Nationals also had a day of leisure when rain prevented the playing of a doubleheader with Boston. The Giants are 2½ games behind Cincinnati."

The headline on the sports page of the *Plain Dealer* the same morning read, "INDIANS MUST SIDETRACK ONRUSHING YANKEES IN CRUCIAL SERIES OPENING TOMORROW." "Every series the Indians play from now on may be termed crucial," Edwards wrote, "but the three game clash with the Yankees that starts tomorrow may be considered crucial to the 'nth' degree as New York comes to town close at the heels of the Indians and striving to win the pennant.

"It is almost imperative that the tribe win two out of the three games to stave off the rush of the Yankees and to remain ahead of Chicago, which should take two out of three games with Boston. True, Boston won three straight from the White Sox recently at Boston, but the White Sox are a stronger team on their own field."

The paper carried a couple of other items of note.

> Carl Mays, New York American League pitcher who threw the ball which resulted in the death of shortstop Ray Chapman of the Cleveland team, did not accompany the Yankees when they left here tonight on their western trip. Col. T.L. Huston, one of the club owners, announced that Mays would not be with the team during the series which opens in Cleveland Thursday, but that he would rejoin the club in Detroit. "We are not taking Mays to Cleveland," said Col. Huston, "not because we think there is any danger of trouble, but out of respect to the feelings of the people there. We don't want to offend them. It is largely a matter of sentiment."[4]

On their way to Cleveland, the Yankees stopped in Pittsburgh for an exhibition game against the Pirates. It proved to be costly as centerfielder Ping Bodie broke his leg sliding into home plate trying to score on a wild pitch in the first inning. Bodie's season was over just as the Yankees were about to begin an important series in Cleveland, because of an effort to make a few extra dollars for a couple of millionaire owners. For the record, New York won, 7–3, and the fans received what they hoped for as Ruth hit a home run. Lanyon made a promise to his readers on the morning of September 9, the day of the series opener.

> The New Yorkers will face a different team than that which they went against on their last visit here, when they took four straight games. The Cleveland club today will be a fighting machine, right on the edge for the best sort of baseball. It is a determined aggregation filled with pep and confidence.
> The Indians did not seem so confident when New York was here before. They took their lickings day after day and came back for more. It is their intention to turn the tables this time and administer the trouncing day after day. Every bit of baseball strategy at their command, every ounce of strength will be put into winning the games of this series. And behind the Indians will be several thousand fans, pulling every minute. Ability, confidence and moral support are assets they have at the start.

May they retain them. The Indians will go in to win every game on its merits. They will play baseball and the best kind of baseball. The Indians are out to win.

And win the Indians did, trouncing the visitors, 10–4, on September 9. It was Doc Johnston's 33rd birthday (he claimed, according to the *News,* to be a mere lad of 27), and he celebrated with two triples and a pair of singles. Edwards gloated in his account:

Boasting of their victorious visit to Cleveland last month, when they won four straight games, the New York Yankees came to town yesterday, confident of repeating to the extent of taking all three games to be played. At 5:31, when yesterday's contest at League Park was completed, the score board showed that Cleveland had won the first battle, 10 to 4.

It was a veritable rout. The New York club does not act like one that can come up from behind and wrest victory out of an impending defeat. Once the redskins acquired a lead of three runs they curled up and called it a day. They were through as far as Thursday was concerned and it mattered not to them whether Cleveland scored ten or twenty runs. They manifested a spirit exactly the reverse of that displayed by the Indians, who twice came from behind and then tied the score and finally went out in front, never to be headed again.

The Indians made Coveleskie's task harder by committing five errors. Ruth played centerfield, substituting for his injured roommate, Bodie. Chicago beat Boston, giving the Tribe a one game lead over the White Sox and a 1½ game advantage over the Yankees.

Also on September 9, the *Press* published a column carrying the byline of Eddie Cicotte, the ace pitcher of the White Sox who was up to his eyeballs in the Black Sox scandal. It was Cicotte, normally a master of control, who threw the pitch that plunked Cincinnati's lead off batter, Morrie Rath, in the first inning of the first game of the 1919 World Series, signaling the gamblers that the "fix" was on.

"If any one case of the three leading American League clubs can step out right now, it will be that club's pennant. I think the White Sox will come thru [sic] and win the pennant, but, of course, I might reasonably be expected to be prejudiced," Cicotte wrote. "Cleveland is the team we expect to have to beat, with due respect to the hard hitting Yanks. Cleveland has the best schedule with a lot of home games late in the season. New York is not a good road team. So we figure the Yanks are most likely to crack as the season approaches the end." It isn't know if Cicotte's words were his own or, like Ruth's, those of a ghostwriter. It also isn't known if his opinion of the Yankees was colored by Ruth's season-long dismissal of the White Sox as legitimate contenders. Regardless, Cicotte's by-line wasn't seen in the *Press* again.

As far as the Yankees being a poor road team, the Indians would've begged to differ. New York may have given up on Thursday's game after falling behind by three runs, but it wasn't ready to concede Friday's or Saturday's contests. Bob Shawkey's easy 6–1 victory over Caldwell on September 10 was his sixth win in seven decisions against the Indians in 1920. Shawkey allowed just 13 runs in those seven games. His only loss to the Tribe had been a 3–2 setback in New York in August, two days after the Chapman incident. Caldwell had out-pitched Shawkey on an afternoon when many of the players were still in a daze. Shawkey made sure it didn't happen again.

The game marked the major league debut of Joe Sewell, a 21-year-old infielder who'd been playing for the University of Alabama just a few months earlier. After Lunte suffered a serious leg injury in the Labor Day doubleheader against the Browns, the Indians found themselves desperate for a shortstop. Evans wasn't the answer. Speaker and Dunn studied the list of players that the club held options to in the minor leagues and came upon Sewell, who was batting .289 for New Orleans. Speaker swallowed hard.

He was convinced, based on what he'd seen of Sewell in spring training, that he wasn't ready for the big leagues. But Speaker was equally convinced that the Indians couldn't hold off Chicago and New York with an outfielder playing shortstop, which was what they had in the willing but overmatched Evans. Sewell received the call.

Once again, Dunn had to ante up. The Indians paid New Orleans $6,000 for the shortstop and surrendered their rights to all of the other players on the Pelicans' roster to whom they held first options. A brass ring was waiting to be grabbed. Now was the time to roll the dice and let the future take care of itself.

"Joe Sewell, the New Orleans recruit, made his major league debut yesterday, replacing Evans in the fifth inning. He was twice at bat failing to make a hit. He fouled out once and grounded to Pipp the last time up. He had no ground balls to handle in the field, but had a wide throw to first in trying to complete a double play in the sixth inning, an error that did no damage," said the game notes. From such inauspicious beginnings Hall of Fame careers are occasionally born. Such was the case with Sewell's.

Chicago beat Boston on that Friday afternoon, leaving the Indians and White Sox in a virtual first-place tie. The Tribe had won two fewer games than Chicago but had also lost two fewer. The Yankees were a half game back. The same game notes that announced Sewell's debut said that "the Indians are confident of making two out of three from the Yankees, as it is their belief that Jim Bagby will outpitch anyone Miller Huggins can send to the mound. Naturally, he bemoans the fact he was unable to bring Carl Mays to town."

Huggins didn't need Mays on September 11 as Hank Thormalen did what the Indians were confident that no one on the Yankee staff could do: outpitch Bagby. As a crowd of 30,805, described by Edwards as "the quietest crowd at League Park this year," looked on, Thormalen shut out the Indians until the ninth inning, when a pair of errors by first baseman Pipp led to two meaningless runs. The Yankees led, 6–0, at the time. The defeat left the Indians with a final season record of 9–13 against the Yankees, who won six of the last seven games they played at League Park. Since late June, the Indians' record against the

Joe Sewell wasn't sure he was ready to play shortstop in the major leagues when he was summoned to Cleveland three weeks after Ray Chapman's tragic death. Sewell became the hardest hitter in baseball to strike out and wound up in the Hall of Fame.

two clubs they were battling for the pennant stood at 7–15. With Boston beating Chicago, the Tribe's loss to New York left the three contenders separated by a scant four percentage points. The Indians held first place by one point over the Yankees.

The weekly Sunday statistics printed on September 12 showed that the Indians had regained the American League lead in team batting average at .302, an honor they'd gladly have traded for a ten-game lead in the standings.

Mails paid a second dividend on that Sunday afternoon, pitching the Tribe past Philadelphia, 5–2. It was his second straight seven-hit, complete game victory. "More than 20,000 fans were present yesterday, demonstrating the two reverses at the hands of the Yankees had not dampened their ardor," said the newspaper game notes. "They were happy when the score board announced Detroit had scored four runs off Carl Mays, but the groan that went up when the same score board recorded five runs for New York in the third could have been heard half a mile away." The Yankees kept on scoring, pounding the Tigers, 13–6. Washington blanked Chicago, 5–0. One percentage point continued to separate the Indians and Yankees. Chicago was a game back.

The Indians squeezed out a 3–2 win over the Athletics on September 13. "Although Joe Sewell made no hits for Cleveland, he had a lot to do with Cleveland's victory," explained the game notes. "In the fifth inning, he smashed a ball back on a line to [Rollie] Naylor. The tall pitcher threw up his hands to cover his face. The ball struck them and fell to the ground. Sewell was thrown out, but Naylor's hands tingled so from the force of the blow that before he completely recovered, Cleveland had made two safe knocks and scored two runs." Coveleskie allowed six hits and shut the Athletics out after the first inning. New York and Chicago also won, so the Indians' lead over the Yankees remained one percentage point, and their lead over the White Sox remained one game.

The National League race had loosened up considerably. The Dodgers led the Reds by five games, by virtue of the fact they'd won nine more games than Cincinnati. The difference between the two teams in the loss column was a single game, with the advantage belonging to Brooklyn. As a wire service story explained it, "as the teams now stand, Brooklyn has fourteen more games to play; Cincinnati twenty-two; and New York eighteen. Should [the Dodgers] win half their remaining games, seven, it will be necessary for the Reds to win sixteen of their twenty-two and the Giants fourteen of their eighteen to tie Brooklyn. On the other hand, if Cincinnati and New York win only half their remaining games, it will be necessary for Brooklyn to win only four more games to capture the pennant."

Philadelphia pounded the Indians, 8–0, on September 14. Caldwell was dispatched to the showers early and Ed Rommel broke even less of a sweat than a knuckleball pitcher normally does. Edwards pointed out that, aside from Shawkey and his six victories, Rommel had been more effective against the Indians than any other American League pitcher. The shutout gave Rommel 25 and two-thirds innings of work against Cleveland for the season. He'd been nicked for just nine hits and two runs.

A fan, apparently frustrated by the hard-hitting Tribe's inability to connect with Rommel's knuckleball, which was thrown with the velocity of flowing molasses, unloaded on the home team in general and its manager in particular. "A bleacherite started knocking the tribe in the seventh inning and then began to abuse manager Speaker, winding up his tirade with profanity. Speaker rushed over to the bleachers to tell the fan what he thought of his actions and was applauded by the remainder of the bleacher patrons. Spoke then sent [ticket manager] Clay Folger to refund the offender's money and have him banished from the ballpark," according to the *Plain Dealer*'s game notes.

While the Indians were being baffled by Rommel, the Yankees whipped Detroit and Washington stopped Chicago. The Yankees led the Tribe by six percentage points by virtue of having won four more games while losing one more. Chicago had one more victory than Cleveland but three more losses, and trailed the Indians by 11 percentage points. The Indians' advantage over both teams was the additional games that they had remaining, all of which potentially could go in the victory column. The Tribe's 52 defeats were fewer than either of the other contenders.

Although Huggins had the Yankees in first place, exactly where his bosses, Ruppert and Huston, expected them to be, rumors continued to swirl about his imminent departure from the Big Apple. According to the *News*, scuttlebutt had him taking the reins of the Browns in 1921. Huggins had managed the Cardinals for five seasons, never finishing higher than third, before taking the Yankees job. "Several members of the pitching staff have resented his giving them instructions, it is understood, and other players have not proved amenable to Huggins' brand of discipline."[5] Ruth particularly chafed under any sort of discipline.

The Tribe wrapped up its dealings with the Athletics for the year with a resounding 14–0 thrashing on September 15. "Jim Bagby pitched for Cleveland," Edwards noted, "and despite the fact the tribe counted fourteen times for him, he persisted in pitching airtight ball as though the score was 1 to 0." With New York and Chicago idle, the Indians gained a little ground on both, moving to within four percentage points of first place and increasing their lead over Chicago to 1½ games.

"The White Sox are cracking," claimed the *Press*. "The pitching staff has suddenly become shot. The infield, especially Risberg, has been piling up so many errors lately that rumors of a shake-up in the line-up are constant. Two out of three games have just been dropped to the second division Washington club, the finale a shutout. The breaks are going against the team and Kid Gleason the manager is in a quandary. Gleason was asked ... how he intends, with his wavering ball club, to start the attack of the confident and powerful leaders. 'It looks like Kerr,' he said. The Kid's remark about not starting Cicotte is significant. The series veteran has been away off form."[6]

In the September 16th edition of the *Plain Dealer* was the headline, "RUTH STANDS TO MAKE A FORTUNE." The story beneath it read:

> When the season opened, Ruth was guaranteed by New York baseball men $500 for every home run he made this season in excess of his 29 record for 1919. To date, he has made twenty more home runs than last year, which nets him the tidy sum of $10,000 under his guarantee, and the season has some three weeks to run.
>
> But that's not all, as the "Pride of the Diamond" nets $35,000 this year from a movie contract, gets $10,000 from a soup company, $5,000 for talking into a phonograph, will draw $20,000 or more as his season's salary and has more than a fair chance to figure in the world series profits, all of which makes him the best paid ball player at date for any one season's profits. Best of all, there is not a fan or player who begrudges the popular star one cent of his income.[7]

According to the above figures, Ruth would earn at least $80,000 between his baseball salary and outside endorsements, with three weeks left in which to hit more home runs at $500 a pop. A New York victory in the World Series would add a few grand to that total. A loss in the World Series would add a little less. A total haul of $85,000 was well within the realm of possibility. This was in an era when the average player's salary was in the low to middle four-figure range. Outside income came from an off-season job, not from making movies, endorsing soup, and voicing one's opinion on various topics of the day into a phonograph, not to mention (sort of) writing a newspaper column.

In the interest of accuracy, the Yankees hadn't exactly been idle while the Indians were romping over the Athletics. About a hundred miles to the west of League Park, New York was losing an exhibition game, 8–7, to the Toledo team of the minor league American Association. Ruth contributed a pair of homers, guaranteeing that the paying customers went home happy. But a team that could've used a rest in a grueling pennant race didn't receive one, as a club's regulars were expected to play most, if not all, of an exhibition game in those days, lest the fans feel cheated.

9. Thank You, Miss Jamieson

The Indians extended their streak of consecutive games played in which one team failed to score to three with a 1–0 victory over Washington on September 16. The Senators' Tom Zachary held the Indians to a run on four hits, but Mails was even better, blanking the visitors on three safeties. Sewell scored the game's only run on a double by O'Neill in the eighth inning, and Mails made it stand up.

Edwards supplied the details:

> Walter Mails and Joe Sewell, two recruits who have been with Cleveland only a few days, put the Indians back in first place yesterday. Now it is up to Stanley Coveleskie, Jim Bagby and Ray Caldwell and the other redskin hurlers and, in fact, the entire tribe to stay where the youngsters put them. They have it in them to win nearly every game against Washington and Boston despite the fact both teams are well equipped with star pitchers and batters.
>
> The fact that ten thousand fans were out yesterday applauding every play demonstrates most emphatically the Cleveland fans are with the Indians. Now the Indians must continue showing the fans they are for Cleveland. The Fifth City has never had a pennant and it is pulling harder than it ever pulled before for a championship. If you are in first place the night of Sept. 25th, it means that the best club is going to win the pennant, and that is CLEVELAND.

September 25 marked the final home game of the regular season. It also marked the conclusion of a three-game series with the White Sox, which would go a long way toward determining the American League's champion.

One of the better than 10,000 fans in attendance at the first game of the Washington series was described in the game notes as follows:

> a new luck bringer. She sat in the stands yesterday when the tribe nosed out the Nationals, 1 to 0. And every man on Tris Speaker's club is certain that her presence turned the game into the right side of the percentage column.
>
> The young lady in question is Miss Edna Mae Jamieson [apparently no relation to Indians' outfielder Charlie Jamieson], who looks after the routine of the busy office. Miss Jamieson has been employed at the park for seven years and, until yesterday, never witnessed a complete game. But with the Indians in second place and battling desperately for the top spot, she felt it a duty to go and dispense some good luck to the tribe. Her presence was so fruitful that it is likely the tribe will want her in the stands daily from now on instead of once every seven years.[8]

In their quest for the pennant, the Indians welcomed all the assistance they could get from every imaginable source. The club's busy office could surely survive without Miss Jamieson's guidance for two hours each afternoon during the rest of the homestand.

Chicago topped New York on that Thursday afternoon. The Indians led the Yankees by three percentage points and the White Sox by 1½ games ... or 13 percentage points.

The Indians took the measure of Washington on September 17, 9–3, as Edna Mae Jamieson cheered them on for the full nine innings. "Miss Jamieson of the Cleveland club's office staff, who mascotted the Indians to victory Thursday, saw her second game in seven years yesterday," reported the game notes. "Her instructions from Jim Dunn are to see every game from now on."[9] There was no word as to whether or not Miss Jamieson objected to being referred to as a "mascot."

With Chicago defeating New York again, the Indians opened up a full game lead on the Yankees. Chicago stayed 1½ back. In the National League, it was all over but for the spraying of championship champagne. The Dodgers had taken a six-game lead over Cincinnati as hopes for an all–Ohio World Series evaporated. "Although Brooklyn has not yet clinched the pennant, it will take almost superhuman effort to nose out [the Dodgers.] The latter have ten more games to play, and if they win seven it would be impossible for New York or Cincinnati to tie them if the Giants and Reds won all their remaining games, fourteen and seventeen, respectively," reported the *Plain Dealer*.

In his column on September 18, Edwards wrote that over the winter the Indians had tried to trade money and pitcher Fritz Coumbe, who threw the slow curveball that Ruth hit over League Park's right field wall, costing the Indians a game and costing Lee Fohl his job, to Sacramento of the Pacific Coast League. That was the team for which Mails had toiled in 1919. When Sacramento was slow in responding to the offer, the Indians sent Coumbe and cash to St. Paul for Dick Niehaus, who pitched out of the Tribe bullpen with limited success in 1920. Sacramento club officials wired their acceptance of Cleveland's offer a day after the trade with St. Paul was completed.

Edwards made the following claim:

> Had Mails been with Cleveland all year, the race would have been settled by this time, as the tribe would be so far in front it could take it easy from now until time to engage in the world's series. It surely has been tough going for Speaker to stick in front without a capable left-hander until now, and he deserves

all the more credit for keeping his team in the race under such a handicap.

But we have Mails with us now and he is going to keep on winning games for Cleveland for the reason he has everything, including confidence and gameness and the knowledge he has a hustling team behind him. He is going to be able to take part in the world's series, also, if the tribe wins as expected, and he should prove to be one of the pitchers who will bother the Robins the most. It will be pretty sweet for Walter to take the National League champions into camp, as he was a member of that team when it won the championship in 1916. [The Dodgers were often referred to as the Robins in honor of their manager, "Uncle" Wilbert Robinson].

The Indians completed a sweep of Washington on September 18, but it wasn't easy, as Edwards told his readers. "Ray Caldwell's masterly hurling allowed Cleveland to make it three straight from Washington yesterday and thus retain its lead over Chicago, which won its third consecutive game over New York. The score was 7 to 5.

"With ordinary support, Caldwell would have won his game rather easily. Because his support had nearly as many holes as a sieve, he had to pitch about the best ball of which he is capable." The "best ball" from Caldwell took the form of a complete game 14-hitter. The Indians' defense added to the population of Senators on the League Park base paths, committing five errors, three by Sewell. The media must not have used the term "winning ugly" in 1920, or surely Edwards would've mentioned the phrase in his game summary. Perhaps the presence of Miss Jamieson, the club's resident good luck charm, enabled the Indians to overcome the sloppy effort. Assuming that Miss Jamieson had followed her boss's orders and sat through the game from start to finish, her record was now 3–0. The Tribe held on to its 1½ games advantage over the White Sox while the Yankees slipped to two games back.

The weekly Sunday statistics printed on September 19 showed that the Indians had fallen behind the Browns in the league batting race, .302 to .300. Individually, Sisler of St. Louis was batting .397. Speaker was second at .390. The Yankees were outscoring Cleveland, 778–749. But the Indians led in the only place it mattered: the standings.

"With Brooklyn having a clear lead of several games in the National League," Edwards wrote on that Sunday morning, "it looks as if a bunch of discards again was about to win the pennant in the older circuit. It is not at all surprising, as aggregations of cast-offs seem to have better luck than their rivals. The majority of the Boston Braves of '14 were discards.

So were the Phillies of '15, the Robins of '16, the Cubs of '18 and the Reds of '19."

Edwards warned Indians fans looking ahead to a Brooklyn vs. Cleveland World Series that "Brooklyn is said to have the best pitching staff in either league, having seven pitchers, all of whom are regarded as first stringers." This had to be cause for concern despite the Tribe's big bats since it is a cherished baseball axiom that "good pitching always beats good hitting."

The Indians needed good pitching to win the first game of their series with Boston on September 19, and they received it. "Jim Bagby, premier hurler of the American League, discovered yesterday that it devolved upon him to keep Cleveland ahead of the White Sox," Edwards wrote in his game summary, "and most skillfully did he execute the task imposed. To win his game, he found it necessary to hold Boston to at least one run [Edwards meant "to hold Boston to no more than one run."] He did better than that. He shut out the Red Sox and Cleveland won 2 to 0. Not only did the clever Georgian keep the redskins the required distance ahead of Chicago, but he won his twenty-ninth game of the year."

Bagby's previous victory, the blanking of the Athletics, had established a new franchise record of 28, eclipsing the high-water mark of 27 set by Addie Joss in 1906. The victory wasn't a typical Babgy outing as the Sarge limited the Red Sox to just three hits. The Indians gave him all the support he needed in the sixth, when a double by Smith scored Speaker and a single by Johnston sent Smith home. The newspaper game notes included these tidbits:

> No overflow crowd was allowed in right field, Tris Speaker making the request of management, that the garden be kept clear so that the Red Sox could not gather a bunch of two base hits into the populace. Boston hit five balls that would have been doubles with the fans on the grass. As it was, all five were caught, four by Smith and one by Speaker. The Indians lost three two sackers for the same reason.
>
> Joe Sewell, who is enjoying his first autumn in the north, sat shivering on the bench prior to the game when coach Jack McCallister remarked to president Dunn, "d'you know, Mr. Dunn, that this is the warmest September we have ever had?"
>
> "Yes, it surely is warm. Great baseball weather," Dunn replied.
>
> "Say," interposed Sewell, "you all don't think this is warm, do you? If this is warm, how cold does it get when it isn't the warmest fall on record?"[10]

Elsewhere on that September Sunday, Chicago beat Philadelphia while the Yankees, smarting from the licking they took in Chicago, continued their freefall in St. Louis, losing to the Browns. New York was three games out.

The Indians bounced Boston again, 8–3, on September 20. Mails wasn't nearly as sharp as in his previous outing, allowing a dozen hits. The Red Sox scored twice in the second inning on four hits and two Cleveland errors, but the Tribe bats made it easy for Mails to notch his fourth victory.

"The outcome of the American League race hinges largely on the outcome of the Cleveland-Chicago series, which begins Thursday," noted the *Plain Dealer* on September 20. "If the Indians win half their remaining twelve games, the White Sox must win six out of nine and the Yankees seven out of eight to tie Cleveland. The White Sox are confident they will overcome the Indians' lead and the Yankees feel sure they will keep pace by taking the Washington series and make the race even closer."

The Indians had done their part by trimming Boston. Miss Jamieson, assuming that she was following Dunn's instructions like a dutiful employee and was watching each game from the stands from the first pitch to the last, was now a perfect 5–0. Chicago swamped Philadelphia and New York edged St. Louis, so the American League maintained the status quo for the day.

Also on September 20, the Indians announced that they were no longer accepting applications for World Series tickets. It was not because they didn't think they'd win the pennant, but because they had received far more applications than they had seats in League Park to sell.

The Indians completed the sweep of the Red Sox with a resounding victory on September 21, which just happened to be their leading home run hitter's birthday. "When it comes to celebrating a birthday, Elmer Smith, right fielder of the Indians, is in a class by himself," wrote Edwards in his account of the contest. "Elmer was 28 yesterday and he made the event memorable by assembling a single, double and a home run, driving in four of his colleagues and scoring twice himself.

"As Elmer is a popular member of the tribe these days, the entire aggregation of Indians turned in to aid him in celebrating the anniversary of the day he made Sandusky famous. As a result of the double celebration, Cleveland vanquished Boston, 12 to 1, thus keeping 1½ games ahead of the White Sox, who refuse to back up an inch." The win went to Coveleskie, who was given the rest of the afternoon off by Speaker after toying with the Red Sox for seven innings. Guy Morton finished up. Edna Mae Jamieson's unblemished record was now 6–0.

As Edwards had noted, the Indians maintained their lead on Chicago, heading into an off day for both clubs. The Yankees beat St. Louis, so the Indians' lead over New York stood at three games, or 24 percentage points. The Tribe had one more victory than the Yankees and five fewer defeats.

"Now for the fourth little world's series to be held in Cleveland this year," said the *Plain Dealer* on September 22, as the city prepared for the invasion by the red hot White Sox. "With the exception of a flying trip here [July] 25th, the White Sox, who come to Cleveland tomorrow for three games, have not played in the Fifth City since May 30th. Upon this series is believed to depend the American League pennant. If Cleveland takes three straight or two out of three, the Indians have the pennant won. If the tribe takes just one game, it still has a better than even chance with the Sox to take the bunting. Three straight defeats for the redskins would hurt more than a little."

Three defeats were exactly what Chicago manager Gleason was certain the Indians had awaiting them. "We'll clean up on the Indians as sure as I'm standing here," Gleason told reporters. "The supposed advantage the Indians have in playing at home does not cut a bit of ice in a big series like this. It doesn't matter where it is played, both teams will be going top speed and, take it from me, we'll win."[11] The cautious Gleason of April had been replaced by a fiery skipper who'd been

Elmer Smith led the Indians with 12 homers in 1920, not counting his historic grand slam in game five of the World Series. Smith's 103 RBI were third behind Tris Speaker's 107 and Gardner's 118.

9. Thank You, Miss Jamieson 149

through a season almost as difficult as the Tribe's. No one will ever know how hard Gleason had to work to keep the White Sox from imploding.

No American League games were scheduled for Wednesday, September 22. The Yankees, however, didn't enjoy a day of rest as the Indians and White Sox did. New York, on its way east after the series in St. Louis, played an exhibition game at Indianapolis and lost, 7–6, making it two straight losses to minor league teams in games that didn't count. Ruth contributed three hits, but Indianapolis pitching kept those hits within the confines of the playing field. In the National League, Pittsburgh swept a doubleheader from Cincinnati, officially dethroning the Reds as league and world champions and dashing hopes for a World Series played entirely within Ohio's borders. What was left of the National League race was between those ancient enemies, the Dodgers and Giants.

The headline above a story in the *Plain Dealer*'s sports section on the morning of September 23 read "SERIES IS FIXED IS QUIZ TESTIMONY: EVIDENCE PRESENTED TO THE JURY THAT 1919 GAMES WERE 'NOT ON THE SQUARE.'"

The article underneath quoted Hartley Replogle, an assistant district attorney for Cook County, Illinois, the county in which Chicago is located, as saying that seven current members of the White Sox were being investigated for consorting with gamblers to throw the 1919 World Series to Cincinnati. Replogle said that none of the Reds were under suspicion.

The headline in the *Press*, above an open letter to Cleveland mayor W.S. FitzGerald and police chief F.W. Smith, demanded that they "DRIVE OUT THE BASEBALL GAMBLERS AND SCALPERS!" The newspaper's editors wrote that "the world series is going to be played in Cleveland," and wanted the city cleansed of the gamblers who'd arranged the fix of the 1919 World Series and who, according to the American League's president, had bet heavily on the Indians to win the pennant.

Ban Johnson claimed to have "heard statements that the White Sox would not dare win the 1920 pennant because the managers of a gambling syndicate alleged to have certain players in their power had forbidden it."[12] In a 1960s interview with Professor Lawrence Ritter, author of the classic book *The Glory of Their Times*, Joe Wood admitted that Eddie Cicotte had confided to him early in the 1920 season that "we don't dare win."[13] Gleason and Charlie Comiskey both knew that something had been fishy about Chicago's eight-game swan dive against the Reds. No one who'd spent a lifetime in baseball, as Gleason and Comiskey had, could've missed the telltale signs. Comiskey and his fellow owners had a vested interest in keeping the story under wraps, but the stench couldn't be covered up indefinitely, particularly with another World Series, on which millions of dollars would be wagered, right around the corner.

"I have nothing to say in the matter from any phase whatsoever, except that we are trying our best to win the pennant, all reports to the contrary notwithstanding," said Gleason.[14]

"Members of the White Sox scoffed at the report," said the *Press*. "They declared no player of the team was in the clutches of the so-called gambling syndicate. They pointed to their overwhelming victory over the Indians Thursday as evidence of their determination to win and promised to repeat Friday."

No one in the crowd of better than 24,000 at League Park on that Thursday afternoon could've guessed from their performance on the field which of the Chicago players were being investigated. Playing like the club that was supposed to lay waste to the Reds the season before, the White Sox clobbered the Indians, 10–3, ending the Tribe's winning streak at seven in a row and Edna Mae Jamieson's personal winning streak at six. It isn't known if Dunn ordered Miss Jamieson to return to her office duties the next day.

The Sox denied Bagby his 30th victory, breaking open a close game with three runs in the sixth inning, one in the seventh, and five more in the eighth. Dickie Kerr held the Indians to eight scattered hits. Kerr could've been an Indian. The Tribe scouted him when he pitched for Milwaukee of the American Association in 1918 but decided that, at a mere 5'7" and 155 pounds, Kerr was too small to withstand the rigors of the major leagues. But he won 13 games as a rookie for Chicago in 1919, plus two more in the World Series, and 21 in 1920. He was out of the major leagues by 1922.

"The crowd yesterday was not as large as expected, and no one was turned away, either," said the game notes. "Probably the reason was many did not wish to stand and remained away altogether rather than take a chance of not getting a seat. Then, too, right field was kept free from an overflow crowd.

"Not only was there a big delegation of Chicago newspapermen present, but there were also baseball writers from Boston, New York and Pittsburg, some of the New York writers giving the Yankees the go-by to take in the Chicago-Cleveland series, apparently figuring New York out of the race."[15] Mathematically, the Yankees still had a shot. Realistically, they didn't. The defeat reduced the Tribe's lead over Chicago to a half game, or six percentage points. The Yankees picked up half a game to trail by two and a half. At the bottom of the game notes was this bit of encouragement for the fans and the Indians: "Today's another day. Let's go!" Edwards remained confident in the Indians:

> "The Indians may have been decisively beaten yesterday, but they have not lost first place, and it is not in the cards that they are to lose it. It is to be regretted that the tribe lost yesterday's game, as by winning Cleveland would be so far ahead of Chicago the White Sox would have little chance of overhauling them. But there are two more games in the series and the Indians are not discouraged in the least. Victories today and tomorrow, or even in only one of the two remaining games, will send the Indians to St. Louis in first place Saturday night.
>
> "Cleveland will win one of the two games, perhaps both. The Indians are too good a ball club to drop three straight to Chicago. The White Sox got every break yesterday. Perhaps Cleveland will have them today. Yesterday was Chicago's day. Today looks like one made to order for Cleveland."

And so it turned out to be, thanks to Mails.

"Walter Mails of San Quentin, California, yesterday demonstrated to the satisfaction of 20,000 Cleveland fans that he is not only the best left-handed pitcher in the American League, but the gamest," wrote Edwards on September 25. "A gamer exhibition of pitching than that displayed by Mails in the fifth inning of yesterday's contest never was witnessed upon any baseball field."

The accomplishment that so impressed Edwards took place with one out. Mails suddenly lost command of his pitches and walked Chicago catcher Ray Schalk, pitcher Red Faber, "a notoriously weak batter," and lead-off man Amos Strunk to load the bases. Mails then composed himself and struck out Buck Weaver and future Hall of Famer Eddie Collins to keep the White Sox from scoring and possibly save the Indians' season. Once he recovered from his brief bout with wildness, Mails retired 14 of the last 15 Chicago batters, and the Indians, scoring single runs in the first and second off Faber, another future Hall of Famer, had a desperately needed 2–0 victory. The Chicago express had been slowed, and the White Sox were guaranteed to leave town in second place, regardless of the outcome of Cleveland's final home game of the year.

Twelve years before Ruth allegedly called his shot in the 1932 World Series by pointing his bat at the bleachers in Chicago's Wrigley Field and then depositing the next pitch among the patrons, Mails did much the same thing before the game with the White Sox. According to the game notes, "Mails was talking to sporting editor Brown of the San Francisco *Call* prior to the game. Just to show what confidence the left-hander possesses, this is what he said to Brown:

'This afternoon's game is won right now. Some of those fellows are going to be lucky to get a foul off me. I'll be the most surprised man in Cleveland if I don't shut them out.'"[16] As the legendary Dizzy Dean would say many years later, it ain't braggin' if you back it up. And Mails did.

Edwards wasn't the only one awed by Mails' performance. Home plate umpire Brick Owens, who had a bird's eye view of Mails' pitches, said, "I never saw a ball take a sharper hop than Mails' fast one did today."[17]

Edwards compared the game to another pitching duel at League Park between Cleveland and Chicago 12 years earlier, also in the heat of a three-way pennant race. On the afternoon of October 8, 1908, Cleveland's Addie Joss squared off against Chicago's spitball ace, Ed Walsh, in a battle of pitchers who would wind up being enshrined in the Hall of Fame. Walsh allowed four hits and struck out 15, but Joss was better, retiring all 27 White Sox batters he faced. Cleveland won, 1–0. Some consider Joss's perfect game, pitched in the closing days of a tense pennant race, to be the greatest pitching performance in the game's history. Mails couldn't duplicate Joss's gem, but he gave the Indians the shot in the arm that they desperately needed.

The Yankees split a doubleheader with Washington that Friday. The Indians' lead over Chicago was a game and a half. The Tribe's lead over the Yankees was back to three games, with Cleveland still having won one more game and lost five fewer.

Coveleskie wasn't brash enough to call his shot as Mails had done, so Edwards, in his column of Saturday, September 25, did it for him. "What Walter Mails accomplished yesterday, Stanley Coveleskie can and will do this afternoon when the Indians encounter the White Sox in the last game of the series that will practically decide the American League pennant. Cleveland leads the White Sox by one and a half games. When the sun sets tonight, the Indians will be on their way to St. Louis, rejoicing in the fact they are two and a half games in the lead. Only an unexpected reversal of form can dislodge the redskins from first place."

Chicago didn't dislodge the Indians from first place, but they sliced a game off their deficit, reducing it once again to a razor-thin half game. The second largest crowd in the history of League Park, 30,625, gathered in the hope that it wouldn't turn out to be the last baseball game in Cleveland in 1920. A White Sox club, playing as if it wasn't aware of the black cloud that hovered over it in the form of the on-going grand jury investigation clipped the Tribe, 5–1. Edwards' game summary was far less upbeat than the article in which he'd confidently predicted the Indians would board the train that would take them to St. Louis to conclude the season on a short western swing with a 2½ game lead.

"Stanley Coveleskie opened the 1920 season at League Park by defeating St. Louis, 5 to 0," Edwards wrote on September 26. "He closed it yesterday by losing to Chicago, 5 to 1. Although defeated, the Indians are still in first place and if the redskins are true prophets they are going to remain in front until the final curtain is rung down one week from today. The Indians went down fighting, but their efforts were wasted energy, for Claude Williams, Chicago left-hander, puzzled them so completely they were almost as helpless as if they had gone to the plate without a bat in their hands."

"I cannot understand how it is we cannot hit Williams," Speaker groused after the game. "Nearly every other club in the league can hammer him. He does not dare start a game against New York anymore, and rarely finishes one against Philadelphia. But he makes us look like amateurs."[18] Williams had Speaker's number that afternoon, holding Spoke hitless in four at-bats. Williams hadn't exactly been pitching batting practice in 1920, winning 22 games, although he sported a 3.91 ERA, the second highest of his career, and didn't record a shutout. No one knew that his victory over the Indians would be the final game Williams would pitch in the major leagues.

The Indians wouldn't face the White Sox or Yankees again unless the race wound up in a tie, necessitating a playoff. Since late June, the Indians had won eight games and lost 17 to the other contenders. After winning nine of their first 12 games against a White Sox team that may, or may not, have lost some or all of those games on purpose, the Indians then lost seven of 10. The Tribe captured the season series, 12 games to 10. Their combined record against the other contenders was 21–23.

While the Tribe was losing to Chicago, New York was beaten by Washington. Here's how the *Plain Dealer* summed up the race as the Indians headed west: "Cleveland can drop two of its eight games to be played and the best Chicago can obtain by winning five straight would be a tie. The New York Yankees, three games behind the Indians and with only four to play, are still a mathematical possibility for first place, but would have a difficult task even capturing second."

It was a confident bunch of ballplayers who left Cleveland on the night of September 25, despite the drubbing they'd taken from their closest pursuer. "The Indians departed for St. Louis last night to start a series of four games today," said the *Plain Dealer.* "They will go from that town to Detroit to play four more. They departed confident they would win at least seven of the eight from the Browns and Tigers and thus retain first place, even though the White Sox should win the five games they have yet to play with St. Louis and Detroit." If Chicago did win all of its remaining games, the Indians would have to win seven of eight to clinch the pennant. Six wins would mean a tie, and five wins would mean another long, cold winter pondering a second straight near-miss.

The first game at Sportsman's Park didn't get off to a promising start. After presenting Caldwell with a 3–0 lead before he'd thrown a pitch, Slim proceeded to retire only the first batter he faced. Before George Uhle could stamp out the fire, the Browns had a 5–3 lead. Uhle pitched shutout ball until the eighth, when Speaker summoned Coveleskie to finish up. The Indians scored three in the third to regain the lead and won, 7–5.

"The Indians plainly showed the tremendous strain under which they are laboring," said the newspaper game notes. "The strain amounted to desperation when they saw the score of the Detroit-Chicago game posted in the second inning, at which time the Browns were leading by two runs. The men concentrated their attack in the third, however, and took a lead that preserved their slender half game margin."

"St. Louisians are anxious to see the Indians win the pennant," the notes continued. "There was a genuine wave of sorrow akin to dismay when it was learned that the White Sox were smothering the Tigers. A Cleveland victory would be popular all over the circuit, Chicago, of course, excepted." And, presumably, New York, which still had a slim mathematical chance for the pennant.

About 23,000 watched the game on a Sunday afternoon. Ruth and the Yankees had been in town the previous Sunday and attracted a gathering of better than 30,000. Chicago smothered Detroit, 8–1. The Yankees beat Washington. Nothing changed atop the American League.

Speaker sent Mails to the mound with just two days' rest on September 27, and Duster held off the Browns, 8–4. Trailing by a run in the sixth, the Indians scored twice to take the lead, and then added two more in the seventh and three in the eighth to give Mails some breathing room. Charlie Jamieson's three-run, eighth-inning home run proved to be icing on the cake.

The *Plain Dealer* reported the following:

> James C. Dunn, owner of the Cleveland Indians, who have the pole in the race for the American League pennant, this morning will have work started on the erection of additional

seats at League Park for world's series fans, if the Indians cop the flag. He is planning on having 6,000 seats installed in a big new pavilion over the right field wall. Two thousand of those will be in the park and 4,000 over the wall. The building permit was issued yesterday.

Decision of the National Commission to open the series next Tuesday came somewhat as a disappointment to Cleveland officials, as it gives barely a week to complete the big job. If, however, Chicago and Cleveland should end the American League season tied for first place, and a special series to determine the championship is required, the commission may put off the opening date. The additional 6,000 seats will give League Park a seating capacity of between 26,000 and 27,000.

A coin flip determined that the World Series would open in the American League champion's park on Tuesday, October 5. The series had been increased in 1919 to a best-of-nine game tournament, to assist the owners in recouping some of the money they'd lost by playing a 140-game schedule due largely to uncertainty about economic conditions after the end of World War I. The schedule had been returned to 154 games in 1920, but the owners saw no reason to return the World Series to its best-of-seven format. As a result of the coin flip, games one, two, three and, if necessary, eight and nine, would be played in the home of the American League pennant winner. The National League winner would host games four, five and, if necessary, six and seven. That plan lasted for all of one day.

In the event of a tie for first place between the Indians and White Sox, it was determined that the championship would be decided in a best-of-three playoff. The first game would be played at League Park, the second at Comiskey Park, and, if a third game was needed, it would be played at a neutral site yet to be chosen.[19]

The National League champion was crowned on September 27. The Giants split a doubleheader with Boston. New York's loss in the second game clinched the pennant for Brooklyn. The Dodgers would have to wait a while to find out who their opponent would be, although it was virtually certain it wouldn't be a "Subway Series" as the Yankees were clinging to their pennant hopes by the skin of their teeth. All three contenders won their games on September 27, so nothing changed.

On September 28, everything changed.

In spite of the torrid pennant race, events on the field took a back seat to events that transpired in the Cook County, Illinois, courthouse where a grand jury had been listening to testimony regarding the alleged fixing of the 1919 World Series. On that fateful Tuesday, the grand jury heard from White Sox pitcher Eddie Cicotte and outfielder Joe Jackson. Both admitted to accepting money from gamblers to lose to Cincinnati. Before the day was over, the grand jury had indicted Cicotte, Jackson, shortstop Swede Risberg, third baseman Buck Weaver, pitcher Lefty Williams, outfielder Happy Felsch and infielder Fred McMullin. Also indicted was Chick Gandil, the ringleader who didn't play in 1920. Comiskey immediately suspended the seven active players.

"JACKSON AND CICOTTE ADMIT GUILT; CLEVELAND ALMOST ASSURED OF PENNANT," blared the front page of the *Plain Dealer* the day after the indictments were handed down. "SEVEN WHITE SOX PLAYERS AND ONE FORMER PLAYER INDICTED BY COOK COUNTY GRAND JURY, FOLLOWING TESTIMONY BY EDDIE CICOTTE AND JOE JACKSON THAT 1919 WORLD SERIES GAMES WERE THROWN," said the bold-lettered miniature headline underneath. "Cicotte and Jackson are held in the custody of deputy sheriffs. Comiskey suspends accused players, declaring that if guilty they are out of baseball for life. Declares he'll go ahead and win pennant if possible with remaining players. Pennant virtually conceded to Cleveland because of wrecking Chicago's machine," screamed the newspaper.

In point of fact, there was no law against fixing baseball games. It was a lousy thing to do, but it wasn't illegal. The seven "Black Sox" were indicted on a charge of willfully defrauding the public, which understandably expected that the players on both teams were trying their best to win the game they'd paid for a ticket to attend.

Cicotte and Jackson weren't the only Chicago players talking, according to the *News*:

> Charges that some of the players who are accused of throwing the world's series to Cincinnati last year have used their efforts to prevent the White Sox from becoming pennant winners this season were made today by several members of the Chicago team, who have not been mentioned in the grand jury testimony. Referring to charges some players purposely lost games this season, one player, who refuses to allow his name to be used, made the following statement: "when we started our last eastern trip, we had every reason to believe we would win the pennant. Suddenly Williams and Cicotte seemed to go bad without any reason. Some of us talked it over and agreed it looked like they were grooving the ball."[20]

Edwards had plenty to say about the not altogether startling turn of events.

The indictment of seven members of the White Sox by a Chicago grand jury, and their subsequent suspension by president Charles Comiskey of the Chicago White Sox means the practical wrecking of the baseball club that won pennants in 1917 and again last year. The indictments also mean that Cleveland is virtually assured of winning the championship this season. While the Chicago team has not been annihilated by the suspension of the seven players, it may be difficult for manager Gleason to win three straight from as strong a team as St. Louis with a line up that will lack such stars as Cicotte, Williams, Weaver, Risberg, Jackson and Felsch.

The Indians, if they win, and it is believed they will, should not be discredited in the least because of the wrecking of the White Sox, their greatest rivals. Let no one say Cleveland won merely because the Chicago team became involved in such a disgraceful scandal, one that has threatened the very foundation of the game — the national game itself. The Cleveland club was on its way to victory before the crisis was reached at Chicago. To get right down to the truth of it, the Indians probably regret that the expose came when it did. They feel they are the best ball club in the American League and would have preferred the White Sox to play the string out with their strongest team in the field.

Tenney got right to the point. "The Sox could not have caught the Indians anyhow, had they been allowed to maintain their full strength to the finish."

Gleason, his heart broken by the betrayal of his players but his spirit intact, vowed to fight the Indians to the final pitch of the final game. "Don't let anyone tell you that Kid Gleason is licked yet," he insisted. "I'll have a pretty good ball club in spite of what has happened. I'll have Ray Schalk to catch. As pitchers I still have Kerr, Faber, [Roy] Wilkinson and [Clarence] Hodge. I can use Ted Jordan on first base, Eddie Collins on second, Harvey McClellan shortstop and switch John Collins to third base. In the outfield I have [Harry] Leibold, Strunk and [Eddie] Murphy, and with those boys, we'll fight to the end."[21]

The revelation that the White Sox had thrown the Series would've come as no surprise to Ray Chapman. "Chapman, who had been friends with Chicago star Shoeless Joe Jackson when the slugger played in Cleveland five years earlier, attended the Series and came back with an uneasy feeling. He told his family that he did not place any wagers on the games, because 'something didn't seem right.'"[22] Today's standard player contracts contain a clause prohibiting wagering on baseball games. That wasn't the case in 1920. Betting on games was as old as the sport itself, and the hired hands took part in it, sometimes with prior knowledge of the outcome.

The White Sox hadn't been scheduled to play on September 28. The Indians were, and they took care of business, refusing to be distracted by the chaos that had broken loose around them. The headlines that went to the White Sox should've belonged to Bagby, who defeated the Browns, 9–5, to become the first and only pitcher in franchise history to post a 30-win season. Bagby was the first American League pitcher to notch 30 victories since Washington's future Hall of Famer, Walter Johnson, won an incredible 36 games in 1913. Only two American Leaguers since Bagby have reached the 30-victory mark in a season: Philadelphia's Hall of Famer Lefty Grove with 31 wins in 1931, and Detroit's Denny McLain, who won 31 in 1968.

Bagby allowed the Browns ten hits and helped his own cause with a second-inning double that put the Tribe ahead to stay, 3–2. "The unstained and unindicted members remaining will never be able to beat out the Indians," said the wire service account of Bagby's historic victory, "and it is extremely doubtful if Chicago, with its full strength, could have nosed out the aggressive redskins. Cleveland played championship baseball in every particular today, and showed that it was eminently fitted to represent the American League in the titular series."

The victory gave the Indians a full game lead over what was left of the White Sox. The Yankees' only hope was that they'd win their two remaining games with Philadelphia while the Tribe dropped its last five games and the White Sox, in their state of disarray, would be swept in their final series in St. Louis. That would have resulted in a three-way tie for first place.

"Permission for the Cleveland Americans to use shortstop Sewell, successor of the late Raymond Chapman, in the world's series if the Indians win the American League pennant, was granted tonight by Charles H. Ebbets, president of the Brooklyn National League champions," reported the *Plain Dealer* on September 29. "Mr. Ebbets' announcement was made in a reply to a telegram from president James G. [sic] Dunn of Cleveland, in which he made a request to use Sewell. The Brooklyn president said he hoped Cleveland is successful in the American League race in view of the indictment of the Chicago American League players."

Because Sewell hadn't joined the Indians until early September, following Lunte's injury, he wasn't eligible to play in the World Series, since the rules required then, and still do, that a player be on a club's roster on August 31 in order to participate in the post season. Dunn appealed to baseball's governing body, the National Commission, which consisted of the two league presidents and August (Garry) Herrman of the Cincinnati club, whose job was to cast the deciding vote since the two league presidents almost always disagreed. The commission decided to drop the matter into Ebbets' lap, and Ebbets felt that he had no choice but to allow Sewell to play, given the unprecedented circumstances that led to his arrival in Cleveland. Baseball didn't need to give the fans another reason to be angry at it following the disclosure of the Black Sox scandal.

Dunn also asked the commission to flip-flop the games of the upcoming World Series, if the Indians won the pennant, since the 6,000 seats he was adding to League Park wouldn't be ready for occupancy by paying customers on October 5. The commission handled this request without assistance and granted it. If the Indians were in the World Series, games four and five and, if necessary, six and seven would be played in Cleveland.

Hartley Replogle in Cook County wasn't the only district attorney investigating rumors of a crooked World Series in late September. The *Plain Dealer* issued this report on September 30:

> New York authorities started an inquiry into rumors that the same group of gamblers [that fixed the 1919 World Series] planned to fix the 1920 series.
>
> Acting on a newspaper story that intimated that members of the Brooklyn Nationals were to be bribed to lose the series to the Cleveland Indians, district attorney Lewis of King's County summoned all members of the Brooklyn team to appear before him Friday morning and at the same time he telegraphed to Chicago to forward any evidence available there. The district attorney was promised full co-operation by Charles H. Ebbets, president of the Brooklyn club, who said he would personally request his players to visit the district attorney's office.
>
> Zack Wheat, captain and left fielder of the team, tonight denied reports that players had been approached in an attempt to "throw" the coming world's series. Asserting there was absolutely no truth in the rumors, Wheat continued "no one has ever approached me and it would not be well for anyone who had. I am sure that none of the other players have been approached. If any person has doubts about the game, they had better come out and see us perform. Perhaps we will be beaten in the series, but we will play the best game we can."[23]

In Chicago, National League president John Heydler told the grand jury that had indicted the Black Sox that "anyone who has even insinuated the 1920 world's series has been fixed ought to be shot, for such reports are just deliberate attempts to hurt baseball."[24]

The Indians completed a four-game sweep of the Browns on September 29th, ending the remote possibility of a three-way tie for first place and eliminating the Yankees from the pennant chase. Coveleskie pitched an eight-hitter and the Indians blasted St. Louis, 10–2. "It was a semi-private exhibition," said the wire service game account. "One of the largest crowds of the season was absent. The temperature took a drop that exceeded even the downward shoot of Coveleskie's spitter, and fewer than 300 were in the stands to view the last stand of the Indians in the far west. Withal, Cleveland extended its lead over the White Sox to one and a half games." The Yankees swept their season-ending doubleheader from Philadelphia, but the results were unimportant. Ruth and company were free to begin their off-season barnstorming tour that would add a few more dollars to the Babe's bank account.

On the morning of Thursday, September 30, the American League standings looked like this:

Cleveland	96–54	.640	—
Chicago	95–56	.629	1½
New York	95–59	.617	3
St. Louis	74–76	.493	22
Boston	72–81	.471	25½
Washington	65–83	.439	30
Detroit	59–91	.393	37
Philadelphia	47–103	.313	49

The Indians had four games remaining in Detroit. Three victories would clinch the pennant, regardless of what the decimated White Sox did in St. Louis. Two victories over the Tigers guaranteed no worse than a first-place tie.

There was no change among the leaders on September 30. Rain postponed the Indians' game, setting up a doubleheader on October 1, the day Chicago's series with the Browns started.

After 5½ months of baseball, nothing had been decided.

10

Cleveland's Time to Win

The Indians, needing two victories to secure the franchise's, and the city's, first pennant, sprinted to a 4–0 lead in the first game of the doubleheader at Navin Field on Friday, October 1, and held it until the eighth behind Uhle's shutout pitching. But Ty Cobb and his teammates, who'd been eliminated from the pennant race some time around Independence Day, weren't about to roll over and play dead. Detroit chased Uhle with a four-run rally in the eighth, forcing Speaker to use Bagby, who was scheduled to start the next day's game, in relief. Timothy Gay says that Cobb, who passed out praise to the opposition sparingly, was one of Bagby's admirers, calling him "the smartest pitcher he'd ever faced."[1] Gay described Bagby's repertoire as including "a nasty fadeaway [later to be dubbed a screwball], and [Bagby] could apply foreign substances to the ball with the best of them."[2] Bagby retired the side in the eighth and pitched through the ninth unscathed, but the Indians' offense was held in check by Detroit's pitching. Bagby surrendered a run in the tenth when Ira Flagstead reached second base after Sewell fielded his ground ball and threw it into the dugout, and then scored on a single by Babe Pinelli, giving the Tigers a 5–4 victory.

"By losing the opening battle, Cleveland was forced to forego the cinching of the American league [sic] pennant for at least another twenty-four hours," read the newspaper account of the game, picked up from a wire service. Even with the Indians on the verge of clinching the city's first pennant, none of Cleveland's papers saw fit to send their beat writers to cover the event. Neither Edwards, nor Tenney, nor Bang would be in the Navin Field press box to report history in the making. "Cleveland got away to a bad start in the second number and the fans, who were rooting like mad for the Indians, groaned in anguish when the score board showed that the misfit Chicago aggregation had obtained an early three run lead on the Browns."

Although Caldwell found himself on the short end of a 2–1 score in the second inning of the second game, the Indians quickly turned things around. Scoring in seven of the game's eight innings, they routed the Tigers, 10–3, giving Caldwell his 20th win of the season and moving a step closer to the pennant. Umpire Brick Owens ended the contest due to darkness after eight innings. It was October, and the sun set too early to allow two full games to be played.

Chicago's early lead on St. Louis didn't hold. The Browns battered Red Faber for five runs in the third inning and held on for an 8–6 victory. With the White Sox' loss, the Indians had clinched no worse than a tie for the pennant. Bagby removed all doubt the next day.

Twirling a nifty 11-hitter, the Sarge was tough in the clutch, as usual. The Indians gave him three early runs to work with, and Cleveland's first pennant was secured on a Saturday afternoon in Detroit. The wire service account of the game appeared in the October 3rd edition of the *Plain Dealer*,

> Manager Tris Speaker and the Cleveland Indians entered the baseball hall of fame at Navin Field this afternoon by riding roughshod over the Detroit Tigers, 10 to 1, thereby earning the right of representing the American League in the world's series against Brooklyn, the best club in the National League.
>
> To Speaker went the credit of retiring the last Detroit batter in the contest that made his club winners of the American League pennant, an honor never before achieved by a team that represented the city of Cleveland. As the great ball player/manager clutched [Clyde] Manion's fly for the final out, 10,000 Detroit rooters jumped to their feet and it seemed as though the roar of applause that followed must have been heard in the sister city across the lake.

Cleveland's response to its first sports championship was muted, according to Edwards. Underneath a headline that read, "BAGBY CROWNS 42 YEAR EFFORT TO REACH TOP; BIG HANDICAPS OVERCOME; MANAGER SPEAKER'S TEAM TRIUMPHS DESPITE NUMEROUS SETBACKS," Edwards wrote the following words:

> When James Bagby pitched the Indians to a 10 to 1 victory over Detroit yesterday, he also was pitching Cleveland to its first big league championship. The triumph gave the Fifth City the American League pennant for 1920.

10. Cleveland's Time to Win

> Could it really be true? That was the question veteran fans on the streets asked each other. Could it actually be true that Cleveland had won a pennant after forty-two years of strenuous effort? The fans did not enthuse. The calm manner in which they received the news that Cleveland had won the deciding game caused transients to ask if Clevelanders were cold-blooded and if they no longer took interest in the national game.
>
> Cold-blooded? No interest? Say, there are no more rabid fans in all the nation than right here in the Fifth City. It was simply a case of inability to believe the truth. Too often they had seen Cleveland's representatives on the diamond come close to winning the pennant, only to lose in the final month, the final week, the final days. They were just dazed. They will awake today.

It had taken 12 long years, but Cleveland finally had the "revenge" alluded to by the *Plain Dealer* following the injustice of 1908. Perhaps then, it was fitting that the pennant-clinching victory came at the expense of Detroit, which had "copped the flag" in 1908 by playing one less game than the schedule called for, while Cleveland had played them all.

Edwards' reference to a 42-year quest for a pennant alluded to Cleveland's first major league team, the Forest Citys, who entered the infant National League, then in its fourth year of existence, in 1879. He could have gone back even further, to a club also known as the Forest Citys that represented Cleveland in the National Association of Professional Base Ball Players (baseball being two words in those days), the first professional league (and that term is used loosely in reference to the National Association) in 1871. The original Forest Citys won ten games and lost 19, finishing seventh in the nine-team association.

The 1872 Forest Citys were even worse, winning six, losing 16, and throwing in the towel about a third of the way through the season. Though professional, there's still some doubt among historians as to whether the National Association constituted a true major league, when measured against the standards set by the leagues that followed it, which may explain why Edwards didn't mention the original Forest Citys while writing the first article of his career that basked in the glow of a championship.

The "new" Forest Citys of 1879 were truly awful, posting a record of 27–55 but managing to stay out of last place because the ball clubs put together by Syracuse and Troy, New York, were even worse. The small town of Troy, New York, just north of Albany on the Hudson River, its population in the most recent census 48,469, was a member of the National League from 1879–1882, as the league either waived or ignored its rule that member cities have populations of at least 75,000. Cleveland remained in the National League through the 1884 season, fielding teams that ranged from good to dreadful. The good teams weren't good enough to seriously challenge for a pennant. The bad teams lost games by scores of 35–4.

Cleveland was without major league baseball in 1885 and 1886. It can be argued that the city was without a major league club in 1887 as well, even though it had been granted a franchise in the American Association, which was a major league at the time. Cleveland's entry finished last, winning just 39 times and finishing a whopping 54 games behind pennant-winning St. Louis. Cleveland's 1888 club improved to sixth, a mere 40 and a half games out of first place, which was again occupied by St. Louis.

The National League re-admitted Cleveland for the 1889 season, replacing Detroit, and Cleveland jumped at the chance to re-join what was considered the stronger of the two major leagues. This was the team that came to be known as the Spiders, because the 1889 crew had so many tall, skinny players. The Spiders made the playoffs three times, winning once, but never captured a National League pennant. Cleveland's American League team had its share of near-misses and found some ingenious ways to avoid winning the pennant when it had the league's best talent, as documented in chapter one. But this did not happen in the tumultuous summer of 1920, when the Indians may simply have been too good to lose.

"My sincere congratulations to you and to all members of the Cleveland ball team," Dunn said in a telegram to Speaker after the clinching. "I am sharpening the tomahawks and I am sure we will scalp the Dodgers. You fought fairly and squarely and deserve the championship."[3] Dunn was the toast of the town. He'd promised a pennant winner within three years of the day he met the press after buying a seventh-place club in January of 1916. It had taken Sunny Jim five years to make good on that promise, but no one was counting.

"Outfielder Jack Graney is the dean of Cleveland players in point of service," noted the *Plain Dealer* in an article profiling each player on the Tribe roster the morning after the pennant was clinched. "He first joined the club at the start of the 1908 campaign and has been here continuously since the start of the 1910 season.

"Next to come was catcher Steve O'Neill, who reported Sept. 15, 1911. Pitcher Guy Morton, second baseman William Wambsganss, and outfielder Elmer Smith were next to arrive. They donned the war paint of the tribe in 1914.

"Those are the only Indians surviving who were members of the club purchased by Dunn in 1916. Pitchers Bagby and Coveleskie, though, had been purchased prior to the sale of the club to Dunn and reported the week afterward." Some of the building blocks had been in place when Dunn arrived, a few arrived very shortly afterward, and Dunn (and Lee Fohl) added to them wisely in 1917, 1918 and 1919. The key acquisition, of course, had been Tris Speaker. Without Speaker's bat, glove, and leadership, there most likely wouldn't have been a baseball revival on the shore of Lake Erie, and almost certainly no pennant or world championship in 1920.

In St. Louis, behind the pitching of Dickie Kerr, the broken-hearted "Clean Sox" defeated the Browns, 10–7. It didn't matter. They were two games behind with only one game left to play. The Indians had one game left, too, and league regulations required them to play it. They lost to Detroit, 6–5, on a hit in the home half of the ninth by Cobb against Bob Clark, Speaker's third pitcher of the day. The game was played in a snappy 88 minutes "in frigid weather" according to the newspaper game notes.

"The Cleveland champions did not exert themselves," said the newspaper game story. "Morton, Uhle and Clark contested themselves by simply lobbing the ball to Nunamaker and the Tigers took advantage of their liberality by fattening up their batting averages. O'Neill and Johnston were allowed to enjoy a rest and Speaker retired, after participating in part of the contest, to allow Joe Wood to obtain a little practice."

When the sun set on Sunday, October 3, the final American League standings showed something that had never before been seen on the season's last day in the league's 20-year existence. Cleveland was on top.

Cleveland	98–56	.636	—
Chicago	96–58	.623	2
New York	95–59	.617	3
St. Louis	76–77	.497	21½
Boston	72–81	.471	25½
Washington	68–84	.447	29
Detroit	61–93	.396	37
Philadelphia	48–106	.312	50

As far as statistics are concerned, after leading the league most of the season in team batting average, the Indians surrendered that crown to St. Louis, .308 to .302. If they were going to surrender a league lead, that was the one they wanted to lose. The Tribe was the league's most prolific offensive team, scoring 857 runs (an average of 5.5 per game) to New York's 838. Edwards had been correct about the Yankee juggernaut finding it more difficult to score away from home, as opposed to the Polo Grounds, on its final two road trips.

Ruth assaulted pitchers in every American League park. He established a new major league record for home runs with a staggering 54, more than any other *team* in either league, except the Philadelphia Phillies. The Indians hit 35 homers. Ruth also led the circuit with 158 runs scored and 137 runs driven in. It still hadn't been enough to power the Yankees to the pennant. That would have to wait another year. But once Ruth and the Yankees started rolling, there'd be no stopping them. The Indians would discover that in 1921. But no one was thinking beyond the Tribe's date with the Dodgers in the World Series.

"Threading their way through knots of silent but admiring fans at Union Station," read a story on the front page of the *Plain Dealer* on the morning after the season finale in Detroit, "manager Speaker and his troop of pennant-winning ball players reached home shortly before midnight last night. Speaker was happy, but too wearied to make a detailed statement, even to friends.

"Of course I'm glad that it's over and that we've won the league flag," Speaker told the crowd. He also said he hadn't yet decided who would start the first game of the World Series at Brooklyn's Ebbets Field in about 36 hours. The newspaper reported that Speaker would assemble his team for a meeting at League Park Monday afternoon to discuss the strategy to be employed against the National League champs, then board a train that wouldn't arrive in Brooklyn until a few hours before the first pitch of game one.

In his column on October 4, Edwards wrote about his introduction to Dunn on that winter day in 1916. "Dunn had lived in Cleveland in the summer of 1908 and he knew the city to be a good baseball town when it had a winning team. He also knew that it had never won a pennant and he was just sentimental enough to wish to be the first man to give it a championship." With help from Speaker, and from Fohl, Dunn had accomplished just that. But the job was only half-finished.

On its editorial page that same day, the *Plain Dealer* heaped kudos on the American League's new champions.

> They have shown that the name CLEVELAND on a team's uniform is no insurmountable obstacle to success.
>
> In the past, sudden and unforeseen misfortunes and handicaps intervened to keep Cleveland from winning. No team that has ever represented Cleveland has suffered so cruelly as the Indians of 1920. No misfortune in the history of professional baseball is comparable to the Chapman tragedy. Few teams could have recovered from such a stunning blow. The Indians did recover, and the spirit of Chapman helped materially to lead them to their final triumph.
>
> Eleven cities are now represented in the two big leagues.

Cleveland is the tenth city to win a championship. Each of the other cities, except Washington, has been honored by a championship in one of the existing leagues or in the old American Association. Providence and Baltimore, cities that have passed from the select class, have also had their pennants. It was time for Cleveland to win.

There was, however, one final indignity the Indians would have to endure, and it continues to this day.

What if the Black Sox scandal hadn't been exposed when it was? What if Cicotte, Williams, Jackson, Weaver, Risberg, Felsch and McMullin hadn't been suspended? The White Sox had been running neck-and-neck with the Indians in September. Could the Indians have held them off had the Sox been at full strength for their final three games?

Baseball historians and fans have pondered those questions since the day that the grand jury indicted the seven players and Comiskey responded by suspending them. The answer, of course, is that we'll never know. We will probably also never know to what extent, if any, the gamblers who fixed the 1919 World Series had their hooks into the Black Sox in 1920. Several of the "Clean Sox" who testified before the grand jury, none of whom were identified in the newspapers, claimed to be certain that their crooked teammates continued tanking games during the 1920 pennant race. And the "Clean Sox" weren't the only ones who suspected the Black Sox of not playing to win every time they took the field.

In the book, *Burying the Black Sox: How Baseball's Cover Up of the 1919 World Series Fix Almost Succeeded,* Gene Carney quoted Yankee shortstop Roger Peckinpaugh, a Clevelander who'd return to his hometown to manage the Indians in 1928, as saying, "you never knew when the White Sox were going to go out there and beat your brains out or roll over and play dead. Somebody was betting on those games [in 1920], that's a cinch. When they wanted to play, you had a hard time beating them, that's how good they were."[4] But how often did they want to play? There are those who insist the White Sox would've left the Indians and Yankees choking on their dust had every member of the team played every game on the schedule to win.

Carney wrote of one allegedly "tossed game" in 1920 in which Weaver's error upset Kerr so much that he demanded of his teammates, "If you fellows are throwing this one, let me in on it."[5] According to Carney, "Rumors of meddling by gamblers cropped up again as the pennant race heated up in September. It appeared that some of the players who tossed the 1919 World Series were at it again, this time tilting things so that Cleveland would win the American League flag.

"Against this background, Eddie Collins met with Charles Comiskey on or around September 2nd. Most sources ... have Collins complaining about crookedness in his teammates, with Comiskey politely listening and then doing nothing about it."[6] Collins was one of the few "Clean Sox" to openly accuse his teammates of not giving a full effort. Most of the other accusations, including the ones made before the grand jury, came from players the press declined to identify. Carney quoted one such story:

"An unidentified White Sox player spoke to a writer from *The Sporting News* after the scandal broke, about the 1920 stretch run. 'Some of us always had believed we were sold out in the World Series. When the [crooked] players showed they meant to beat us out of getting in on this one we decided to act. Cicotte was told that he would have to win a certain game or he would be mobbed on the field by the honest players on the team. He won it.'"[7]

Carney wrote that "Sox shortstop Harvey McClellan and catcher Byrd Lynn told the Chicago *Tribune* that they now recalled seeing teammates toss three games to Boston on a late-season eastern road trip. They claimed the crooked Sox kept one eye on the scoreboard 'more than even the average player in a pennant race,' losing games on purpose to keep the race close."[8] Peckinpaugh's comment would indicate the Black Sox had been throwing games long before the stretch run.

When the indictments were handed down, those not indicted celebrated with dinner at a downtown Chicago restaurant. As sportswriter/umpire Billy Evans had noted during spring training, Chicago's ability to contend depended on Gleason's ability to maintain, if not a harmonious clubhouse, at least a clubhouse in which open warfare didn't break out. Said one of the honest Sox, "No one will ever know what we put up with this summer. I don't know how we ever got along. I know there were many times when things were about to break into a fight, but it never got that far."[9]

In his history of the team, Franklin Lewis quoted American League president Ban Johnson as saying that the gamblers who fixed the World Series had placed heavy bets on the Indians to win the pennant and were pressuring the Chicago players to drop out of the race to allow the Indians to win. "Did the series in League Park look as if the White Sox were deliberately throwing the games?" Lewis asked. It didn't, nor did the next two games against Detroit, both of which the White Sox won. Nonetheless, there are those who will forever insist that had all of Chicago's players been in it to win, the Indians would've been fighting the Yankees for second place. Who's to say they're wrong?

In a search for evidence that the Black Sox did put forth less than full effort at times during the 1920 season, a look back at the first two and a half months may prove enlightening. As already noted, the schedule-maker pitted the Indians and White Sox against each other a dozen times during the season's first six weeks. If the same gamblers who had paid off the Sox to throw the World Series had money on the Indians, as Johnson claimed, the White Sox had a golden opportunity to help the Tribe get off to a quick start, and they did, losing nine of those 12 games. As for the assertion of McClellan and Lynn that the Black Sox kept their eyes on the scoreboard and, when noticing that the Indians had lost or were losing, steered the White Sox to a defeat (or, at least, tried to) to keep the race close, it's worth noting that only three times between April 14 and June 30 did both clubs lose on the same day.[10]

For what it's worth, the Indians were rained out five times on days the White Sox were also scheduled. It's reasonable to believe the White Sox knew of the postponements before taking the field, or learned of them via the scoreboard, and realized an opportunity to gain ground with the Indians idled was presenting itself. Chicago lost all five games.

On the morning of June 30, having just taken two of three from Cleveland at Comiskey Park, the White Sox were 37–26, five and a half games out of first place. They'd play .648 ball the rest of the way, winning 59 and losing 32, including five of their seven remaining games with the Indians. The Tribe would play at a .611 pace for the rest of the season, winning 55 and losing 35.

So what might've happened had the scandal broken a few days later and the Black Sox not been suspended? On the day the seven Chicago players were banned, the Indians beat St. Louis and had a record of 95–54. Chicago was one game behind with a record of 95–56. The next day, with the White Sox not scheduled, the Indians defeated the Browns again to improve to 96–54 and increase their lead to a game and a half. Cleveland had four games remaining in Detroit. The White Sox had three games to play in St. Louis.

The Indians split those four games in Detroit. At full strength, and with "Clean Sox" Faber and Kerr starting two of the games, Chicago stood a strong chance of sweeping the Browns, which would've resulted in a first-place tie. However, if the Indians had needed to win the season's final game in order to clinch the pennant, they wouldn't have mailed it in. There's no way Speaker would've started Morton in a game of that importance, especially with Coveleskie available on three days' rest. The Tigers had to rally in the ninth against the rarely used Clark to win a game that the Indians showed up to play only because of schedule requirements. Had the pennant been on the line that Sunday afternoon, the outcome may have been different.

Then again, it may not have been. Coveleskie, while a Hall of Fame pitcher, wasn't invincible. He lost 14 games in 1920 and might've been beaten by Detroit on that frigid day. Who knows?

It's interesting that a best-of-three playoff would've broken a tie. The National League used such a format, until the advent of the wild card, but the American League didn't. And never has. There have been five ties in American League history, and each has been broken by a one-game, winner-take-all playoff. The Indians participated in the first, defeating Boston at Fenway Park for the 1948 pennant. The second playoff also took place at Fenway Park, with the Yankees edging the Red Sox for the Eastern Division title in 1978. The Seattle Mariners beat the California Angels in a one-game playoff to win the 1995 Western Division championship. Central Division titles were decided in one game playoffs in consecutive seasons when Chicago beat Minnesota in 2008 and the Twins defeated Detroit in 2009. How might a best-of-three playoff between the Indians and White Sox have turned out in 1920?

Chicago's chances seemed good given the momentum the White Sox had built and the way the Indians had faltered against the other contenders in July, August and September (8–17 against the White Sox and Yankees). Having used Bagby on Saturday and Coveleskie on Sunday (based on the assumption that Speaker, needing to win the season's final game to win the pennant, would've turned to Coveleskie), who would've been Speaker's starter? Caldwell was a 20-game winner, but he was clearly the shakiest of Cleveland's "big three." Caldwell's ERA of 3.86 was considerably higher than Bagby's 2.89 or Covey's 2.49, and Caldwell would've had only two days' rest, most likely eliminating him. Mails was well-rested and had baffled the White Sox once, but he was high-strung and Speaker may not have wanted to entrust a crucial playoff opener to a nervous novice with limited experience. Mails' response when Speaker tabbed him to start the third game of the World Series (see the next chapter) justified any trepidation the manager may have had about starting him in a playoff game. But what other choice would he have had? If Gleason had Williams available, it may have been a moot point. Or maybe not. The Indians had routed Williams, 7–2, back in July at League Park. With Williams being one of the Black Sox, there's no way of knowing if he had an off performance or hadn't given his best effort. Risberg committed two key misplays in the seventh, when the Indians turned a 3–2 lead into a 6–2 lead. Were they legitimate errors or intentional flubs to assist Williams in losing the game?

Would there have been a travel day between games one and two, allowing Speaker to send Bagby to the mound on three days' rest to either try to wrap up the series or keep the Indians alive? Who would've been Gleason's choice, and would it have mattered? Gleason had four 20-game winners from whom to choose in Williams, Cicotte, Faber and Kerr. Speaker, of course, had a 30-game winner and a pair of 20-game winners on his staff, plus a red hot pitcher in Mails, who won seven games in September, including a dominating shutout of the White Sox.

If the clubs split the first two games, it's probably safe to assume that the third game would've been played either in Detroit or St. Louis, neutral sites within easy traveling distance. Also assuming no off day for the trip, Speaker could've gone with his ace, Coveleskie, on three days' rest. If Gleason had opened with Williams and Kerr (keep in mind that Cicotte hadn't pitched well in September), he could've opposed Covey with either Faber, in a match-up of Hall of Fame-bound spitballers, or with Cicotte, who won 21 games despite slumping down the stretch (and Cicotte was one of the Black Sox, so one has to view any poor performances with that knowledge).

Given all the factors to be considered, Chicago's chances would have been favorable in a three-game playoff, even with the first game set for League Park. Packed houses hadn't intimidated the Sox when they took two of three from the Tribe in late September. And even though both teams would've entered the playoff with clean slates, one can't forget the Indians' miserable showing against the White Sox and Yankees in July, August and September. That 8–17 mark was difficult to ignore.

It didn't come to a playoff, so we'll never know. But the 1920 Indians will never be completely able to shake the sniping from historians who insist that Chicago would've caught them in the season's final days had the scandal not exploded when it did. Nor will they ever be able to escape the charges by skeptics that they were unworthy champions who wouldn't have been in first place had the Black Sox not continued throwing games into the 1920 season, an accusation that, in all likelihood, with all the participants now deceased, will never be proven or disproven.

There's another question to consider: would the playoff have been on the square? If Johnson was correct about the gamblers who'd fixed the 1919 World Series having bet heavily on the Indians, who's to say they wouldn't have tried to fix the playoff? Would the Black Sox have defied them and risked potentially deadly consequences? In the film, *Eight Men Out*, based on Eliot Asinof's book of the same name about the Black Sox scandal, Williams is warned that his wife will be killed if he doesn't blow the eighth game of the World Series. Carney suggests that one of the reasons that all of the Black Sox were tight-lipped about the scandal was because they feared for their lives, even decades later.

For the record, Mike Sowell in *The Pitch That Killed* wrote that if the grand jury had handed down the indictments after the season ended and Chicago had won the pennant, the White Sox would've been stripped of their championship and the World Series would have been cancelled. The Indians, as runners-up, wouldn't have been called upon to "pinch-hit."

There's another factor that some the historians, who insist the Indians wouldn't have won the pennant without assistance from the White Sox, haven't considered, and that's the Chapman factor. The only rough stretch that the Indians encountered in 1920 occurred in August, when they dropped 12 of 16 games. The slump started with the five-game losing streak that Bob Clark's victory over St. Louis ended to before the club embarked on the fateful eastern road trip that began in the Polo Grounds on August 16. It continued for 11 more games, including the game in which Chapman suffered the fatal injury. The Indians lost seven of those 11 contests. The entire stretch may have been the kind of slump that any team encounters during the course of a six-month season, but it isn't unreasonable to think that the team was affected, physically and emotionally, during those 11 games by the strain of dealing with Chapman's death.

For the sake of argument, let's consider what may have happened had Chapman ducked away from Mays' fatal pitch, and the game (which the Tribe won) had continued without incident. On the heels of the five consecutive losses, the Indians would've had a two-game winning streak. If Bagby had indeed weakened under the mental strain after pitching eight strong innings in the second game, removing that strain may have allowed the Sarge to keep the Yankees off the scoreboard in the ninth and preserve the Tribe's 3–2 lead, and the winning streak would've reached three in a row. Caldwell's 3–2 victory over Bob Shawkey the following day would have run the string to four.

With no interruption in the schedule to allow the team to return to Cleveland for Chapman's funeral, the Indians may well have won four of five from the Red Sox in Fenway rather than losing four of five. From Boston, they may have gone to Philadelphia and won two of three instead of the reverse. The Indians had dominated the Red Sox and Athletics all season and could reasonably have been expected, under normal conditions, to continue doing so. If the Indians had won six of the 11 games that included and followed the game in which Chapman was fatally injured, they would have won 100 games rather than 98. Had they won seven, exactly matching their full-season winning percentage of .636, they would have won 101. Then the White Sox would have been too far behind when the scandal broke for the suspensions to make any difference.

For what it's worth, during the 11-game stretch in question, while the Indians were posting a 4–7 record, the White Sox, who had moved into first place, played just seven times and won only three. Could it have been that the Black Sox were making sure they didn't get too far ahead of the Tribe? That will never be known.

Baseball historians will argue about the 1920 American League season for as long as the game is played. The Indians may have been the beneficiaries of chicanery, or, as the *Plain Dealer* phrased it, it may simply have been "time for Cleveland to win."

11

There's No Place Like Home

One had to like Jim Dunn.

According to his biographers, Timothy Gay and Charles Alexander, there were many reasons why Joe Lannin had been willing, perhaps even eager, to part with Tris Speaker in the spring of 1916. The main reason was Speaker's refusal to accept a $9,000 salary cut. Just weeks after buying the Indians and announcing he'd spend money to build the club into a contender, Dunn did just that by paying Lannin $55,000 to take Speaker off his hands, and then giving him a more generous deal than Lannin had offered.

Dunn could've hidden behind the nameless team official who decided, apparently without authorization, that the free tickets issued to 16,000 school kids for use when the Yankees came to town for a four-game showdown in August wouldn't be honored on those dates after all. Dunn could have sold those tickets for big money to fans clamoring to see those games. But a promise was a promise, and 16,000 Cleveland school children saw those contests with New York for free.

On the day after the Indians polished off Brooklyn in the seventh and final game of the World Series, the *Plain Dealer* buried this item in its sports section:

> James C. Dunn, owner of the Cleveland baseball club, has a remarkably good memory. Fifty Clevelanders stand ready to swear to that. Anthony Carlin, president of the Anthony Carlin Rivet Works, says.
>
> Four years ago, when Mr. Dunn came here from Iowa and bought the Cleveland club, Mr. Carlin gave a dinner in Dunn's honor. Again, a year later, Mr. Carlin brought the group

together. On both occasions, Mr. Dunn said substantially these words, which nearly all present promptly forgot. "We're going to bring Cleveland its first championship with the Indians, and when we do, I am going to have every man and woman here as my guest at the first world's series game in Cleveland." Early last week, Mr. Carlin received a telephone call from Mr. Dunn, asking for a list of all those who had been present at those dinners. Then came tickets for everyone, and with each ticket a personal invitation signed by Mr. Dunn.[1]

How, exactly, did the Indians arrive at the moment when that story could be printed, namely, the day after they'd defeated the Dodgers and made good on Dunn's promise to win not only the pennant but the world championship?

"INDIANS FAVORITES AT OPENER TODAY" was the headline atop the front page of The *Plain Dealer* on the morning of Tuesday, October 5. The Indians had won 98 games, the Dodgers 93. The oddsmakers established the Tribe as a 6–5 favorite "and according to quotations in Wall Street, several thousand dollars have been placed on the series here."

"There are those who insist that inasmuch as the White Sox didn't play fair in the last world's series they probably 'laid down' during the 1920 playing season," Ed Bang told his readers on the day of the first World Series game. Bang didn't react to the scandal with the same shock and indignation as his counterparts, Edwards and Tenney, as evidenced by the next statement. "That's possible, but it's a poor sport indeed who will try to deprive the Indians of the credit that is their just due. They have been afflicted with sickness, injury and even two deaths but they stuck gamely to their task of trying to finish in front and success crowned their efforts."

"We are going to Brooklyn confident that we will win," Speaker told newspaper reporters shortly before the Tribe's train pulled out of Union Station the night before the first game. "The series against them will be no harder than our long struggle during the American League season, and we won there. The team is in the best of physical condition and filled with determination to defeat the National League champions."[2]

Speaker's decision to stop in Cleveland after the season's final game for a strategy session, rather than taking a train from Detroit to Brooklyn to arrive the day before the game and give his club a chance to familiarize itself with Ebbets Field, the Dodgers' home, took most observers by surprise.

"Manager Speaker's action in not bringing the Indians to the battlefield until the morning of the first scrap was a big surprise to nearly all baseball men, as it is the first time in the history of the world's series clashes that a manager has not had his team on the job the night before. They agree, though, that Spoke must have had some good reason and that, as he generally is right, he must be right this time," wrote Edwards. It would've been hard to argue with the manager who'd just won the franchise's first pennant.

Another unconventional decision that could've been debated, but wasn't, involved scouting. The *Press* reported that the Dodgers had scouts following the Indians throughout September, which remains standard operating procedure to this day for a team with a chance to qualify for post season competition. The Indians, however, "were the first in some years to go into a world series without having had scouts to look over the enemy and report on their batting weakness, their style of play, directions in which their hitters are accustomed to smite the ball, and all the other details which are supposed to help in outlining the plan of action for the series."

Speaker's explanation was simple. "We were too busy winning out the American League pennant to pay any attention to the fellows we'd have to fight if we won that pennant. But I don't figure we shall suffer for lack of scouting on the Brooklyn team as several of us who came to Cleveland from the Red Sox have seen most of the Brooklyn team in action from having played that ball club in the series of 1916."[3] Four of Brooklyn's regular position players, shortstop Ivy Olson (a former Indian), third baseman Jimmy Johnston, centerfielder Hy Myers and left fielder Zack Wheat were holdovers from the Dodgers' 1916 pennant winners. Among the pitchers, only Sherrod Smith and Rube Marquard had been on Brooklyn's 1916 staff. Speaker was satisfied that Gardner and Wood learned enough about the Dodgers in that five-game series, and remembered enough about them four years later, to provide an adequate scouting report. Or maybe he didn't want to clutter the minds of his weary players with what we'd call today "too much information."

"The Cleveland team goes into the world's series with a clean bill of health," said Ban Johnson on the eve of the opening game. "Practically every club in the league was under surveillance this season and I am proud to say the Indians are entirely free from suspicion, but they are not the only club."[4] Since Johnson didn't issue a clean bill of health for the entire league, did that mean at least one American League team wasn't free from suspicion? Which team or teams hadn't been under surveillance during the season, and why not? Did the gumshoes not follow, oh possibly, the White Sox for fear they might find something they didn't want to know about and, more importantly, didn't want the fans to know about?

Speaking of the White Sox, one of the telegrams congratulating Speaker on piloting the Tribe to the pennant came from Chicago second baseman Eddie Collins. "Congratulations upon winning the American League pennant," it read. "I want to assure you that none of the remaining members of the White Sox begrudge your club the honors you have honestly won, and furthermore, we are pulling for you to beat Brooklyn. Best of luck to you."[5]

"Show me the man who can pick the winner of a world's series and I'll show you a good guesser," Babe Ruth wrote on the eve of the opener. "I can't find enough difference between the Robins and the Indians to pick a winner, altho I am pulling for the Indians to win. If there is any edge at all in a comparison of these two champion ball clubs, I think it is with Cleveland."[6] Speaking of expert opinions, columnist Earle Ferris of the *Press* observed that "Eddie Cicotte hasn't signed up to write the world series for any newspaper."

"It was a happy, singing, laughing bunch of Indians that blew into New York today, all ready for the first world series in which a Cleveland ball club ever participated," Tenney wrote on October 5. "They were all chock full of confidence in their ability to clean up on the Dodgers."

The World Series was America's premier sporting event, and it attracted the crème de la crème of the sportswriting fraternity. On the front page of the *Plain Dealer,* beneath the headline trumpeting the Indians' 3–1 victory in the opener, Damon Runyon described the scene at Ebbets Field.

"It has been a cold day," Runyon wrote, "much too cold for baseball. The Brooklyn ball yard is set in a sort of pocket which sucks in all the chilly drafts of Flatbush." These drafts were made chillier by the Dodgers' loss. Runyon noted that the Indians wore new blue uniforms while the Dodgers wore "dingy white."

The Indians drew first blood in the second inning when George Burns' fly ball fell behind first baseman Ed Konetchy, who then compounded his mistake by throwing the ball wildly into left field when he tried to nail Burns at second. Burns scampered home with the first run of the series. Joe Wood then walked, went to third on a single by Joe Sewell, and scored on Steve O'Neill's double. The Indians made it 3–0 in the fourth with Wood's blast "hitting the bleacher fence on the bound, six inches from being a home run." (Balls that bounced into the stands counted as home runs in 1920). Wood scored on O'Neill's second double against Marquard, the Cleveland native who was Dodger manager Wilbert Robinson's somewhat surprising choice to open the series. Burleigh Grimes, Jeff Pfeffer,

Leon Cadore, Al Mamaux, and Smith won more than the ten victories Marquard posted, and since the Dodgers had clinched the pennant relatively early, Robinson had plenty of time to arrange his pitching rotation to his liking. Robinson, however, wanted a lefty to start the first game in Ebbets Field, which, like League Park, had a short right field. The wall in Brooklyn was 297 feet from home plate, seven feet further than the wall at League Park, and Robinson knew that Speaker would load his line up with right-handed hitters against the southpaw Marquard. Robinson liked his chances with Burns, Wood and Evans swinging for a left-field wall that was far more distant than the right-field barrier.

Edwards could be excused if he viewed the first game with mixed emotions. According to Franklin Lewis, Edwards had noticed Marquard pitching on Cleveland's sandlots in 1907. He brought the lefty to the attention of the Indians' owner, Charles Somers, and manager Napoleon Lajoie. Two scouts accompanied Somers and Lajoie to watch Marquard pitch, and their verdict was unanimous: the 18-year-old wasn't a major league prospect.[7]

Tris Speaker (right) and "Uncle" Wilbert Robinson chat before a World Series game at Ebbets Field. After his Indians bested Robinson's Dodgers, Speaker called Robinson "a grand fellow," for whom he would've liked to have been able to root.

Marquard signed with Indianapolis of the American Association and was sent briefly to the Canton, Ohio, team of the Central League to learn his craft. He did so well that he quickly returned to Indianapolis, which sold his contract to the New York Giants for the then princely sum of $11,000 in 1908. Marquard struggled, winning just nine games while losing 18 in his first three seasons. It looked as if Lajoie and the Cleveland scouts had known about what they spoke. Marquard was labeled "The $11,000 Lemon" by the New York press. He shook off that nickname by winning 73 games from 1911 to 1913, including a league-record 19-game winning streak in 1912. The Giants won the pennant each season, with Marquard and Christy Mathewson combining for a formidable left-right pitching punch. Marquard won 201 games and was elected to the Hall of Fame in 1971. Edwards never got over the belief that those games should have been won in a Cleveland uniform.

The three runs that the Tribe scored against Marquard were more than enough for Coveleskie, who limited Brooklyn to five hits and a harmless seventh-inning run on Wheat's double and consecutive groundouts. As Ruth had been during the season, Wheat was hired by a newspaper wire service to put his thoughts on paper after each game, with those thoughts being carried by papers around the country, including the *Plain Dealer* in Cleveland. Such columns were almost always ghost-written by professionals, with the players usually (but not always) telling the writer what they thought of the game, and the writer putting those thoughts into printable (coherent?) form. Among those sharing their thoughts with the public was Giants' manager John McGraw, who grudgingly confessed that "It is dishonest in a way, because few of the players write or dictate their stuff, and some never see it. I have never written a line of my articles myself, though I have looked over them before they went into print. For a long time, I refused to allow the use of my name. Then, when I saw that everyone else was getting the money while posing as authors, I decided that I would be foolish to refuse it."[8] It isn't known how authentic the thoughts appearing under Wheat's by-line were.

"The Indians had all the breaks today," Wheat complained after the first game. "They had their hits when hits meant runs. We had just as many hits, but they did not come at the right times."

"The result of the game goes to show that I was not boasting when I contended that Cleveland would display just as good pitching as Brooklyn," Speaker said. "They would have us believe that Brooklyn has the real pitching market cornered. It is my belief that the pitching in the American League is every bit as good as that in the National and our batting average of .302 was deservedly earned."⁹ Though Speaker and his troops grew tired of hearing about the Dodgers' mound strength, the numbers were revealing. Brooklyn's 2.62 ERA was the lowest in the major leagues. The Indians' ERA of 3.41 wasn't even the lowest in the American League.

The result of the first game meant something else to Edwards. "That means that unless precedents are upset, Cleveland will win the baseball classic, for only once has the team that won the inaugural contest failed to emerge from the series as a world's champion." Edwards' history was faulty. In the first World Series played in 1903, Pittsburgh won the first game but lost a best-of-nine series to Boston, five games to three. In 1911, the Giants won the first game but, despite the presence of both Mathewson and Marquard, lost the Series to Mack's Athletics. And in 1915, the Phillies took the first game from Speaker's Red Sox and then dropped four in a row. The correct count showed the team winning the first game of the Series had prevailed 13 times in 16 tries, which still boded well for the Indians.

Notebook in hand, Tenney ventured into both club's locker rooms after each game to pose questions to the key participants. He found Robinson in a sour mood. "We did not get a single break in the entire game," the Brooklyn manager groused. Breaks, or the lack of them, would be a recurring theme of the World Series. "Every break there was went Cleveland's way. I want to say I do not believe Coveleskie will be as successful against us the next time we tackle him."¹⁰

Even amid the euphoria of the franchise's first pennant and first victory in a World Series game, the mundane but critical business of running a baseball team persisted. The *Press* reported on October 6 that "C.C. Hamilton, star pitcher on the Iowa University nine, has been signed by the Cleveland Indians." Like the overwhelming majority of prospects a team signs, Hamilton never made it to the major leagues.

In his column of October 6, Ruth wrote that "until the playing of the first game for the world's championship, I have refused to make any out-and-out predictions as to the winner of the big series. Enough has happened now to venture an opinion. If Brooklyn cannot win with Rube Marquard in the box, Brooklyn cannot win the series." The Babe didn't explain why he expected Marquard, a ten-game winner, to out-duel Coveleskie, who'd won 24 games during the regular season.

Robinson went with his ace, 23-game winner Burleigh Grimes, in the second game. Not many managers have been able to hold back a 31-game winner for the second contest of a World Series, but Speaker enjoyed that luxury with Bagby. Sarge was gone after six innings with Uhle mopping up in relief. The Indians were as baffled by Grimes' spitball as the Dodgers had been by Coveleskie's. Brooklyn evened the Series with a 3–0 victory, as both teams managed seven hits.

"Each club has now taken one game and henceforth it looks like a real battle," wrote Harry Cross in the game account carried on the front page of the *Plain Dealer*. "The Indians were always menacing and many times were on the verge of driving their tomahawks home." They didn't, however, and after two games, the tone of the Series had been set. The visiting team couldn't hit its way out of a paper bag, even if it had posted a .302 batting average during the regular season (or, as in the Dodgers' case, .277).

The 1920 Series marked the first time that brothers had played against each other in the fall classic, as Tribe first baseman Doc Johnston's brother, Jimmy, scored Brooklyn's first run of the game in the first inning when he singled off Bagby, stole second, and raced home on a double by Wheat. A single by Grimes and a double by Tommy Griffith plated the second Dodger run in the third, and Brooklyn made it 3–0 in the fifth on a single by Olson, who took second on a groundout and scored on Griffith's single. That concluded the day's scoring.

"The Indians were whitewashed, and you can't win ball games unless you score some runs," Edwards noted. "That ten redskins were left on the base paths is ample evidence that timely hitting was not one of the tribe's long suits this afternoon."

"We could not hit with men on bases and Brooklyn had two batters who could. That is the best reason I know for explaining why we lost,"[11] Speaker said after the game.

Wheat's column was considerably more upbeat than it had been the previous day. "Today's game was a typical Dodgers comeback," he wrote. "It's the season's history repeated. We have always been able to come back the next day after a run of bad luck like we had yesterday and, in fact, as our pennant shows, we've done better than that. I consider today's a right good game." The 24,559 fans who watched the game undoubtedly agreed, even if they didn't always know who was at bat.

"The visiting fans are wondering where Charley Ebbets gets his announcers," said the *Plain Dealer*'s game notes. "The one he had yesterday was only recently introduced to the English language, while the one employed this afternoon had such a cold no one could understand him. Possibly Charley will have some individual with a hare lip manipulating the megaphone today." This was a time long before the era of public address systems blaring information, and more, throughout ballparks.

Meanwhile, back in Cleveland, newspaper pictures showed anxious fans lined up outside of League Park to purchase tickets for the spiffy new temporary bleacher section in right field. "Eight windows at League Park opened simultaneously yesterday morning, starting the stampede for tickets to the world's series games in Cleveland," said the accompanying story. "It was not a wild stampede, however, as tickets were given only to those who had been notified by mail that the pasteboards awaited them — for a slight consideration ranging from $26.40 to $52.30. Only two tickets to each game were sold to each applicant, and the applicant was required to buy tickets to all four games.

"Bleacher tickets will go on sale the day of each game. The new right field stand along Lexington Avenue N.E. will seat 2,000 additional fans." It would also make possible some history in the fifth game.

Among the players Tenney interviewed after the second game was Duster Mails, who was his usual loquacious and confident self. "I am sure I will be able to beat the Brooklyn Dodgers whenever I am called upon," he told Tenney. "I should not be surprised if I shut them out, for they don't look to me to be as tough as the Chicago White Sox, whom I whitewashed in that last crucial series. I will be ready to go right in there and give this Brooklyn bunch all that is coming to them, whenever I am called upon, and the sooner the call comes the better I will be suited."[12]

According to Lewis, Speaker planned to start Mails in the third game but didn't tell the lefty because of his tendency to be hyperactive. The two men shared a cab to Ebbets Field, and Speaker smiled but said nothing when Mails repeated what he'd said to Tenney the day before, telling his manager he was certain he could beat the Dodgers if Speaker would give him the chance.

Speaker told Mails in the clubhouse that he'd have the opportunity to beat his former team and then went about his business preparing for the game. He was stunned when one of his coaches, Jack McCallister, told him that Mails was begging off due to a sore arm. Caldwell, who had just finished pitching batting practice, heard the conversation, which was peppered with expletives from Speaker directed at his suddenly reluctant pitcher, and offered to start. Speaker took him up on it, but that wasn't the way a manager wanted to choose his starter for the third game of a World Series.

After the Indians were retired without scoring in the first inning, it was Caldwell's turn to be stunned. No sooner had he walked Ivy Olson, Brooklyn's lead-off batter, than he heard a popping sound coming from the outfield. Mails, without being instructed to, was warming up in the

Cleveland bullpen and throwing hard. The noise stopped after Johnston bunted Olson to second and Sewell booted Griffith's slow roller. Mails had now sat down and was holding his left arm in apparent pain.

Singles by Wheat and Hy Myers ended Caldwell's day with the Indians down by two. Slim's one-third of an inning pitched remains the shortest stint by a starting pitcher in World Series history. A furious Speaker summoned Mails and, in the words of Lewis, ordered him to "pitch, and pitch with everything you've got in you!" But it was too late. The mighty Cleveland bats produced just a run and three hits against Dodgers left-hander Sherrod Smith, and Brooklyn won, 2–1.

In Ruth's words, "Brooklyn had the pitching again Thursday, and Brooklyn won. As a result, Cleveland's chances in the series don't look so good and I don't look so good as a prophet."

"Manager Wilbert Robinson and his players, full of confidence and fight, started for Cleveland tonight, to meet the American League champions on their native heath Saturday," wrote Cross in the *Plain Dealer*'s front page game story. "With an advantage of two games to one in the season's supreme baseball argument, the Dodgers are now favored to capture the big sporting classic."

"OUTPLAYED TRIBE IS ZACK'S VERDICT: DODGERS CAPTAIN, JUBILANT, DECLARES NOTHING CAN STOP BROOKLYN CLUB NOW," read the headline above Wheat's column the morning after the third game. "We just naturally outplayed them all the way around, I thought," Wheat stated succinctly. He also expressed remorse at costing Smith a hard-earned shutout. "I'm sorry I was the cause of preventing Smith from getting a shutout, for I don't think they would have gotten a run otherwise." The Indians' only tally was registered in the fourth inning, when Speaker doubled to left and Wheat misplayed the ball, allowing it to roll though his legs. Before he could retrieve it, Speaker had circled the bases.

"The Indians are behind the Dodgers now in everything but errors," said the newspaper game notes. "They have Brooklyn tied for boots with two each. The Dodgers lead in games won, runs registered and hits made. They trail in the number of strikeouts and are behind in the giving of bases on balls." In the words of Wheat, through three games, the Indians were being outplayed all the way around, although by a narrow margin. The Tribe had only been outscored 6–4, and both games that Cleveland lost could've gone the other way with a timely hit. The pitchers hadn't exactly been torched by the Dodger bats.

Both managers talked to reporters after the game. "We will win the series," Speaker pledged as he departed Ebbets Field. He credited Brooklyn's victory to better teamwork. "The Brooklyn players were up on their toes and certainly played great baseball, while our men in the field did not do so well today."[13]

"The clubs are very evenly matched," Robinson said, "but I think we have the edge on Cleveland in respect to pitchers."[14] Based on the results of the first three games, who could argue?

Speaker could.

Jim Dunn wasn't his usual sunny self as he rode back to Cleveland with his manager, bemoaning the fact that the Series would be returning to Ebbets Field, a place with which Dunn had become too familiar. Speaker assured his boss that wouldn't happen. "We're going to win four straight at home," he predicted, promising Dunn that home cooking was all that his club needed to get untracked.[15] And four victories was all that it needed to win the world championship.

Edwards agreed with Speaker. "Just wait until the Indians get the Robins in their own base hit orchard, the park where the tribe collected the swats that gave them a batting average of .302," he wrote. "The series is not over by a long shot. The tribe, which has not struck its true batting gait here [Ebbets Field], is sure to come to its own when it returns to its familiar stomping ground." The oddsmakers didn't see the situation that way. The Indians had gone from 6–5 favorites to 7–5 underdogs, even though the next four games (if four games were necessary) would be played in League Park.[16]

Wheat's picture didn't accompany his newspaper column. Otherwise, he may not have been approached by a scalper offering to sell him a ticket to each of the four games at League Park for $100. "Zack was too astonished to say a word," reported the *Plain Dealer*. But the incident may have given Wheat's teammate Marquard an idea. Rube was picked up by Cleveland police shortly after the Dodgers' arrival for trying to scalp his World Series ducats. Marquard pitched three scoreless innings in the fourth game, but the affair embarrassed Ebbets sufficiently to result in Marquard's trade to Cincinnati in December of 1920. Rube's lapse in judgment was the closest thing to a scandal that the 1920 World Series would produce.

"SPEAKER CONFIDENT ON EVE OF GAME," said the newspaper headline when the series shifted to Cleveland. Below it, Speaker was quoted as saying, "We have just begun to fight. They had us down a few times during the American League season, but they could not keep us down. Brooklyn has us down now, but it cannot keep us there."[17]

For a club that had survived the death of its ace pitcher's wife, the tragic death of its beloved shortstop, a drag-out brawl between its manager and catcher, the rampaging bat of Babe Ruth, an attempt by a former player to convince a member of the pitching staff to jump his contract and defect to an outlaw league, and the taunts of those who insisted the White Sox would've caught them had the Black Sox scandal not broken at a most opportune moment, trailing two games to one in the World Series with the opposing team's star player declaring inevitable victory in his newspaper column was not too large a concern for the Indians.

"I am not going to offer any alibis beyond that while we have batted hard we have hit in hard luck," Speaker continued. "Brooklyn has been lucky enough to poke a few balls just outside our reach. We have hit the ball harder than Brooklyn but right at someone. I was told today that Brooklyn resorted to the old stuff of fixing the third base line so that bunts would roll foul, that the [pitcher's] box had been elevated and the diamond soaked. I don't take stock in any of these rumors. We were beaten because we could not hit the ball safely. Brooklyn won because it was able to get a few lucky breaks."[18] It sounds like Speaker concurred with Wheat about clutch hitting being a matter of luck rather than skill, at least when the Dodgers were doing it.

On the subject of luck, the Dodgers may have exhausted theirs due to the penuriousness of their owner after the third game in Brooklyn. As mentioned earlier, no professional athletes are more superstitious than baseball players, and almost anything can be considered a good luck charm. In 1919, the White Sox hired a hunchback named Eddie Bennett to serve as their "mascot," and a pennant followed. In 1920, the Dodgers lured Bennett away from Chicago, and Bennett's presence contributed to another pennant. For those considering this utter nonsense, consider what happened to the Dodgers after Ebbets declined to pay for a train ticket and lodging in Cleveland for Bennett and left him behind in Brooklyn.[19]

Cleveland hosted its first World Series game on Saturday, October 9, and 25,734 loud fans watched giddily as the Indians evened things at two games apiece with a 5–1 victory. Richard T. F. Harding provided a description in the *Plain Dealer*:

> Cleveland made the world's series stand at two all by beating Brooklyn, 5 to 1, yesterday afternoon at League Park, and more than 25,000 rooters who saw the contest went away satisfied that nothing short of dire misfortune can keep the Indians from winning the world's championship.
> So far as the end result was concerned, the game was over at the end of the first inning in which Cleveland scored two runs by following a base on balls with two definite business-like hits

and a sacrifice fly that Myers, the Brooklyn centerfielder, had no chance to throw to the plate in time. As the first three players to face Coveleskie had retired without a struggle, the contest, even at that early stage, began to look one-sided.

The Indians padded their lead with a third-inning run on singles by Wambsganss, Speaker and Burns. Brooklyn scored its only run in the fourth on a single by Jimmy Johnston and a double by Griffith, who was becoming a royal pain for Tribe pitchers. The Indians ended the offense for the day with a sixth-inning run produced by singles off the bats of Coveleskie, Evans and Wambsganss. Among those cheering the Tribe's exploits was Jenny Speaker, who had arrived with a delegation from Hubbard, Texas, to watch her son perform.

"The Indians yesterday displayed their true form," wrote Edwards. "The Indians of yesterday were the Indians who won the American League pennant, not the luckless athletes who lost two out of three games at Brooklyn." Never has there been a better example of how sports is a matter of individual perspective.

"WE'LL WIN THREE NOW," SAYS WHEAT, read the headline above the Dodger outfielder's analysis of the fourth game. "Cleveland got the jump on us, and just as all the games in this series have gone, the team that got the jump won. Then Cleveland got all the breaks." Wheat went on to assure Dodger fans, and warn Tribe supporters, "We are going back to Brooklyn, but we are not going to take the Cleveland team with us. We are going back with the world's championship."

In their spare time, to ease the tension of trying to win the biggest prize in professional sports, two of the participants decided to engage in some friendly competitive recreation. "Doc Johnston of the Indians and brother Jim of the Robins are to meet in some billiard exhibitions while the teams are here," said the newspaper game notes. Perhaps taking a cue from his ex-teammate, Joe Harris, "Doc has just purchased a billiard room to keep him busy during the off-season." The newspaper neglected to mention who won the World Series of billiards between the Johnston brothers.

Game five of the 1920 World Series remains one of the most historic contests ever played. The fireworks started early.

After Bagby disposed of the Dodgers in the top of the first inning, the Indians made quick work of their second game nemesis, Grimes. Jamieson and Wambsganss led off with singles. Speaker sacrificed but was safe when Grimes slipped and fell while fielding his bunt. That brought up the Tribe's clean up hitter, Elmer Smith, who did what a clean-up hitter is paid to do: clean the bases.

11. *There's No Place Like Home*

The 1920 World Series was historic for many reasons, one of which involved brothers oposing each other for the first time. Wheeler (Doc) Johnston (left) was the Indians' first baseman. His brother, Jimmy, was the Dodgers' third baseman.

Smith deposited Grimes' fourth pitch "far over the right field wall, over the screen, over the temporary bleachers,"[20] as Lewis described it, for the first grand slam in World Series history. Unlike earlier in the season, when Smith's grand slam against Carl Mays at League Park gave Bagby a 4–0 lead over the Yankees that he couldn't hold, the fifth game, with eight innings still to be played, had been decided. The Dodgers were done. But the fun had only started.

In the fourth inning, with Johnston and O'Neill on base, Bagby connected with a Grimes pitch and sent it into the first row of the temporary seats in right-center field. The Indians had a 7–0 lead and Bagby owned the first World Series homer ever hit by a pitcher.

As if that wasn't enough fodder for the record books for one game, Wambsganss pulled off another first in the fifth inning. Not one to overly exert himself with a big lead and the bases empty, even in the World Series, Bagby surrendered singles to Pete Kilduff and Otto Miller leading off the inning. "Batters, two and three in a row, were forever singling off Bagby," Lewis noted. Robinson chose not to bother pinch-hitting for pitcher Clarence Mitchell, who had replaced Grimes after Bagby's homer and who'd batted a respectable .234 during the regular season. Mitchell smoked a line drive that seemed headed for right field before Wambsganss leapt and snared it. He then took a few steps and touched second base before Kilduff could scramble back, and tagged Miller, who was too surprised to even try to return to first. The fans were surprised, too. League Park was silent for several seconds before erupting in cheers as the crowd realized what it had witnessed: the first (and, through the 2011 season, the only) unassisted triple play in World Series history.

After all that, the Indians had enough energy left to add one more run in their half of the fifth, when Brooklyn third baseman Jack Sheehan muffed Speaker's grounder and Tris came around to score on singles by Smith and Gardner. Any additional heroics probably would've been too much for the delirious but exhausted crowd to stand. The Dodgers broke through for a meaningless ninth-inning run to break Bagby's shutout and make the final count, Indians 8, Brooklyn 1.

"We gave future teams playing in the world series something to shoot at," beamed Speaker in the victorious clubhouse. "It was one of the most remarkable games I ever took part in, and must have been a great game to watch. It surely was one of which I could feel proud to have participated in."[21]

After the game, Smith talked about the pitch that he slammed over the right field wall. "It was a straight fast one about chest high," he told Tenney. "I could see it going up and on as I raced for first base and then when it went over I slacked up and took my time."[22] Bagby, too, according to eyewitness accounts, took his time circling the bases after his historic home run, in order to properly savor the moment.

"That sure is a ball club," said Dunn, who was feeling much sunnier than he'd felt on the train returning from Brooklyn. "The baseball writers will have something to send their papers tonight."[23] One of the things that writers had to send their papers was Wheat's column.

"Everything was against us yesterday," the Brooklyn outfielder moaned. "Bagby had horseshoes and, despite thirteen hits, we could only score one run." In other words, it was a typical outing by the Sarge. "We are due for some breaks. Cleveland can't have all the breaks in this series. A little luck has got to come our way. Yesterday's game is over. What we have to do is think about today's, and we are not going to let Cleveland get any further advantage than they have now. You watch us."

That advantage was three games to two. If the Series did return to Brooklyn, the Dodgers would be taking the Indians along with them to continue the hostilities, despite Wheat's assurance to the contrary.

There may have been more to the Indians' ability to solve the mystery of Grimes the second time around than the fact they were playing at home. In his book, *The Brooklyn Dodgers: An Illustrated Tribute,* author Donald Honig quotes the future Hall of Fame pitcher (and the last to throw a legal spitball) as blaming a teammate, and some eagle-eyed Indians, for his woes that afternoon.

"We had a fellow named Pete Kilduff playing second base. He's out there and he can see the catcher's signs. Before each pitch, he's picking up some sand and putting it in his glove. If it's not a spitter, he drops the sand. If it's going to be a spitter, he keeps it in his glove. He's doing that, you see, so if the ball is hit to him, he'll get some of the wet off of it so it won't slip when he throws it.

"Christ, I don't know why the hell he had to do that. Fellows were throwing it from short, from third. Anyway, it didn't take long for somebody to pick that up, and all the hitters had to do was watch Kilduff."[24] Grimes said he eventually confronted Kilduff about the habit but Kilduff didn't have much to say. A pitcher tipping his pitches is one thing. A teammate tipping pitches is another.

Grimes shook off the rough treatment that he received on that history-making Sunday afternoon. "They won't get me next time," he promised. "I feel sure of that for I know I won't have two bad games in succession."[25] Grimes would get the chance to prove it in game seven.

Among the fans attending the sixth game was Secretary of War Newton D. Baker, the former Cleveland mayor whose decision not to completely exempt major league baseball from the "work or fight" order in 1918 put an early end to a season that might, had it been played to its scheduled conclusion, have resulted in an Indians pennant. A picture of a smiling Baker graced the newspaper's sports section, and he was said to be "perfectly satisfied with the result."

With the series being a best-of-nine game tussle, "Yesterday's game was the last in which the players share in the receipts [26,684 witnessed the historic contest], and the tabulation of the figures shows that if Cleveland wins the world's series each player will receive approximately $4,395," noted the *Plain Dealer.* "If Brooklyn wins, the National League athletes will get only $3,951 each. The discrepancy is due to the fact that Brooklyn's share must be split among twenty-seven men, while only twenty-two Clevelanders will be rewarded."

How could the Indians top their performance in the fifth game? They couldn't, of course, so they, and the 27,174 fans who occupied every corner of League Park, had to settle for a 1–0 Tribe victory. Again, Brooklyn's Sherrod Smith was brilliant, holding the Indians to seven hits. But this time, Mails overcame his jitters and pitched a three-hit shutout, shaking off three errors that his teammates committed behind him.

"I would pitch my arm off for Tris Speaker if need be," Mails said in the happy clubhouse after the squeaker. "I didn't need to strain myself in this game as I kept going along easy." Mails wasn't content with a mere World Series shutout. "If it wasn't for Olson, Neis and [Konetchy] getting singles, I'd have had a no-hit game to my credit."[26] Bernie Neis, a rookie outfielder, actually wasn't partially to blame for Mails' falling short in his bid for immortality. Mails held Neis without a hit in two at-bats. (The Dodgers' third hit was stroked by Hy Myers.) Mails' three-hit shutout had been bettered only twice in World Series annals, and it had been done on consecutive days in 1906, when Ed Walsh of the White Sox blanked the cross town Cubs on two hits, 3–0, in the third game, and Mordecai (Three-Finger) Brown of the Cubs returned the favor the next day, 1–0. Ed Ruelbach of the Cubs had limited the White Sox to a single hit in the second game of the Series, but the "Hitless Wonders," who were almost held hitless that day, managed to scratch out a run in a 7–1 defeat. Mails' whitewashing of the Dodgers had placed him in some fast company.

The Tribe reached Smith just once, in the sixth, when Speaker singled and scored on a double by Burns. Billy Evans, the American League umpire who spent his off-seasons as the sports editor of a national news wire service, wrote a syndicated column that was picked up by the *Plain Dealer* analyzing each game of the series. Evans' analysis of the sixth game pointed out how close Speaker came to being sent back to third base on Burns' hit.

> There came mighty near being an argument over the run Speaker scored. Some Cleveland fans in the temporary seats in left field almost spoiled the true value of Burns' hit. The ball struck the temporary fence, caromed off and was fielded by Myers. As the ball shot off the fence, a half dozen Cleveland fans leaned over the railing and frantically grabbed for the ball. All were anxious to obtain it as a souvenir. Had it been touched by any of the fans, Speaker, who was on first, would have been held at third. It might have meant the ball game. Brooklyn made the claim that it had been touched, but it was not allowed

and rightly, as the ball rebounded with such speed from the fence that there wasn't a chance for a spectator to touch it.

Evans praised the work of the umpires in the series. Two of the arbiters assigned to the games, Bill Klem of the National League and Tommy Connolly of the American League, were eventually enshrined in the Hall of Fame, as was Evans. Hank O'Day and Bill Dineen also worked the Series.

Burns was born in Niles, Ohio, meaning that two of the major contributors to the Indians' pennant and world championship, Burns and Elmer Smith, were natives of northern Ohio.

In only four seasons have four victories not been enough to claim the World Series, and 1920 was one of them. The first World Series in 1903 had been a best-of-nine affair, as were the Series of 1919, 1920 and 1921. The owners returned to the best-of-seven format in 1922 and have stayed with it ever since. Thus, despite their four victories, the Indians hadn't won anything yet. But the Cleveland papers were convinced they would.

Edwards delivered this assessment:

> Unless the age of miracles is revived, Cleveland will win the deciding game of the world's series at League Park this afternoon. The statement was made possible yesterday by the stoutheartedness of John Walter (Duster) Mails, the Indians' only southpaw pitcher who was the hero in Cleveland's 1 to 0 victory over Brooklyn.
>
> Mails, however, was not the only hero of the game. While he was the biggest factor in the Indians' defense, it was George Burns who saw to it that the game did not go into extra innings by driving a terrific two-base hit to the center field bleachers and driving in Speaker all the way from second base in the sixth inning.

"There is little doubt that the 1920 series will end this afternoon with Cleveland winning, five games to two," said an unattributed article on the front page of the *Plain Dealer*. "Cleveland has all the advantage, especially in confidence. The Indians know they have to win but one more game to take the title. Brooklyn must win three straight." That was just what the Dodgers were going to do, in the opinion of their manager.

"Beat? I should say not," snarled Robinson, some of the old Oriole in him on display. "We haven't been hitting and that's the only trouble. We're going out there tomorrow and smash into those Indians so hard they'll wish they'd never seen a world's series, and when we get back to Brooklyn, Cleveland won't have a chance. We're not beaten until Cleveland wins five, and that will never happen. We'll hit from now on. If Coveleskie pitches tomorrow, we'll drive him out of the box despite his two victories."[27]

Wheat, in his next-to-last column, was far more subdued. "This is our only chance to stay in, and we want that game," he wrote. So did the Indians, and the 27,525 fans who packed League Park to watch them obtain it.

To prepare the fans for the eagerly anticipated victory celebration, *Plain Dealer* cartoonist Don Wootton offered these suggestions: if the Indians win ...

"Don't give away all your money (it may come in handy some time). Don't let someone near you tear off all your clothes (it may be a long way home). Don't swallow your scorecard. Don't throw away your derby (they cost about $10). Don't lose all your voice applauding." The last admonition may have been the most difficult to live up to, as there was plenty for Tribe fans to applaud, Robinson's bluster notwithstanding.

Edwards' front page game story appeared on October 13:

> The better the day, the better the deed. On October 12, 1492, Christopher Columbus discovered America and paved the way for the organization of the American Baseball League. On October 12, 1920, the Cleveland Indians, no relation to those discovered 428 years ago, won the world's baseball championship. It was a long time to wait, but the prize was worth waiting for.
>
> For forty-two years or more Cleveland has been striving to win a major league pennant. Year after year it was doomed to disappointment. Yesterday, Columbus Day, its ambitions were realized for, in addition to the championship of the American League, Cleveland has acquired the honor of being the home of the world's baseball champions.

The Indians blanked Brooklyn in game seven, 3–0, behind Coveleskie's third straight complete game, five-hit victory, shrugging off Robinson's insistence that his Dodgers would drive Coveleskie from the mound and return the Series to Ebbets Field.

The Tribe scored the only run that Covey would need in the third inning when Gardner singled off Grimes, who had returned to the mound on one day's rest, went to third on Johnston's single, and scored on a delayed double steal of home. In the fifth, Jamieson beat out an infield hit, stole second and scored on Speaker's triple. The game's, and the Series', final run came home in the seventh, when O'Neill doubled but was caught in a rundown as Coveleskie tried to sacrifice him to third. O'Neill stayed in the rundown long enough to let Covey reach second, and he scored on a double by Jamieson.

"With proper breaks, only one run would have been made off me," Grimes grumbled after the game. "But that would have been plenty to beat me the way Covey was going."²⁸

Indians 3, Brooklyn 0. Speaker had been right. The Indians wouldn't be heading back to Brooklyn after all.

"They met a champion ball club from an older league and battered it to a mushy pulp," wrote *Plain Dealer* columnist Frank G. Menke, whose analysis was a bit exaggerated. For the seven games, the Tribe had outscored the Dodgers, 21–8, but five of the games had been close, Cleveland battering Brooklyn into a "mushy pulp" only in game five. For a team with a supposedly inferior pitching staff, the Tribe's ERA was a microscopic 0.89, compared to Brooklyn's stingy 2.59 ERA. Indian pitchers held the Dodgers to a .205 batting average, which would've been lower had Brooklyn not smacked Bagby for 13 hits in the fifth game.

Stan Coveleskie was the true ace of the Indians' staff, even though Jim Bagby won more games. Coveleskie wrote his name in the history books with three complete game victories in the World Series.

The Indians (who'd scored 197 more runs than the Dodgers during the regular season) didn't exactly tear the cover off the ball either, batting .244 with two home runs.

As Grimes noted while the Dodgers packed for the long trip back to Brooklyn, "We couldn't expect to win when we made eight runs in the entire series. We lost this series because we weren't hitting."²⁹ The key to the Series had been the Indians winning the first game at Ebbets Field. Cleveland's record of 47–29 away from League Park had been the best in the major leagues in 1920; Brooklyn's road record of 44–32 had been tops in the National League. After the Tribe's victory in the first game, the home team won the six remaining games because the visitors simply couldn't score. The Indians scored four runs in three games at Ebbets Field. That, thanks to Coveleskie, was enough to win one of them. The Dodgers scored a measly two runs in four games at League Park. Not surprisingly, that wasn't enough to win any of them.

After handing the ball used to record the final out to his mother, Speaker made a series of remarks:

> From the start, I never had any doubt of our being able to win the world championship. The American League campaign was what gave us the trouble, but the fact we had to fight it right out to the finish helped us against Brooklyn. We were playing at top speed when the regular season ended and we kept going at the same gait until we won the world's series.
>
> All the boys have felt the same way. They know we are a good ball club and have known it right along. When we lost two in a row in Brooklyn, none of us was discouraged because we knew we had a better ball club than Brooklyn and would win if all the breaks were not against us. I presume some thought I was over confident when I predicted four straight. Nothing of the kind. I knew my boys and they came through just as I expected.
>
> We defeated a good club, one that played cleanly and honestly, a bunch of good sportsmen. They fought us hard all the way but never resorted to rough tactics. They have a wonderful man as manager in Wilbert Robinson. He is a grand fellow. I sure would like to have had the chance to pull for him.
>
> It has been a long time Cleveland has been waiting for its first pennant winner and I am happy that the honor was reserved for me and that I and my boys were also able to bring a world's championship here also.[30]

In his last column, Wheat praised the club that had bested his Dodgers. "They beat us and they beat us fairly and squarely. Tris Speaker deserves all the credit that can be given him, both for his playing and for his generalship in the series. The entire Cleveland team deserves the championship, but to Speaker should go the bulk of the praise for the handling of the Cleveland team here and in Brooklyn. Give the Cleveland team credit for a clean cut victory. We have no excuses. The other team won." Wheat, however, didn't concede that the better team had won.

If Robinson never visited Cleveland again, it would probably have been too soon. His Orioles had been vanquished by the Spiders some 25 years

An aerial view of Cleveland's tiny League Park, circa 1936. The park hadn't changed at all since 1920, except that the temporary right field bleachers, installed for the World Series, were gone. Lights were never installed at League Park. Tris Speaker was convinced his club would not lose a World Series game at home, and he was right.

earlier in the National League's Temple Cup playoffs, losing all three games played in Cleveland, and now the Indians had defeated his Dodgers, who lost all four games played in Cleveland.

"Cleveland has a wonderful ball club, and Tris Speaker and his men certainly deserve the splendid support they received from the city," Robinson said. "It was a well-fought and honestly played series. We did our best, but we couldn't hit Cleveland pitching. That's about all there is to say."[31]

Before leaving town, Robinson denied rumors that he'd leave the Dodgers to manage the Yankees in 1921, as rumors also continued to swirl that Miller Huggins would be dismissed. Robinson managed Brooklyn for 11 more seasons, retiring after the 1931 campaign. He had, however, won his last pennant. Robinson and his old Oriole friend and teammate, John McGraw, shared one thing in common. Neither had much success in the postseason. In addition to losing the Temple Cup together in 1894 and '95, McGraw's Giants won ten pennants but only three world championships. Robinson's Dodgers won two pennants and lost both World Series. Somehow, despite a managerial record of nearly an even .500 (1,399 wins and 1,398 defeats), Robinson was elected to the Hall of Fame for his 17 seasons at the helm of the Dodgers.

The Dodgers wouldn't win another pennant until 1941. Baseball has its "Curse of the Billy Goat," which has allegedly kept the Cubs out of the World Series since 1945, and the "Curse of the Bambino," which supposedly plagued the Red Sox from the January day of 1920 that they sold Ruth to the Yankees until they won the 2004 World Series. Since Brooklyn would spend the next 20 years wandering aimlessly through the second division of the National League, maybe it was the victim of the "Curse of the Neglected Mascot?" Perhaps angry at Ebbets for leaving him behind when the Dodgers departed for Cleveland, leading the World Series two games to one, Eddie Bennett left Brooklyn for Manhattan, where he served as the Yankees' mascot in 1921. The result: a pennant. The Dodgers slipped to fifth.[32]

"Stanley Coveleskie, pitching ace, always has a laugh stored away for an interviewer," wrote the *News* on October 13. Coveleskie had plenty to laugh about, having joined Pittsburgh's Deacon Phillippe and Babe Adams; his teammate Wood; Jack Coombs of the Athletics; and Red Faber of the White Sox as pitchers winning three games in a single World Series. Phillippe had done it in the first World Series in 1903 (he also lost two games), Adams did it in 1909, Coombs in 1911, Wood in 1912 and Faber in 1917. Though an impressive accomplishment, which wouldn't be duplicated until 1946, winning three games in a single World Series was far more common in an era of four-man pitching rotations, when managers thought nothing of sending a starter to the mound on two or three days' rest or even less, as in the case of Grimes, who got the nod from Robinson in an effort to stave off elimination on just one days' rest. Speaker turned to Coveleskie to wrap up the championship on just two days rest after he'd started and won the fourth game, rather than giving the ball to Caldwell. How many times has a 20-game winner pitched just one-third of an inning in a seven-game World Series?

"Of course, Covey is as straight-faced as they make them, but he gives the laugh nevertheless. After his first victory over the Dodgers, Covey said 'I didn't try very hard. I didn't have to bear down.' After the second triumph, he vouch-safed the information that 'I could beat them guys four times if Spoke said the word.' And after Tuesday's shutout victory he queried as to the number of hits he allowed and when given the information he said 'two runs in twenty-seven innings ain't so bad but they got too many hits today—five—but then my arm wasn't quite right.' What would he have done if his arm had been good?" the newspaper asked.[33]

11. There's No Place Like Home

Ed Bang had one final bouquet to toss to the world champions. "Honesty and righteousness triumph in the long run," he wrote. "That was never better exemplified than in the case of our Indians in their long drive for the pennant and the world's championship. Theirs was a hard row to hoe, harder than any team that has ever won a pennant." Thus, the accolades that poured in from around the country were well-deserved.

The Indians' office was swamped with congratulatory telegrams. One came from President Woodrow Wilson, asking, "May I not congratulate you on your honest and sincere efforts?" Another came from the man who hoped to succeed Wilson, Ohio Governor James M. Cox, the Democratic nominee for president, who wired that "Ohio is proud of your victory." Cox (who, being from Dayton, may have been a Reds fan) didn't fare as well as the Indians. He'd be defeated by the Republican candidate, Ohio's junior U.S. Senator, Warren G. Harding, in the largest popular vote landslide in history (60 percent to 34 percent) about three weeks later.

There's no record of a congratulatory message from Harding, but it wasn't because he wasn't a baseball fan. Almost a decade earlier, Harding had been impressed with the performance of a pitcher named Wilbur Cooper, who was toiling for a low minor league team, of which Harding was a part-owner in Harding's home of Marion, some 100 miles southwest of Cleveland. Harding recommended Cooper to the Naps, who weren't as impressed and declined to sign the left-hander.[34] Cooper signed with Pittsburgh and spent 15 seasons in the major leagues, winning 216 games, including a National League-leading 22 victories in 1921. Between Cooper and Marquard, the Naps had tossed away 417 victories. No wonder it took Cleveland two decades to win a pennant!

In the late summer of 1920, befitting a much simpler era, the Chicago Cubs had stopped by Marion to play the local team in an exhibition game. Harding tossed the first pitch before retiring to the stands to watch the Cubs trim the locals, 3–1.

A city's first sports championship requires a celebration, and Cleveland scheduled one for October 13. The party at Wade Park in University Circle drew an estimated 25,000 to 30,000 revelers and quickly degenerated into mass chaos, as such gatherings often do. A makeshift dais had been set up for Mayor W.S. FitzGerald and the players. A row of chairs was lined up in front of the dais for the relatives and friends of the dignitaries. The occupants of those chairs soon had to run for cover as wave after wave of fans raced to the dais to touch or, if the fan was lucky, shake hands with his or her favorite Indian.

The *Plain Dealer* covered the proceedings. After the first rush, an attempt was made to resume the program.

> Mrs. Carl W. Kettleman, Tris Speaker, Wheeler Johnston and Joe Wood sang 'Watching the World Go By.' From that time on, the program was abandoned. When Johnston, Stanley Coveleskie and Dunn leaned over the railing to shake hands with those nearest the stands a new rush began. Then those on the platform started to plead with the fans to go home.
>
> For half an hour, officials in charge pleaded with the crowd to go home, but repeated assurances that the ball players themselves had gone were without avail. Thousands, hoping to reach the stand to shake hands with the diamond stars, or at least see them at close range, were pushing from the rear, and those nearest the platform were caught in the crush. So far as could be learned, no one was seriously injured.

A smaller celebration was planned for Milan, Ohio's favorite son, grand slam hero Smith. "A royal reception in all that implies will be accorded to Elmer Smith, Indian outfielder, upon his arrival in Milan ... where, as heretofore, he will pass the winter at the home of his father, playing basketball, shooting rabbits and doing odd jobs about the home place," said the *Plain Dealer*. On a January day in need of brightening with some baseball information, Edwards had engaged in some whimsy while telling his readers about Smith's humble beginnings.

"It is understood that Elmer was born in Sandusky," Edwards wrote. "As an infant, he did not seem to enthuse over that town and at the age of 2 years he informed his parents that he wanted to live in Milan [about 10 miles to the south.] As he could not be swayed from his purpose, his parents decided to accompany him to Milan." Both Sandusky and Milan were proud to claim Smith as one of their own, particularly after he sent Grimes' pitch soaring over League Park's right field wall in the first inning of the fifth game of the World Series.

Parties weren't needed for northern Ohio to show its support for, and appreciation of, its world champions. Tribe fans had already done that by establishing a new franchise attendance record of 912,839 during the regular season, an average of 11,703 per game. That figure would've established an American League single season record, easily eclipsing the mark set by the 1905 White Sox, had not the Yankees drawn the astronomical total of 1,289,422 fans to watch Ruth do his thing. Another 107,337 fans had paid their way into League Park to watch the World Series. The Cleveland club had come a long way since it finished in seventh place in the American League's inaugural season of 1901 and drew just 131,380 fans, the lowest total in the major leagues, causing league president Ban Johnson to warn, as he searched for a team to move to St. Louis, that "the franchises of Cleveland or Baltimore may be shifted." Baltimore's franchise was moved to New York, becoming the Yankees. Cleveland's franchise stayed put.

When Speaker held his season-ending meeting with his players, a number of them asked to borrow their uniforms, and the manager knew why. Speaker reminded "his boys" that the National Commission prohibited members of the world championship team from collecting extra cash by participating in unsanctioned exhibition games, from which the National Commission wouldn't receive a cut, hence its aversion to them, and any player caught doing so would have $500 deducted from his World Series share. "Some of the Indians who had requested the loan of uniforms decided they did not want them when they were reminded of the $500 fine," it was noted in the newspaper.

There were no restrictions on members of the world champions receiving goodies from admirers, and the Indians benefited from the spoils that go to the victors. Included in the haul was "a black leather belt with a handsome silver buckle, engraved with the player's initials. They were gifts of the O.R. Rust Company, 1225 West 6th Street, the manufacturers," according to a newspaper story.

Jim Dunn took advantage of the good feelings that permeated the Tribe's clubhouse as the players basked in the glow of a hard-earned world championship to make sure that all of his boys were satisfied for 1921. Before the players scattered to their off-season homes, Dunn signed each of them to a contract for the coming season. He also presented them with a bonus equaling ten percent of their 1920 salary as a reward for a job well done.

One person who didn't share in the booty was Larry Gilbert, whom the Indians had wooed but failed to win over while in New Orleans for spring training. "Larry Gilbert, who preferred to stick to his garage and gasoline business here to joining the Indians in the spring, and thereby lost the opportunity of splitting the world's series money is now regretful of his stand," reported the *Plain Dealer*.

"'Never again. I will play baseball hereafter,' says Gilbert, who had shared in the series money with the Boston Braves in 1914." Gilbert would play baseball, but never again in the major leagues. Gilbert, nonetheless, played an important role in the Indians' march to the pennant. In September, with Ray Chapman's successor, Harry Lunte, injured and finished for the season (Lunte would make a token appearance in the World Series), and with Joe Evans incapable of handling the shortstop's job, the Indians, in desperation, had purchased the contract of Joe Sewell from New Orleans. Speaker was skeptical of Sewell's readiness to play the infield's most important position for a pennant contender, and he wasn't alone. Sewell himself doubted that he belonged in the major leagues and didn't want to report to Cleveland.

Sewell's New Orleans teammate, Gilbert, who'd passed up the chance to play in Cleveland six months earlier, talked him into it.[35]

12

Aftermath

If it was good enough for John McGraw, it was good enough for Jim Dunn.

In the spring of 1906, McGraw outfitted his New York Giants in uniforms with the words "WORLD CHAMPIONS" written on the shirts. After refusing to play the American League champion Boston Pilgrims following the 1904 season, referring to the Pilgrims as champions of a "minor league," McGraw and Giants owner John T. Brush bowed to pressure from both the public, which wanted to see a showdown between the two league champions, and his players, who didn't appreciate being denied the opportunity to make money by participating in a postseason series. On the strength of one of the greatest pitching performances of all time from Christy Mathewson, who authored three shutouts, the Giants had disposed of the AL champion Athletics in five games in the 1905 World Series, legitimizing McGraw's claim that the NL champs of 1904 were the rightful world champions, even if they hadn't earned the title on the diamond. And he wasn't too modest to brag about the accomplishment.

Dunn's Indians were the world champions, and he wanted to make sure that no one forgot it during the summer of 1921. When the season opened, the Tribe sported new uniforms. Gone was the familiar block "C" on the chest. In its place were the words "World's Champions." It's a sports cliché that the defending champion has a target on its back the following season, but Dunn put the target on his player's chests. According to Whitey Lewis, the players didn't feel embarrassed by wearing the designation on their work clothes. In fact, Lewis wrote, they felt that they deserved to boast of their status as the best baseball team on the planet. It's reasonable to assume that the uniforms greatly annoyed the Tribe's opponents in 1921.

If the rest of the American League needed any additional incentive to knock the Indians off their perch, staring at those uniforms for nine innings surely provided it.

In addition to new uniforms, the Indians almost had a new center fielder and a new manager in 1921. Possibly exhausted by the triumphant but traumatic 1920 season, or perhaps wanting to leave the game while on top, Speaker wanted to retire after winning the world championship, according to Charles Alexander. Dunn talked him out of it.[1]

Speaker and Dunn were convinced the Indians would repeat, and so were many of the "experts" who'd accurately forecast the Tribe's 1920 championship. Less than a week after the Indians had dispatched the Dodgers, the *Press* reported that the Cardinals would send their star second baseman, Rogers Hornsby, the National League's batting champion, to the Giants for a staggering $200,000 — twice the amount the Yankees paid for Ruth, not counting Ruppert's $350,000 loan to Harry Frazee. The story declared that Hornsby's addition all but guaranteed a pennant for the Giants in 1921 and would set up a Giants-Indians World Series. In the opinion of at least one writer, the other 14 major league clubs would be participating in the 1921 season only for exercise.

The story didn't carry a by-line, but the author proved to be a partially proficient prognosticator. Although the Cardinals were then cash-strapped and playing second fiddle to the Browns, management decided that selling the club's best player wasn't the way to make inroads with the populace. Hornsby stayed in St. Louis, and the Giants won the 1921 pennant without him.

The 1921 American League pennant race was another frantic duel between the Indians and Yankees. Chicago, decimated by the eternal banishment of the eight Black Sox by newly appointed Commissioner Kenesaw Mountain Landis, plunged to seventh place. St. Louis and Washington finished above .500 but never seriously challenged Cleveland and New York.

Speaker, who was sidelined by a knee injury during the closing weeks of the season, still batted .362 and drove in 74 runs. He managed to keep the Indians nipping at the heels of the powerful Yankees despite the dramatic declines of Bagby and Caldwell. Bagby's victory total dropped from 31 to 14, and Caldwell won just six times in 1921 after posting 20 victories the previous season. Uhle, Mails, and spitball artist Allan Sothoron, acquired on waivers from Boston, which had picked him up following his release by the Browns, combined for 42 victories to pick up some of the slack.

With less than two weeks remaining in the season, the Indians arrived in New York for a four-game series, trailing the Yankees by just two percentage points. With a hobbled and frustrated Speaker contributing just one hit in 13 at-bats, the Indians lost three of the four games ending the race. The world champions had been dethroned. The Indians finished the season with a record of 94–60, four and a half games out of first place.

Speaker believed for the rest of his life that the Indians were the better team and should have won a second consecutive pennant. So does Mike Sowell — with a caveat. In the book *Play It Again, Baseball Experts on What Might Have Been,* Sowell says that had Ray Chapman lived, and had Chapman not retired after the 1920 World Series, the Indians would have captured the 1921 pennant. "With Sewell's bat and Chapman still in the line-up, Cleveland would have improved on its 94–60 record and won 100 games in 1921, beating out the Yankees for the AL pennant. Cleveland was in first place as late as September that season and having Chapman could have made the difference. They would have gone on to beat the New York Giants in the 1921 World Series."[2] Sowell doesn't say where Speaker would've found the pitching to notch those six additional victories, since he had to scramble to offset the loss of productivity from Bagby and Caldwell, whose combined win total shrank from 51 to 20. Chapman couldn't have helped there. Chapman, of course, didn't live, and the Indians, despite a valiant effort, weren't able to postpone the dawning of the Yankee dynasty by one more season.

As sportswriter Heywood Hale Broun would pen later in the decade, "The Ruth is mighty and shall prevail." And so he did. The Indians had withstood Ruth's record-setting 1920 offensive onslaught. The Babe's 1921 season, still considered by many historians to represent the single greatest individual offensive performance in the sport's annals, was too much for them to overcome. Ruth batted .378, hit 59 home runs, drove in 171 runs and scored 177. His slugging average of .846 is the second highest ever recorded, eclipsed only by his .847 slugging average of 1920. For good measure, Ruth threw in 44 doubles, 16 triples, and 144 bases on balls.

It was too much for mere mortals to compete with, even the world champions.

No one could have foreseen that the Yankees' 1921 American League pennant would be the first of a phenomenal 43 league championships. No one could have foreseen that the Indians, who'd waited 20 years for their first pennant, would have to wait 28 seasons for their next one. They'd come close only twice during that drought, finishing three games behind the Yankees in 1926 and one game in back of Detroit in 1940.

The 1920 world champions began to scatter as the seasons passed. Coveleskie, who contributed 23 victories to the Indians' bid to repeat in 1921, would pitch in the World Series again. Traded to Washington after the 1924 season, Covey posted a 20–5 record for the 1925 pennant-winning Senators. Coveleskie carried a 2–1 lead into the eighth inning of the second game of the World Series but was victimized by shortstop Roger Peckinpaugh's two errors, two of eight miscues Peckinpaugh, the league's Most Valuable Player, would commit during the Series. Outfielder Kiki Cuyler's two-run homer gave the Pirates a 3–2 victory. Given the chance to pitch the clincher, as he had in 1920, Coveleskie was driven from the box in the seventh inning of the fifth game, when the Pirates snapped a 2–2 tie and went on to win, 6–3. There would be no clincher for the Senators, who lost the Series in seven games. Coveleskie was inducted into the Hall of Fame in 1969 on the strength of his 215 career victories (and three in the 1920 World Series), 162 of which were won in an Indians uniform.

O'Neill, Covey's sturdy catcher, became a coach and then a manager, as many catchers do. He managed the Indians for the final 60 games of 1935 through the 1937 season, and led Detroit to the 1945 pennant and World Series championship. In 14 seasons as a major league manager with the Indians, Tigers, Red Sox and Phillies, O'Neill's teams won 56 percent of their games (1,040–821) and never once lost more than they won.

Gardner, the steady third baseman, enjoyed the best season of his 17-year career in 1921. At age 35, Gardner hit .319, scored 101 runs and drove in 115 while missing just one game. In three seasons with the Indians, the durable Gardner had played in 446 of 447 games. Combining the 1920 and 1921 campaigns, he'd driven in 233 runs despite hitting just six home runs. Never a power threat, Gardner swatted only 27 homers in his career. He showed signs of age in 1922, hitting .285 in 137 games. After playing in just 52 contests in 1923 and 38 in 1924, Gardner retired.

Sewell, the emergency shortstop, wore a Cleveland uniform for a decade before spending the last three years of his career with the Yankees. His ability to put his bat on the ball is legendary. In 7,132 career at-bats, Sewell struck out just 114 times. On only two occasions did he strike out twice in one game. Sewell posted a lifetime batting average of .312 and joined Coveleskie in the Hall of Fame in 1977.

The 339 and two-thirds innings he pitched in 1920 took a toll on Bagby's stout right arm. After his 31-victory season, Bagby won just 18 more games for the Indians. He finished his career with Pittsburgh in 1923.

12. Aftermath

In typical Bagby fashion, he pitched 68 innings and allowed 95 hits for the Pirates, but managed to win three of his five decisions. Bagby's son, Jim Junior, would pitch for the Indians from 1941 to 1945.

As for the other World Series heroes, Elmer Smith enjoyed a productive 1921 season, batting .290, again pacing the Indians with 16 homers and driving in 84. On Christmas Eve of 1921, Smith was sent to the Red Sox along with George Burns and Joe Harris, the reluctant first baseman who never agreed to contract terms with the Tribe for 1920 or 1921 (but was still considered Cleveland's property due to the reserve clause), in exchange for first baseman Stuffy McInnis, who'd anchored the infield of the Athletics' 1910 to 1914 dynasty. It was the second time that the Indians had traded Smith, who was shipped to Washington in 1916 and re-acquired in 1917. Smith bounced from Boston to the Yankees (striking out twice in as many at-bats in the 1922 World Series) to Cincinnati and retired after the 1925 season.

Hometown hero Bill Wambsganss, who missed just one game in 1920, was limited to 107 contests in 1921, but his batting average increased by 41 points. Wambsganss and Sewell formed the Tribe's keystone combination through 1923, although Wambsganss played in just 101 games in his final season with the Indians. In January of 1924, Wamby and O'Neill were sent to the Red Sox in a deal that returned Burns to Cleveland as the front office gradually broke up the 1920 world champions. Wambsganss retired after playing sparingly for the Athletics in 1926.

Although he spent only the month of September with the Indians, there probably would have been no pennant flying above League Park in 1921 without the contributions of Mails. As a follow-up, Duster posted a 14–8 record for the 1921 Tribe, but his ERA soared to 3.94 and, according to both Henry Edwards and Franklin Lewis, the seeds of his demise as a major leaguer were sewn when Ty Cobb discovered his Achilles heel. Cobb, a notorious bench jockey, learned that his barbs aimed at Mails had their desired effect. Mails heard each word and allowed the jockeying to distract him. Every team in the American League followed Cobb's lead. Mails possessed "rabbit ears," and couldn't let go of the taunts from his opponents go in one and out the other. Driven to distraction by verbal assaults from opposing dugouts, Mails' record plunged to 4–7 in 1922, earning him his release by the Indians. Mails didn't return to the big leagues until 1925, when he won seven and lost seven for the Cardinals. He retired with a career mark of 32–25.

Speaker was among the first players to earn Hall of Fame recognition. He was elected as part of the class of 1937, and was present at the first induction ceremony in Cooperstown, New York, in 1939. His 792 doubles are still the major league record. Speaker stands sixth on the all-time list with 223 triples. His 3,514 career hits and .345 lifetime batting average place him fifth in both categories. Speaker's bat and leadership were instrumental in securing Cleveland's first World Series title. He eventually made the city his off-season home and should have finished his distinguished career in a Tribe uniform. But that wouldn't happen.

Shortly after leading the Indians to a surprising second-place finish in 1926, Speaker abruptly resigned as manager and announced his retirement. Though his average slipped to .304, Speaker had driven in 86 runs and had given no indication that he was ready, at age 38, to hang up his spikes.

Within weeks, an even more startling announcement came from Detroit, where Ty Cobb was given his unconditional release after 22 years in a Tigers uniform. Cobb hadn't enjoyed the success that Speaker had in his five seasons as Detroit's manager and was relegated to part-time status in 1926, but still batted .339 and had likewise given no indication that he was ready to call it a career.

Baseball fans everywhere, particularly in Cleveland and Detroit, wanted answers that the sport would have preferred not to provide. But the circumstances that led to the departures of two of the game's greatest players couldn't be swept under the rug.

In the fall of 1926, Commissioner Landis received a correspondence from Hubert (Dutch) Leonard. Since his hiring to clean up baseball after the Black Sox scandal, Landis had spent much of his time putting out fires pertaining to gambling accusations. Leonard's correspondence started another conflagration.

Leonard won 139 games during his 11-year career, spent with the Red Sox and Tigers. He'd come out of a three-year retirement in 1924 to aid Cobb's beleaguered pitching staff, only to be placed on waivers the following year despite an 11–4 record. Cobb thought Leonard was lazy and wasn't impressed with his bloated 4.51 ERA. Leonard swore revenge on Cobb and added Speaker to his list when Speaker declined to claim Leonard on waivers for the Indians.

Leonard's revenge took the form of letters written by Cobb and Joe Wood in 1919, detailing bets allegedly placed by Wood, Cobb, and Leonard on a supposedly fixed game late in the season between the Tigers and Indians at Navin Field. The White Sox had clinched the pennant, the Indians were assured of finishing second, and Detroit was fighting the Yankees for third place, which would mean a small share of the World Series players' pool. After the game of September 24, Cobb, Wood, Leonard and Speaker allegedly met under the Navin Field stands to talk baseball, and Cobb expressed the hope that his Tigers could grab third place. Speaker was supposed to have assured Cobb that the Tigers would win the next day, a charge Speaker denied. Wood's letter left no doubt that wagers were placed by himself and Leonard on the game of September 25. Speaker's name wasn't mentioned in either Cobb's or Wood's letter, a fact that wasn't lost on Landis as he investigated the matter.

The Tigers won the game, 9–5, with the *Plain Dealer's* wire service account noting that "it did not seem like a real championship game ... with nothing really at stake, pitchers [Bernie] Boland and Myers did not appear to exert themselves, and the batsmen simply hit the ball to unfrequented sections of the park."

If there was chicanery involved, it failed. Detroit finished a half game behind the Yankees and out of the money.

Landis probed Leonard's accusations cautiously, since the spotless reputations of two legendary players were on the line. The commissioner took a dim view of Leonard's refusal to come to his Chicago office and confront the men he was accusing. That forced Landis to visit Leonard's home in California to conduct his interrogation. Leonard may well have feared that Cobb, who proved throughout his career to be as handy with his fists as he was with a bat, would've assaulted him.

Landis exonerated Speaker and Cobb, declaring that "by no decent system of justice" could he have found them guilty of fixing the game in question. Wood, by that time, had retired and was baseball coach at Yale University and thus not subject to Landis's jurisdiction. Leonard crawled back into the woodwork, in spite of overwhelming evidence that the game of September 25, 1919, in Detroit hadn't been played on the square. The reputations of two of baseball's greatest stars had been restored, and Speaker rescinded his retirement, signing with Washington for 1927. Cobb hooked on with the Athletics, and Speaker joined him in 1928. Both had arrived at the end of the line and retired following the season.

The Indians, without Speaker, plunged from second place to sixth in 1927. Who knows how the franchise's fortunes would've changed if he'd been permitted to retire an Indian, as he should have? Landis, meanwhile, had endured his fill of investigating accusations of fixed games. After issuing his ruling in the Speaker/Cobb/Leonard affair, the commissioner announced that he wanted to hear no more about any game that may not have been on the level played before he took office in 1921.[3]

Dunn, the man who promised Cleveland a world championship baseball team and then delivered, made good on a second promise the day of the first World Series game to be played in the city. He re-christened the Indians' home park Dunn Field, as he had vowed to do as soon as he made good on the promise of a pennant. Dunn owned the team until his death in June of 1922 at age 57. His widow, ably assisted by the trusted and beloved Barney Barnard, operated the club until November of 1927, when it was sold to a group of wealthy Clevelanders known as "the millionaires," headed by Alva Bradley. Soon thereafter, the name of the Indians' playground reverted to League Park.

Bradley and "the millionaires" owned the team until July of 1946, when it was sold to Bill Veeck, whose promotional genius took Cleveland by storm. By 1948, Veeck didn't need gimmicks to lure fans to Municipal Stadium. A championship-contending team kept the turnstiles spinning, although Veeck's give aways and stunts didn't do any harm. A year after the Indians drew a record-shattering 2,620,627 fans while winning the World Series, Veeck sold the team to a group of Clevelanders and departed in search of new challenges. So many years later, Veeck remains a hero to Cleveland's long-time baseball fans who wait patiently for another world championship.

Just as Cleveland has forgotten Charles Somers, without whose money the American League may have faded into oblivion as other challengers to the National League had done, so has the city forgotten Sunny Jim Dunn, who accomplished the one thing Somers, and all Indians owners save for Veeck, couldn't: bringing a World Series triumph to the city at the mouth of the Cuyahoga River during the incredible summer of 1920.

Appendix A: 1920 Indians Statistics

Batting

Player	G	AB	H	R	2B	3B	HR	RBI	AVG
George Burns	44	56	15	7	4	1	0	13	.268
Ray Chapman	111	435	132	97	27	8	3	49	.303
Joe Evans	56	172	60	32	9	9	0	23	.349
Larry Gardner	154	597	185	72	31	11	3	118	.310
Jack Graney	62	152	45	31	11	1	0	13	.296
Charlie Jamieson	108	370	118	69	17	7	1	40	.319
Doc Johnston	147	535	156	68	24	10	2	71	.292
Harry Lunte	23	71	14	6	0	0	0	7	.197
Les Nunamaker	34	54	18	10	3	3	0	14	.333
Steve O'Neill	149	489	157	63	39	5	3	55	.321
Joe Sewell	22	70	23	14	4	1	0	12	.329
Elmer Smith	129	456	144	82	37	10	12	103	.316
Tris Speaker	150	552	214	137	50*	11	8	107	.388
Chet Thomas	9	9	3	2	1	0	0	0	.333
Bill Wambsganss	153	565	138	83	16	11	1	55	.244
Joe Wood	61	137	37	25	11	2	1	30	.270

*AL leader

Batting average: .303
At-bats: 5,196
Hits: 1,574
Runs: 857*
Doubles: 300*
Triples: 95
Home runs: 35

Source: *Cleveland Indians Encyclopedia*

Pitching

Player	G	GS	IP	H	BB	SO	W–L	ERA
Jim Bagby	48*	39*	339.2	338*	79	73	31*–12	2.89
Joe Boehling	3	2	13	16	10	4	0–1	4.85
Ray Caldwell	34	33	237.1	286	63	80	20–10	3.86
Bob Clark	11	2	42	59	13	8	1–2	3.43
Stan Coveleskie	41	38	315	284	65	133*	24–14	2.49
George Ellison	1	0	1	0	2	1	0–0	0.00
Tony Faeth	13	0	25	31	20	14	0–0	4.32
Duster Mails	9	8	63.1	54	18	25	7–0	1.85
Guy Morton	29	17	137	140	57	72	8–6	4.47
Tim Murchison	2	0	5	3	4	0	0–0	0.00
Elmer Myers	16	7	71.1	93	23	16	2–4	4.77
Dick Niehaus	19	3	40	42	16	12	1–2	3.60
George Uhle	27	6	84.2	98	29	27	4–5	5.21
Joe Wood	1	0	2	4	2	1	0–0	22.50

*AL leader (Bagby also led AL in innings pitched)

Complete games: 94 (Bagby 30*, Coveleskie 26, Caldwell 20, Mails 6, Morton 6, Clark 2, Myers 2, Uhle 2)
Innings pitched: 1,377
Hits allowed: 1,448
Bases on balls: 401
Strikeouts: 466
Shutouts: 11 (Bagby 3, Coveleskie 3, Mails 2, Caldwell 1, Morton 1, Clark 1)
Saves: 7 (Coveleskie 2, Niehaus 2, Morton 1, Myers 1, Uhle 1)
Earned run average: 3.41

Source: *Cleveland Indians Encyclopedia*

1920 World Series Statistics

Batting

Player	G	AB	H	R	2B	3B	HR	RBI	AVG
Les Nunamaker	2	2	1	0	0	0	0	0	.500
Jim Bagby	2	6	2	1	0	0	1	3	.333
Charlie Jamieson	6	15	5	2	1	0	0	1	.333
Steve O'Neill	7	21	7	1	3	0	0	2	.333
Tris Speaker	7	25	8	6	2	1	0	1	.320
Elmer Smith	5	13	4	1	0	1	1	5	.308
Joe Evans	5	13	4	0	0	0	0	0	.308
George Burns	4	10	3	1	1	0	0	2	.300
Doc Johnston	5	11	3	1	0	0	0	0	.273
Larry Gardner	7	24	5	1	1	0	0	2	.208
Joe Wood	4	10	2	2	1	0	0	0	.200
Joe Sewell	7	23	4	0	0	0	0	0	.174
Bill Wambsganss	7	26	4	3	0	0	0	1	.154
Stan Coveleskie	3	10	1	3	0	0	0	0	.100
Duster Mails	2	5	0	0	0	0	0	0	.000

At-bats: 217
Hits: 53
Doubles: 9
Triples: 2
Home runs: 2
Runs: 21
Batting average: .244

Pitching

Pitcher	G	IP	H	R	ER	BB	SO	W–L	ERA
Stan Coveleskie	3	27	15	2	2	2	8	3–0	0.67
Duster Mails	2	15.2	6	0	0	6	6	1–0	0.00
Jim Bagby	2	15	20	4	3	1	3	1–1	1.80
George Uhle	2	3	1	0	0	0	3	0–0	0.00
Ray Caldwell	1	.1	2	2	1	1	0	0–1	27.00

Innings pitched: 61
Hits allowed: 44
Runs allowed: 8
Earned runs: 6
Bases on balls: 10
Strikeouts: 20
Earned run average: 0.89

Source: *Cleveland Indians Encyclopedia*

Appendix B: 1920 Indians Game by Game

Date	Opponent	Score	Record	Place	GB
4/14	ST. LOUIS	5–0	1–0	1st	—
4/17	ST. LOUIS	4–5	1–1	2nd	1
4/18	DETROIT	11–4	2–1	2nd	½
4/19	DETROIT	7–6	3–1	3rd	1
4/20	DETROIT	11–10	4–1	3rd	1
4/22	at St. Louis	11–3	5–1	2nd	1
4/24	at St. Louis	10–1	6–1	3rd	1
4/25	at St. Louis	1–4	6–2	3rd	1
4/27	CHICAGO	3–2	7–2	3rd	1
4/28	CHICAGO	5–4	8–2	1st	—
4/29	CHICAGO	1–6	8–3	3rd	1
5/1	at Detroit	9–3	9–3	3rd	1
5/2	at Detroit	5–2	10–3	2nd	1
5/3	at Detroit	1–5	10–4	3rd	1
5/4	at Detroit	1–2	10–5	3rd	1
5/5	at Chicago	3–2	11–5	3rd	1
5/6	at Chicago	3–2	12–5	2nd	1
5/7	at Chicago	1–6	12–6	3rd	1
5/8	at Chicago	10–6	13–6	1st	—
5/9	at Chicago	4–3	14–6	1st	—
5/10	ST. LOUIS	7–3	15–6	1st	—
5/12	at Boston	9–7	16–6	1st	—
5/15	at New York	0–2	16–7	1st	—
5/16	at New York	8–2	17–7	1st	—
5/18	at New York	0–11	17–8	1st	—
5/19	at New York	5–0	18–8	1st	—
5/20	at Philadelphia	10–4	19–8	1st	—
5/21	at Philadelphia	9–4	20–8	1st	—
5/22	at Philadelphia	4–1	21–8	1st	—
5/23	PHILADELPHIA	1–2	21–9	1st	—

1920 Indians Game by Game

Date	Opponent	Score	Record	Place	GB
5/26	at Washington	9–13	21–10	2nd	½
5/28	CHICAGO	13–6	22–10	1st	—
5/29	CHICAGO	7–8	22–11	1st	—
5/29	CHICAGO	8–1	23–11	1st	—
5/30	CHICAGO	8–6	24–11	1st	—
5/31	DETROIT	9–5	25–11	1st	—
5/31	DETROIT	7–3	26–11	1st	—
6/1	DETROIT	10–11	26–12	1st	—
6/2	DETROIT	8–5	27–12	1st	—
6/3	DETROIT	3–6	27–13	1st	—
6/4	ST. LOUIS	6–7	27–14	1st	—
6/5	ST. LOUIS	0–6	27–15	1st	—
6/6	ST. LOUIS	2–6	27–16	1st	—
6/6	ST. LOUIS	2–1	28–16	1st	—
6/8	PHILADELPHIA	7–5	29–16	1st	—
6/9	PHILADELPHIA	6–1	30–16	1st	—
6/10	PHILADELPHIA	7–2	31–16	1st	—
6/11	PHILADELPHIA	5–2	32–16	1st	—
6/12	NEW YORK	5–4	33–16	1st	—
6/13	NEW YORK	0–14	33–17	1st	—
6/14	NEW YORK	7–1	34–17	1st	—
6/15	NEW YORK	10–2	35–17	1st	—
6/18	WASHINGTON	9–2	36–17	1st	—
6/19	WASHINGTON	1–5	36–18	1st	—
6/20	BOSTON	9–10	36–19	1st	—
6/21	BOSTON	3–2	37–19	1st	—
6/22	BOSTON	13–5	38–19	1st	—
6/23	BOSTON	7–6	39–19	1st	—
6/25	at Chicago	3–6	39–20	1st	—
6/26	at Chicago	7–12	39–21	1st	—
6/27	at Chicago	4–1	40–21	1st	—
6/28	at St. Louis	7–4	41–21	1st	—
6/28	at St. Louis	9–6	42–21	1st	—
6/29	at St. Louis	5–4	43–21	1st	—
6/30	at St. Louis	8–10	43–22	1st	—
7/2	at Detroit	10–3	44–22	2nd	½
7/3	at Detroit	7–3	45–22	2nd	½
7/4	at Detroit	11–3	46–22	1st	—
7/5	at Chicago	3–5	46–23	1st	—
7/5	at Chicago	5–6	46–24	1st	—
7/6	at Chicago	4–5	46–25	2nd	2
7/8	at Washington	4–2	47–25	1st	—
7/8	at Washington	9–6	48–25	1st	—
7/9	at Washington	8–4	49–25	1st	—
7/10	at Washington	7–2	50–25	1st	—
7/10	at Washington	1–2	50–26	1st	—
7/11	at Washington	4–0	51–26	1st	—
7/13	at Philadelphia	4–3	52–26	1st	—
7/14	at Philadelphia	5–3	53–26	1st	—

Appendix B

Date	Opponent	Score	Record	Place	GB
7/15	at Philadelphia	5–1	54–26	1st	—
7/16	at Philadelphia	4–5	54–27	1st	—
7/17	at Boston	5–2	55–27	1st	—
7/17	at Boston	5–2	56–27	1st	—
7/19	at Boston	10–6	57–27	1st	—
7/19	at Boston	4–5	57–28	1st	—
7/20	at Boston	9–8	58–28	1st	—
7/21	at New York	3–4	58–29	1st	—
7/22	at New York	3–11	58–30	1st	—
7/23	at New York	3–6	58–31	2nd	½
7/24	at New York	4–2	59–31	1st	—
7/25	CHICAGO	7–2	60–31	1st	—
7/27	WASHINGTON	5–4	61–31	1st	—
7/27	WASHINGTON	6–19	61–32	1st	—
7/28	BOSTON	8–0	62–32	1st	—
7/29	BOSTON	9–3	63–32	1st	—
7/30	BOSTON	13–4	64–32	1st	—
7/31	BOSTON	2–1	65–32	1st	—
8/1	WASHINGTON	5–8	65–33	1st	—
8/2	WASHINGTON	2–0	66–33	1st	—
8/3	WASHINGTON	10–5	67–33	1st	—
8/4	WASHINGTON	3–11	67–34	1st	—
8/6	PHILADELPHIA	1–2	67–35	1st	—
8/7	PHILADELPHIA	9–1	68–35	1st	—
8/8	PHILADELPHIA	5–0	69–35	1st	—
8/9	NEW YORK	3–6	69–36	1st	—
8/11	NEW YORK	4–7	69–37	1st	—
8/12	NEW YORK	1–5	69–38	1st	—
8/13	NEW YORK	2–4	69–39	1st	—
8/14	ST. LOUIS	3–5	69–40	1st	—
8/15	ST. LOUIS	5–0	70–40	1st	—
8/16	at New York	4–3	71–40	1st	—
8/18	at New York	3–4	71–41	1st	—
8/19	at New York	3–2	72–41	1st	—
8/21	at Boston	0–12	72–42	2nd	1½
8/21	at Boston	0–4	72–43	2nd	1½
8/23	at Boston	2–1	73–43	2nd	2
8/23	at Boston	3–4	73–44	2nd	2
8/24	at Boston	2–7	73–45	2nd	2
8/25	at Philadelphia	1–2	73–46	2nd	2½
8/26	at Philadelphia	2–3	73–47	2nd	3½
8/27	at Philadelphia	15–3	74–47	2nd	2½
8/29	at Washington	2–3	74–48	3rd	2½
8/30	at Washington	8–2	75–48	3rd	1½
8/31	at Washington	7–1	76–48	2nd	½
9/1	at Washington	9–5	77–48	1st	—
9/3	DETROIT	0–1	77–49	1st	—
9/4	DETROIT	12–3	78–49	1st	—
9/5	DETROIT	4–3	79–49	1st	—

Date	Opponent	Score	Record	Place	GB
9/6	ST. LOUIS	7–2	80–49	1st	—
9/6	ST. LOUIS	6–5	81–49	1st	—
9/9	NEW YORK	10–4	82–49	1st	—
9/10	NEW YORK	1–6	82–50	1st	—
9/11	NEW YORK	2–6	82–51	1st	—
9/12	PHILADELPHIA	5–2	83–51	1st	—
9/13	PHILADELPHIA	3–2	84–51	1st	—
9/14	PHILADELPHIA	0–8	84–52	2nd	½
9/15	PHILADELPHIA	14–0	85–52	2nd	½
9/16	WASHINGTON	1–0	86–52	1st	—
9/17	WASHINGTON	9–3	87–52	1st	—
9/18	WASHINGTON	7–5	88–52	1st	—
9/19	BOSTON	2–0	89–52	1st	—
9/20	BOSTON	8–3	90–52	1st	—
9/21	BOSTON	12–1	91–52	1st	—
9/23	CHICAGO	3–10	91–53	1st	—
9/24	CHICAGO	2–0	92–53	1st	—
9/25	CHICAGO	1–5	92–54	1st	—
9/26	at St. Louis	7–5	93–54	1st	—
9/27	at St. Louis	8–4	94–54	1st	—
9/28	at St. Louis	9–5	95–54	1st	—
9/29	at St. Louis	10–2	96–54	1st	—
10/1	at Detroit	4–5	96–55	1st	—
10/1	at Detroit	10–3	97–55	1st	—
10/2	at Detroit	10–1	98–55	1st	—
10/3	at Detroit	5–6	98–56	1st	—

Notes

Chapter 1

1. Lewis. *The Cleveland Indians*, p. 32.
2. Macht. *Connie Mack and the Early Years of Baseball*, p. 169.
3. Voigt. *The League That Failed*, p. 292.
4. Lewis, p. 34.
5. Cleveland *Plain Dealer*, January 11, 1916.
6. Cleveland *Plain Dealer*, January 1–15, 1916.
7. Lewis, p. 77.
8. Alexander. *Spoke: A Biography of Tris Speaker*, p. 107.
9. Gay. *Tris Speaker: The Rough and Tumble Life of a Baseball Legend*, p. 167.
10. Alexander, p. 113.
11. Cleveland *Plain Dealer*, July 8, 1918.
12. Cleveland *Plain Dealer*, July 12, 1918.
13. Cleveland *Plain Dealer*, July 21, 1918.
14. Lewis, p.100.
15. Ibid., p. 102.
16. Gay, p. 183.
17. Cleveland *Plain Dealer*, July 19, 1919.

Chapter 2

1. Cleveland *Plain Dealer*, March 30, 1920.
2. Ibid.
3. Cleveland *Plain Dealer*, March 4, 1920.
4. Cleveland *News*, March 8, 1920.
5. Cleveland *Plain Dealer*, March 3, 1920.
6. Cleveland *Plain Dealer*, March 1, 1920.
7. Cleveland *Press*, March 4, 1920.
8. Cleveland *News*, March 8, 1920.
9. Cleveland *Plain Dealer*, April 1, 1920.
10. Cleveland *Press*, March 2, 1920.
11. Cleveland *Press*, March 9, 1920.

12. Cleveland *Press,* March 23, 1920.
13. Cleveland *Plain Dealer,* March 20, 1920.
14. Cleveland *News,* March 26, 1920.
15. Cleveland *News,* March 18, 1920.
16. Gay, p 6.
17. Alexander, p. 42.
18. Gay, p. 23.
19. Cleveland *Plain Dealer,* April 4, 1920.
20. Cleveland *Press,* March 25, 1920.
21. Cleveland *Press,* March 20, 1920.
22. Cleveland Press, March 26, 1920.
23. Cleveland *News,* April 9, 1920.
24. Cleveland *Press,* April 7, 1920.

Chapter 3

1. Reference books such as *The Baseball Encyclopedia* and *Total Baseball* spell Sothoron's first name "Allen." However, stories in the three Cleveland papers used to research this book spelled it "Allan," which is why I have chosen to use that spelling. Similarly, reference books spell Stan Coveleskie's name without the "e" on the end, but because the newspapers spelled it "Coveleskie" throughout the 1920 season, I have done the same.
2. Cleveland *Press,* April 17, 1920.
3. Cleveland *Plain Dealer,* April 27, 1920.
4. Cleveland *Plain Dealer,* May 1, 1920.
5. Cleveland *Press,* April 16, 1920.
6. Reisler, Jim: *Babe Ruth: Launching the Legend,* p. 29.

Chapter 4

1. Cleveland *News,* April 23, 1920.
2. Reisler, p. 146.
3. Cleveland *Plain Dealer,* May 10, 1920.
4. Cleveland *Plain Dealer,* May 12, 1920.
5. Cleveland *Plain Dealer,* May 15, 1920.
6. Cleveland *Press,* March 15, 1920.
7. Reisler, p. 84.
8. Sowell, Mike. *The Pitch That Killed,* p. 101.
9. Cleveland *Plain Dealer,* May 29, 1920.

Chapter 5

1. Cleveland *Plain Dealer,* June 2, 1920.
2. Cleveland *Press,* June 7, 1920.
3. Cleveland *Plain Dealer,* June 10, 1920.
4. Cleveland *Plain Dealer,* June 14, 1920.
5. Ibid.

Chapter 6

1. Cleveland *Press,* July 8, 1920.
2. Cleveland *Press,* July 12, 1920.
3. Cleveland *Press,* July 14, 1920.
4. Cleveland *Press,* July 18, 1920.
5. Cleveland *Plain Dealer,* July 17, 1920.
6. Cleveland *Press,* July 26, 1920.
7. Lewis, p. 104.
8. Cleveland *Plain Dealer,* August 1, 1920.

Chapter 7

1. Cleveland *Press,* August 2, 1920.
2. Cleveland *Press,* August 4, 1920.
3. Egan. *Baseball in the Western Reserve,* p. 121.
4. Thorn. *Total Baseball,* p. 1982.
5. *The Baseball Encyclopedia,* 9th ed., p. 2208.
6. Cleveland *Plain Dealer,* August 7, 1920.
7. Cleveland *Plain Dealer,* August 11, 1920.
8. Cleveland *Plain Dealer,* August 13, 1920.
9. Cleveland *Plain Dealer,* August 16, 1920.

Chapter 8

1. Sowell, p. 63.
2. Ibid. p. 62.
3. Ibid. p. 82.
4. Ibid. p. 82.
5. Ibid. p. 174.
6. Ibid. p. 178.
7. Cleveland *News,* August 18, 1920.
8. Gay, p. 198.
9. Ibid.
10. Ibid.
11. Ibid.
12. Bresnahan. *Play It Again: Baseball Experts on What Might Have Been,* p. 62.
13. Thorn, p. 133.
14. Bresnahan, p. 67.
15. Cleveland *Press,* August 24, 1920.
16. Lewis, p. 113.

Chapter 9

1. Cleveland *Plain Dealer,* September 2, 1920.
2. Cleveland *Plain Dealer,* September 4, 1920.
3. Cleveland *Plain Dealer,* September 6, 1920.
4. Cleveland *Plain Dealer,* September 8, 1920.
5. Cleveland *News,* September 14, 1920.
6. Cleveland *Press,* September 15, 1920.

7. Cleveland *Plain Dealer,* September 16, 1920.
8. Cleveland *Plain Dealer,* September 17, 1920.
9. Cleveland *Plain Dealer,* September 18, 1920.
10. Cleveland *Plain Dealer,* September 20, 192.0
11. Cleveland *Press,* September 23, 1920.
12. Cleveland *Press,* September 24, 1920.
13. Gay, p. 204.
14. Cleveland *Press,* September 24, 1920.
15. Cleveland *Plain Dealer,* September 24, 1920.
16. Cleveland *Plain Dealer,* September 25, 1920.
17. Ibid.
18. Cleveland *Plain Dealer,* September 26, 1920.
19. Cleveland *Press,* September 27, 1920.
20. Cleveland *News,* September 29, 1920.
21. Cleveland *Press,* September 29, 1920.
22. Sowell, p. 81.
23. Cleveland *Plain Dealer,* September 30, 1920.
24. Ibid.

Chapter 10

1. Gay, p. 173.
2. Ibid.
3. Cleveland *Plain Dealer,* October 3, 1920.
4. Carney. *Burying the Black Sox,* p. 17.
5. Ibid., p. 226.
6. Ibid., p. 225–226.
7. Ibid., p. 227.
8. Ibid.
9. Ibid., p. 226.
10. Cleveland *Plain Dealer,* April 14–June 30, 1920.

Chapter 11

1. Cleveland *Plain Dealer,* October 13, 1920.
2. Cleveland *Plain Dealer,* October 5, 1920.
3. Cleveland *Press,* October 4, 1920.
4. Cleveland *Plain Dealer,* October 5, 1920.
5. Ibid.
6. Cleveland *Press,* October 4, 1920.
7. Lewis, p. 124.
8. Adler. *Mack, McGraw, and the 1913 Baseball Season,* p. 211.
9. Cleveland *Plain Dealer,* October 6, 1920.
10. Cleveland *Press,* October 6, 1920.
11. Cleveland *Plain Dealer,* October 7, 1920.
12. Cleveland *Press,* October 6, 1920.
13. Cleveland *Plain Dealer,* October 8, 1920.
14. Ibid.
15. Lewis, p. 127.
16. Cleveland *Plain Dealer,* October 8, 1920.

17. Cleveland *Plain Dealer*, October 9, 1920.
18. Ibid.
19. Spatz and Steinberg, *1921: The Yankees, the Giants, and the Battle for Baseball Supremacy in New York*, p. 57.
20. Lewis, p. 130.
21. Cleveland *Plain Dealer*, October 11, 1920.
22. Cleveland *Press*, October 11, 1920.
23. Cleveland *Plain Dealer*, October 11, 1920.
24. Honig. *The Brooklyn Dodgers: An Illustrated Tribute*, p. 36.
25. Cleveland *Press*, October 11, 1920.
26. Cleveland *Press*, October 12, 1920.
27. Cleveland *Plain Dealer*, October 12, 1920.
28. Cleveland *Press*, October 13, 1920.
29. Ibid.
30. Cleveland *Plain Dealer*, October 13, 1920.
31. Ibid.
32. Spatz, p. 57.
33. Cleveland *News*, October 13, 1920.
34. Spatz, p. 123–124.
35. Alexander, p. 161.

Chapter 12

1. Alexander, p. 184.
2. Bresnahan, p. 67.
3. Alexander, p. 250.

Bibliography

Books

Adler, Richard. *Mack, McGraw, and the 1913 Baseball Season*. Jefferson, NC: McFarland, 2008.
Alexander, Charles C. *Spoke: A Biography of Tris Speaker*. Dallas: SMU Press, 2007.
Bresnahan, Jim. *Play It Again: Baseball Experts on What Might Have Been*. Jefferson, NC: McFarland, 2009.
Carney, Gene. *Burying the Black Sox*. Dulles, VA: Potomac Books, 2006.
Egan, James M., Jr. *Baseball on the Western Reserve*. Jefferson, NC: McFarland, 2008.
Gay, Timothy M. *Tris Speaker, The Rough and Tumble Life of a Baseball Legend*. Lincoln: University of Nebraska Press, 2005.
Honig, Donald. *The Brooklyn Dodgers: An Illustrated Tribute*. New York: St. Martin's Press, 1981.
Lewis, Franklin. *The Cleveland Indians*. New York: G.P. Putnam's Sons, 1949.
Macht, Norman L. *Connie Mack and the Early Years of Baseball*. Lincoln: University of Nebraska Press, 2007.
Reisler, Jim. *Babe Ruth: Launching the Legend*. New York: McGraw-Hill, 2004.
Schneider, Russell. *The Cleveland Indians Encyclopedia*. Norwalk, CT: The Easton Press, 2002.
Sowell, Mike. *The Pitch That Killed*. New York: Macmillan, 1989.
Spatz, Lyle, and Steve Steinberg. *1921*. Lincoln: University of Nebraska Press, 2009.
Stang, Mark. *Indians Illustrated: 100 Years of Cleveland Indians Photos*. Wilmington, OH: Orange Frazier Press, 2000.
Thorn, John. *Total Baseball*, 6th ed. New York: Total Sports, 1999.
Voigt, David Q. *The League That Failed*. Lanham, MD: Scarecrow Press, 2008.

Newspapers

Cleveland News: January–February 1916; April–October 1919; March–October, 1920.
Cleveland Plain Dealer: October 1908; January–February 1916; April–October 1918; April–October 1919; March–October 1920.
Cleveland Press: January–February 1916; April–October 1919; March–October 1920.

Index

Adams, Babe 196
Alabama 80
Albany, New York 163
Alphonse and Gaston 90
American Association (major league) 8, 102, 167
American League 8–10, 13, 15, 19, 22, 31–32, 37, 50, 53–54, 58, 62, 65, 72–74, 79–81, 84, 94, 99, 102–103, 110, 115, 119, 140, 147–149, 151, 154–155, 158, 161, 165, 168, 170, 173, 175, 179–180, 185–187, 192, 201
Anson, Pop 86
Anthony Carlin Rivet Works 174
Anthony, Idaho 31
Argonne Forest 69
Armour, Bill 66
Atlantic Ocean 21

Bagby, Jim 18, 34–35, 42, 51, 54, 60, 66, 68, 70–74, 76, 78–80, 86–89, 92, 96, 105, 108, 120, 129–130, 139, 141, 143, 146, 158, 161, 164, 170, 172, 180, 186–188, 193, 202, 203, 204, 205
Bagby, Jim, Jr. 52, 205
Baker, Newton D. 19–20, 189
Baltimore (American Association) 103
Baltimore, Maryland 167, 199
Baltimore Orioles 5, 6, 7, 11, 45
Bancroft, Dave 123
Bang, Ed 29, 34–35, 43, 46, 51, 58, 68, 114, 117, 161, 175, 197
Barnard, Ernest L. 14, 42, 81, 208
Barnes, Ross 86
Barrow, Ed 47, 51, 115, 125
Baseball Writers Association of America 123

Bennett, Charley 49
Bennett, Eddie 185, 196
Bennett Park 49
Big Apple 88, 141
Birmingham, Joe 12, 18
"Black Sox" 18, 45, 51, 61, 90, 137, 159, 167, 169–173, 202, 208
Bodie, Ping 136
Boland, Bernie 207
Bonaparte, Napoleon 69
Boston, Massachusetts 8–10, 54–55, 58, 84, 86–87, 121–122, 136, 150, 172
Boston Beaneaters 9
Boston Braves 9, 29, 50, 67–68, 135, 145, 155, 199
Boston Red Sox 13, 15–17, 19–20, 22–23, 29, 33, 37, 43, 45, 50–51, 53–54, 58, 61, 63, 72–73, 78, 86–87, 89, 90, 92, 94–95, 98, 100, 102, 104, 115, 117, 121, 124, 129, 131, 133, 136–138, 143, 146–147, 170, 172, 180, 196, 202, 204–205
Boudreau, Lou 25, 96
Bradley, Alva 25, 208
Bradley, Bill 73
Bradley, George 102
Brooklyn, New York 166, 175
Brooklyn Dodgers (or Robins) 6, 16, 33, 36–37, 50, 67, 85, 88, 133, 135, 140, 144–146, 155, 158–159, 163, 166, 174–196, 202
Brooklyn Superbas 6
Broun, Heywood Hale 203
Brouthers, Dan 86
Brown 152
Brown, Mordecai 190
Browning, Pete 86

225

226 Index

Bruce, John 14
Brush, John T. 7, 201
Buffalo, New York 8
Burke, Jimmy 38, 44, 64
Burkett, Jesse 6, 86
Burns, George 72, 99, 177–178, 186, 190–191, 205
Burns, John 15
Bush, Donie 134

Cadore, Leon 50, 178
Caldwell, Ray 53, 54, 58, 60, 66, 68, 71–74, 78–79, 89, 91–93, 100–101, 105, 109, 121, 127, 129–130, 133, 138, 143, 145, 161, 170, 172, 182, 196, 202, 203
California 207
California Angels 170
Calvary Cemetery 122
Cantillon, Joe 11
Canton, Ohio 179
Carlin, Anthony 174–175
Carrigan, Bill 16
Casey at the Bat 88
Castle, M.H. 111
Cedar Avenue 102
Central League 179
Central Powers 22
Chance, Frank 107, 130
Chapman, Ray 16, 18, 27, 41, 50, 57, 59, 70, 73, 85, 88, 91, 104, 113–119, 121, 124, 127, 132–133, 136, 138–139, 157, 172, 199, 203
Chase, Hal 68
Chicago, Illinois 46, 51, 54, 58, 64, 66, 73, 78–79, 89, 94, 99, 159, 168
Chicago Cubs 15, 20–21, 67, 107, 146, 196–197
Chicago *Tribune* 51, 168
Chicago White Sox 11, 15, 18, 20, 26, 31–33, 37, 41, 44, 51–54, 56, 59, 60–61, 71, 73–74, 77–80, 83–84, 87, 89, 90, 92, 96, 98–102, 104, 106, 108–110, 112, 121–122, 124–128, 131, 133, 135–142, 144, 146–158, 160–161, 168–169, 172, 181, 185, 196, 198, 202, 206
Chicago White Stockings 102–103
Cicotte, Eddie 61, 137–138, 149, 156–157, 167, 168, 171, 177
Cincinnati, Ohio 6, 36–37, 67, 99–100
Cincinnati Reds 6, 32–33, 35–37, 67–68, 73, 88, 99, 135, 137, 140, 144, 146, 149–150, 158, 184, 205
Clark, Bob 91, 96, 100–101, 111–112, 125–126, 165, 169, 172
Clarke, Fred 86
"Clean Sox" 45, 165–169

Cleveland Athletic Club 13
Cleveland Blues 10
Cleveland Bronchos 67
Cleveland Forest Citys 102–103, 163
Cleveland Municipal Court 6
Cleveland Municipal Stadium 208
Cleveland Naps 10–12, 68, 124, 197
Cleveland Naval Reserves 132
Cleveland Spiders 5–7, 164, 194
Cobb, Ty 15, 50, 52, 86, 161, 205–207
Collins, Eddie 46, 90, 151, 168, 177
Collins, John 157
Columbus, Christopher 192
Columbus, Ohio 8
Comiskey, Charles 15, 32, 149, 156, 168
Comiskey Park 26, 53, 73, 77–78, 98, 101, 155, 169
Comstock, C.B. 13
Connolly, Tommy 116, 191
Cook County, Illinois 149, 155
Coombs, Jack 196
Cooper, Wilbur 197
Cooperstown, New York 206
Coumbe, Fred 23–26, 144
Coveleskie, Stan 18, 34–35, 38, 39, 51, 53, 55, 57, 64, 66, 68, 70–71, 73–74, 76–78, 80, 83, 86, 89–90, 92, 104, 108, 115, 124, 127–128, 130, 137, 140, 143, 147, 152, 160, 164, 169, 170, 179–180, 181, 186, 192, 194, 198, 204
Coveleskie, Mrs. Stan 60
Cox, James M. 197
Cross, Harry 181, 183
Crowder, Enoch 19–20
"Curse of the Bambino" 196
"Curse of the Billy Goat" 196
Cuyahoga County Common Pleas Court 6
Cuyahoga River 208
Cuyler, Kiki 204

Daly, Kathleen (Chapman) 113–114, 117, 121
Daly, Martin 113–114
Dauss, Hooks 134
Davis, Dixie 135
Dayton, Ohio 197
dead ball era 9
Dean, Dizzy 152
Delahanty, Ed 86
Dempsey, Jack 69, 125
Des Moines baseball club 72, 91, 131
Detroit, Michigan 8, 46, 49, 58, 92, 101, 136, 154, 160, 163, 166, 169, 171, 175, 206–207
Detroit Tigers 11–12, 15, 32–33, 41–42,

Index

48, 50, 54, 62–64, 68, 76–77, 79, 90, 92, 104, 110–112, 120, 124, 132, 135, 140–141, 154, 160–161, 165, 168, 170, 204, 206–207
Dineen, Bill 191
Duffy, Hugh 86
Dugan, Joe 87
Dunlap, Fred 102
Dunn, James C. "Jim" 14–18, 20, 22, 25, 28, 33, 38, 41, 69, 81–82, 105, 109, 121, 131–133, 144, 146, 150, 154, 158, 163, 166, 174–175, 184, 188, 198–199, 201, 202, 208
Dunn Field 208

East Ohio Gas Company 113
Ebbets, Charles H. 158, 181, 185, 196
Ebbets Field 166, 175, 178, 182–184, 192–193
Edwards, Henry P. 13, 24, 26–29, 35, 38, 42, 47, 51, 56–58, 60, 65–66, 68, 71–73, 77–79, 85, 89–90, 94, 96, 98–101, 104, 106–108, 111, 121, 124, 131, 133, 135, 137, 139–141, 143, 145–147, 151–152, 156, 161, 166, 175–176, 179–181, 184, 191, 205
Eliot, T.S. 62
Ellison, George 91
Enosburg Falls, Vermont 43
Erickson, Olaf 71
Euclid Avenue 113
Europe 22
Evans, Billy 32, 168, 190
Evans, Joe 29, 77–78, 85, 134, 138, 178, 186, 199

Faber, Red 45, 51, 151, 157, 161, 169, 171, 196
Faeth, Tony 130
Federal League 13, 15–16
Felsch, Oscar "Happy" 51, 78, 156–157, 167
Fenway Park 20, 54, 68, 83–84, 87, 124–125, 170, 172
Ferris, Earle 177
FitzGerald, J.V. 79–80
FitzGerald, W.S. 149, 197
Flagstead, Ira 161
Flatbush 177
Fohl, Lee 18, 22–26, 53–54, 64, 70, 109–110, 144, 165–166
Folger, Clay 141
Franklin, Pennsylvania 58, 63, 74, 82
Frazee, Harry 83, 115, 121, 202
Freud, Sigmund 27
Fullerton, Hugh 36–37

Gallia, Bert 65
Gandil, Chick 18, 31, 156
Gardner, Larry 22, 43, 57, 77, 84–85, 89, 95, 123, 135, 176, 188, 205
Gerber, Wally 128
Germans 69
Gilbert, Larry 29, 34, 36, 199–200
Gleason, Kid 32–33, 44, 51, 90, 142, 148–150, 157, 168, 170–171
Grand Rapids, Michigan 7–8
Graney, Jack 17–18, 20, 27, 51, 57, 122, 134–135, 164
Griffith, Tommy 181, 183
Griffith Stadium 77, 130
Grimes, Burleigh 177, 180, 186–189, 192–193, 196, 198
Grove, Lefty 158
Gwinner, Ed 13

Hamilton, C.C. 180
Hanlon, Ned 6
Harding, Richard T.F. 185
Harding, Warren G. 197
Harris, Bucky 87
Harris, Joe 19, 28, 34–35, 58, 63, 74, 82, 86, 105
Harris, Sam 14
Hawley, Davis 7, 12
Henry, John 117
Herrmann, Garry 158
Hess, Otto 66–67
Heydler, John 63, 159
Hildebrand, George 57, 125
"Hitless Wonders" 11, 190
Hodge, Clarence 157
Hofbrau syndicate 13
Hogarty, John 14
Holy Grail 29
Hooper, Harry 79, 87
Hotel Statler 41
Hotel Winston 114
Hornsby, Rogers 202
Howard, Ivy 18
Hoyt, Waite 124
Hubbard, Texas 186
Hudson River 163
Hudson, Wisconsin 64
Huggins, Miller 52, 91, 139, 141, 195
Hunt, Marshall 48, 79
Huston, Tillinghast 32, 52, 115, 136, 141

Indianapolis (American Association) 149, 179
Indianapolis, Indiana 7–8
Iowa 15, 174
Iowa University 180

Jackson, Joe 45–46, 49, 68, 86, 105, 156–157, 167
Jamieson, Charlie 22–23, 36, 42, 72, 80, 143, 154, 186, 192
Jamieson, Edna Mae 143–145, 147, 150
Jasper, Henry 23
Jennings, Hughie 11, 32, 52
Johns, Petie 127
Johnson, Ban 7–9, 12–14, 16, 19, 63, 65, 95, 115, 119, 149, 168, 171, 176, 199
Johnson, Walter 11, 71, 158
Johnston, Doc 35–36, 50, 57, 63, 84–85, 123, 137, 146, 165, 186–187, 192, 198
Johnston, Jimmy 181, 186
Jolson, Al 95
Jones, Sam 16
Jordan, Ted 157
Joss, Addie 124, 146, 152
Judge, Joe 87

Kaiser Wilhelm 20
Kansas City, Missouri 8, 97
Keefe, Dave 83
Keeler, Willie 86
Kennard Street 102
Kentucky 114
Kerr, Dickie 53, 77, 150, 157, 165, 168–169, 171
Kettleman, Mrs. Carl W. 197
Kilbane, Johnny 69
Kilduff, Pete 188–189
Kilfoyl, John 7, 9, 12
Killilea, Henry 10
King's County, New York 159
Klem, Bill 191
Klepfer, Ed 18, 27
Konetchy, Ed 177, 190

Labor Day 133–135, 138
Lajoie, Napoleon 10, 12, 16, 59, 68, 73, 86, 109, 178
Lake Erie 106, 165
Landis, Kenesaw Mountain 19, 202, 206–208
Lannin, Joe 15–16, 174
Lanyon, James 88, 103, 117, 131, 136
League Park 6, 9, 17, 20–21, 23, 29, 38, 42, 44–45, 49, 51, 53, 56–57, 60, 64, 69, 71–73, 90–91, 105, 100, 155, 121, 131–132, 134, 139, 142, 144–145, 147, 150, 152, 155, 159, 166, 168, 170–171, 181, 184–185, 188, 190, 192, 194, 198, 205, 208
Leibold, Harry 157
Leonard, Hubert "Dutch" 132, 206–207
Lewis 159

Lewis, Duffy 120
Liebhardt, Glenn 53
Loftus, Tom 8
Logan, Walter 132
Louisville, Kentucky 7
Louisville Colonels 103
Lunte, Harry 116, 123, 134–135, 138, 158, 199
Lynn, Byrd 168–169

Mack, Connie 9, 12, 41, 64, 74, 83, 104, 180
Magee, Lee 67–68
Mails, Duster 126, 130, 134, 140, 143–144, 147, 151–152, 154, 170–171, 181, 183, 190–191, 202, 205
Mamaux, Al 178
Manhattan Island 26, 196
Manion, Clyde 162
Maranville, Rabbit 123
Marion, Ohio 197
Marquard, Rube 176–178, 180, 184, 197
Martin, Pat 57–58
Maxwell, Robert 31, 57, 62, 84
Mays, Carl 56, 108, 110, 113, 115–116, 119–120, 136, 139, 140, 172, 187
McAleer, James 109
McCallister, Jack 146, 182
McCarthy, Pat 15
McClellan, Harvey 157, 168–169
McCormick, Jim 102–103
McGraw, John 56, 179, 195, 201
McInnis, Stuffy 95, 205
McLain, Denny 158
McMahon, Jane 114
McMullin, Fred 156, 167
McNichols, Walter 110
McRoy, Bob 16
Memorial Day 59, 63
Memphis, Tennessee 36
Menke, Frank G. 193
Milan, Clyde 87
Milan, Ohio 198
Miller, Otto 188
Milwaukee (American Association) 150
Milwaukee, Wisconsin 8, 10
Milwaukee Brewers 10
Minnesota Twins 170
Minuit, Peter 26
Mitchell, Clarence 188
Mogridge, George 87
Moran, Pat 36
Morton, Guy 42, 50, 54, 58, 72, 74, 76, 79–82, 84, 88, 91, 95, 101, 110, 124, 129–130, 147, 164–165, 169
Mudville 88

Murphy, Charles 15
Murphy, Eddie 157
Myers, Elmer 22–23, 50, 53, 69, 71, 83, 100, 129–131, 207
Myers, Hy 176, 183, 186, 190

National Association of Professional Base Ball Players 9, 163
National Commission 14, 155, 158, 199
National League 5–9, 29, 36–37, 49–50, 58, 85, 102–103, 133, 140, 149, 155, 159, 163, 166, 170, 175, 180, 189, 194–195, 202, 208
Navin, Frank 49
Navin Field 49, 68, 76, 161, 206–207
Naylor, Rollie 140
Neis, Bernie 190
New Orleans, Louisiana 14, 28, 31, 33, 155
New Orleans Pelicans 30, 33–34, 138, 200
New York, New York 55, 86, 92, 108, 113, 121, 138, 150, 177, 203
New York *Daily News* 48
New York Giants 22, 33, 56, 133, 135, 140, 144, 149, 155, 179, 195, 201–203
New York *Times* 57
New York Yankees 26, 32, 35–37, 41, 47–48, 50, 54–56, 61–63, 66, 68–73, 77–80, 83–84, 86–90, 96, 98–102, 104, 108–110, 112, 115, 120, 124–127, 131, 133, 135–141, 144, 146–148, 150, 152–154, 158, 160, 165–167, 174, 196, 198–199, 202, 205
Niehaus, Dick 58, 79, 96, 130–131, 144
Niles, Ohio 191
Nunamaker, Les 42, 70–71, 165

O'Day, Hank 191
Odenwald, Ted 64–65, 71–72, 91, 131
O'Doul, Lefty 52, 205
Oeschger, Joe 50
Ohio 88, 91, 99, 108, 197–198
Ohio Supreme Court 6
Oil City, Pennsylvania 63, 74
Oil League 63, 74, 82
Olson, Ivy 176, 181–183, 190
O'Neill, May 69
O'Neill, Steve 18, 20, 24–25, 28, 42, 69–70, 72, 122, 125, 164–165, 177, 187, 192, 204–205
O'Neill, Tip 86
O.R. Rust Company 199
Orr, Dave 86
Owens, Brick 56, 152, 161

Pacific Coast League 107, 126, 130, 144

Peckinpaugh, Roger 25, 87, 167–168, 204
Pennock, Herb 124
Pennsylvania 35, 92
Pfeffer, Jeff 177
Philadelphia, Pennsylvania 8–10, 57–58, 83–84, 87, 125–127, 172
Philadelphia Athletics 12, 20, 22–23, 33, 41, 56–59, 66, 74, 79–80, 83–84, 90, 94, 104, 106, 121–122, 125–126, 140–142, 146–147, 153, 158, 160, 172, 196, 205, 207
Philadelphia Phillies 35, 50, 57, 135, 146, 165, 180, 205
Philadelphia *Public Ledger* 31
Phillippe, Deacon 196
Pioneer Alloys Company 113
Pinelli, Babe 161
Pipp, Wally 116, 120, 138–139
Pittsburgh, Pennsylvania 10, 136, 150
Pittsburgh Pirates 57–58, 64, 136, 149, 196, 204–205
Polo Grounds 50, 55–56, 68, 84, 86–89, 91, 98, 101, 106–107, 111–112, 115, 120, 126, 165, 172
Portland, Oregon 126
Providence, Rhode Island 167

Quayle, John H. 13
Quinn, Jack 55

Rath, Morrie 137
Replogle, Hartley 149, 159
Rice, Grantland 17
Risberg, Swede 31, 90, 141, 156–157, 167, 170
Robinson, Wilbert 145, 177–178, 180, 183–184, 191–192, 194, 195
Robison, Frank 5, 6, 8
Robison, Stanley 6
Rockefeller, John D. 113
Rommel, Ed 83, 140–141
Roosevelt, Franklin D. 19
Roth, Bobby 18, 20, 22, 85
Rowe, Dave 102–103
Ruelbach, Ed 190
Runyon, Damon 177
Ruppert, Jacob 52, 69, 115, 141, 202
Russell, Allen 79
Ruth, Babe 23–25, 32–33, 36, 45, 47–48, 50, 52, 54, 56, 63, 66, 68–69, 77–78, 83–84, 87–90, 98, 101, 104, 106–108, 136–138, 141–142, 149, 151, 160, 165–166, 177, 180, 196, 198, 203

Sacramento (Pacific Coast League) 144
St. Louis, Missouri 8, 10, 58, 66, 73, 92,

98, 102, 149, 151–153, 160, 169, 171, 199, 202
St. Louis Browns 10, 32–33, 38–39, 41, 43, 54, 64, 74–75, 79, 83–84, 90, 94, 105–106, 109–110, 128, 131, 133–135, 138, 141, 145, 147–148, 154, 158–161, 165, 169, 172, 202
St. Louis Cardinals 141, 202, 205
St. Patrick's Day 34
St. Paul (American Association) 144
Sandusky, Ohio 147, 198
San Francisco *Call* 152
San Quentin, California 151
Schalk, Ray 151, 157
Schneider, G.A. 13
Scott, Everett 114
Scullen, William A. 124
Seattle Mariners 170
Sewell, Joe 138–140, 143, 145, 146, 158, 177, 200, 204
Shamokin, Pennsylvania 64
Shawkey, Bob 56, 87, 138, 140, 172
Sheehan, Jack 188
Shibe Park 57, 83, 122, 126
Shocker, Urban 65
Sinclair, Harry 13–14
Sisler, George 105, 111, 133, 145
Slocum, W.J. 88–89, 120
Smallwood, Percy 117
Smith, Charlie 66–67
Smith, Elmer 27, 36, 41, 73–74, 99, 108, 121, 135, 146–148, 164, 186, 188, 198, 205
Smith, F.W. 149
Smith, Sherrod 176, 178, 183, 190
Smyth, Harper Garcia 132
Somers, Charles W. 7–9, 12, 14, 178, 208
Sothoron, Allan 36, 38–39, 44, 65, 202
Southern League (Association) 30, 34, 36
Speaker, Jenny 28, 186
Sportsman's Park 154
Stahl, Jake 13
Stallings, George 68
Standard Oil Company 113
Stenzel, Jake 86
Stick to the Finish Club 41, 46
Strunk, Amos 157
subway series 155
syndicate baseball 6, 9
Syracuse, New York 163

Telling, W.E. 13
Templar Motors 53, 64, 128
Temple Cup 5–6, 195
Tenney, Ross 29–30, 51, 82, 90, 98, 107, 119–120, 122, 126–128, 135, 157, 161, 175, 177, 180
Texas 114
Thayer, Ernest L. 88
Thomas, Chester 124
Thomas, Fred 16
Thompson, Sam 86
Thormalen, Hank 139
Tinker, Zachary 8
Toledo (American Association) 142
Toledo, Ohio 69
Troy, New York 163
Turbeyville, Fred 37
Turner, Terry 18, 73

Uhle, George 27, 41–42, 63, 66–67, 69, 71–72, 79, 84, 87–88, 108, 111–112, 128–130, 161, 165, 202
Union Association 103
Union Station 166, 175
United States Census Bureau 74
University of Alabama 138
University Circle 197

Vaughan, Irving 51, 53
Veach, Bobby 76
Veeck, Bill 208
Vick, Sam 52
Vitt, Oscar 25

Wade Park 197
Wall Street 175
Walsh, Ed 152, 190
Walsh, Tom 15
Wambsganss, Bill 17–19, 27, 57–60, 70, 84–85, 87, 122–123, 135, 164, 186, 205
War Department 19–20
Washington, D.C. 7–10, 46, 49, 58, 81, 84, 87, 101, 127, 130–131
Washington Senators (Nationals) 11–12, 33, 58, 63, 71, 74, 77–80, 83, 87, 90–92, 94, 96–97, 101, 105, 107–108, 117, 124–125, 140–145, 147, 152–153, 204–205, 207
Waterloo 21
Weaver, George "Buck" 46, 51, 151, 156–157, 167, 168
Weeghman Park 20
Weilman, Carl 65
Wellington, Duke of 69
Western League 7
Wheat, Zack 159, 176, 179–186, 188, 192, 194
Whitman, Burt 124
wild card 5
Wilkinson, Roy 157

Willard, Jess 69, 125
Williams, Lefty 45, 77, 90, 153, 156–157, 167, 170–171
Wilson, Woodrow 197
Wisconsin 71
Witt, Whitey 87
Wood, Joe 36, 57, 90, 96–97, 101, 114, 122, 149, 165, 176–178, 196, 198, 206, 207
Woodland Bards 14
Wootton, Don 192
World Series 17, 21–22, 29, 31, 33, 36, 43, 47, 55, 57, 81, 91, 100, 104–105, 115, 133, 137, 142, 147–151, 159, 166, 168, 174–178, 180–184, 186–189, 191, 192, 195, 198, 199, 201, 204, 206
World War I 18, 155
Wrigley Field 20, 151

Young, Cy 6
Young, Ralph 134
Young Furniture 53

Zachary, Tom 143

www.ingramcontent.com/pod-product-compliance
Lightning Source LLC
Chambersburg PA
CBHW030106170426
43198CB00009B/515